Mac OS X
fast&easy

Lisa A. Bucki

A DIVISION OF PRIMA PUBLISHING

A Division of Prima Publishing

Prima Publishing, colophon, and fast & easy are registered trademarks of Prima Communications, Inc. PRIMA TECH is a trademark of Prima Communications, Inc., Roseville, California 95661.

Apple, the Apple logo, AppleWorks, Charcoal, Chicago, ClarisWorks, ColorSync, ImageWriter, "keyboard" Apple logo, LaserWriter, LocalTalk, Mac, Macintosh, Mac logo, "Moof" and Dogcow logo, QuickTime, Sherlock, TrueType, and VideoSync are trademarks of Apple Computer, Inc., registered in the U.S. and other countries. Balloon Help, Extensions Manager, Finder, iMac, iMovie, Think different, and ViewEdit are trademarks of Apple Computer, Inc. "AOL" and the AOL triangle logo are registered trademarks of America Online, Inc. EarthLink and EarthLink logo are trademarks of EarthLink Network, Inc. Microsoft, Microsoft Internet Explorer logo, and Outlook are registered trademarks of Microsoft Corporation in the United States and/or other countries. Netscape and Netscape Navigator are registered trademarks of Netscape Communications Corporation in the U.S. and other countries. Quicken is a registered trademark of Intuit, Inc., in the United States and other countries. Adobe, the Adobe logo, Acrobat, and the Acrobat logo are either registered trademarks or trademarks of Adobe Systems Incorporated in the United States and/or other countries. Stuffit and Stuffit Expander are trademarks of Aladdin Systems, Inc.

Important: If you have problems running Mac OS X, go to Apple's Web site at http://www.apple.com. Prima Publishing cannot provide software support.

ISBN: 0-7615-1984-X

Library of Congress Catalog Card Number: 99-64755

Printed in the United States of America

00 01 02 03 04 DD 10 9 8 7 6 5 4 3 2 1

Publisher:
Stacy L. Hiquet

Associate Marketing Manager:
Heather Buzzingham

Managing Editor:
Sandy Doell

Acquisitions Editors:
Jawahara K. Saidullah,
Kevin Harreld

Project Editor:
Brian Thomasson

Technical Editor:
Brian Thomasson

Copy Editor:
Gabrielle Nemes

Interior Layout:
Danielle Foster

Cover Design:
Prima Design Team

Indexer:
Johnna VanHoose Dinse

Check the Web for Updates

To check for updates or corrections relevant to this book visit our updates page on the Web at http://www.prima-tech.com/support.

Send Us Your Comments

To comment on this book or any other PRIMA TECH title, visit our reader response page on the Web at http://www.prima-tech.com/books/book/comment.

How to Order

For information on quantity discounts, contact the publisher: Prima Publishing, P.O. Box 1260BK, Rocklin, CA 95677-1260; (916) 787-7000. On your letterhead, include information concerning the intended use of the books and the number of books you want to purchase.

To my husband Steve, who's a Mac guy from way back, and to my dog Bo, who keeps my feet warm while I work.

Acknowledgments

Everyone involved with this project deserves a round of thanks for once again maintaining the high standards that yield a great book. In addition to that general "thank you," I would like to specifically thank publisher Stacy Hiquet and acquisitions editors Jawahara Saidullah and Kevin Harreld for offering me the opportunity to work with and write about this exciting new operating system from Apple. Project editor and technical reviewer Brian Thomasson worked hard to kick the project off on a good foot and keep it rolling to the end, working with a team of Prima folks to bring the final book together. Finally, thanks to the unsung heroes from Prima who handle such tasks as proofreading, indexing, and page layout; these people play a key role in bringing you an attractive and readable text.

About the Author

An author and publishing consultant, Lisa A. Bucki has been involved in the computer book business for more than 10 years. She wrote *Photoshop 6 for Windows Fast & Easy, Photoshop 6 for Mac Fast & Easy, Get Your Family Online with AOL 5.0 In a Weekend,* and *Managing with Microsoft Project 2000* for Prima Tech. She wrote *PCs 6-in-1, Easy Quicken Deluxe 99* and *Easy Quicken Deluxe 2000, Easy Works Suite 2000, Sams Teach Yourself Works Suite 99 in 24 Hours, Easy Microsoft Home Essentials 98,* and *Que's Guide to WordPerfect Presentations 3.0 for Windows* for Que and Sams, divisions of Macmillan Computer Publishing. She wrote *Learning Computer Applications: Projects and Exercises* and three other books for education publisher DDC, and *Excel 97 Power Toolkit* for Ventana. She also was the lead author for the *SmartSuite Millennium Edition Bible* (IDG Books Worldwide). For Que, she was a contributing author for *Special Edition Using Microsoft Office 97, Special Edition Using SmartSuite 97, The Big Basics Book of PCs* (both editions) and the *The Big Basics Book of Excel for Windows 95.* For Alpha Books, a former Macmillan imprint, she wrote the *10 Minute Guide to Harvard Graphics,* the *10 Minute Guide to Harvard Graphics for Windows,* and the *One Minute Reference to Windows 3.1.* Bucki has written Web-based tutorials covering Windows Me, Windows CE 2.11, Microsoft Works Suite 2000, Microsoft PhotoDraw 2000, and Microsoft MapPoint 2001. She has contributed chapters dealing with online communications, presentation graphics, multimedia, and numerous computer subjects for other books, as well as spearheading or developing more than 100 computer and trade titles during her association with Macmillan. For Que Education & Training, Bucki created the Virtual Tutor CD-ROM companions for the *Essentials* series of books. Bucki currently also serves as a consultant and trainer in the Asheville, NC area.

Contents at a Glance

PART I
MEET AQUA...**1**

Chapter 1 Getting Started with Mac OS X 3

Chapter 2 Working with Menus and Dialog Boxes 11

Chapter 3 Working with Finder (and Other) Windows 25

Chapter 4 Working with Folders and Files 43

Chapter 5 Getting Help When You Need It 73

PART II
WORKING WITH APPLICATIONS **83**

Chapter 6 Using the Dock and Applications 85

Chapter 7 Working in the Classic (Mac OS 9) Environment 99

PART III
CUSTOMIZING MAC OS X **111**

Chapter 8 Setting up the Desktop 113

Chapter 9 Changing Essential System Preferences 127

Chapter 10 Working with Printers 151

PART IV
JUMPING ONLINE 169

Chapter 11 Setting up the Connection 171

Chapter 12 Corresponding with Mail 183

Chapter 13 Traveling the Web 205

Chapter 14 Snooping for Content with Sherlock 225

Chapter 15 Downloading and Installing Software 235

PART V
BECOMING A MULTIMEDIA MASTER 249

Chapter 16 Jamming with iTunes 251

Chapter 17 Using QuickTime Player 269

Chapter 18 Working with Other Features 287

PART VI
BASIC MAINTENANCE
AND TROUBLESHOOTING 315

Chapter 19 Emergency Startup Measures 317

Chapter 20 Tackling Disk Issues 327

Chapter 21 Managing Users 337

Appendix Installation Notes 351

Contents

Introduction xv

PART I
MEET AQUA 1

Chapter 1 **Getting Started with Mac OS X** 3

Starting up 4
Looking at the New Desktop 4
Reviewing Mac OS X Features 6
Putting the Mac to Sleep and Waking It up 8
Shutting Down 9
 Using a Menu to Shut Down 9
 Using the Power Button to Shut Down 10

Chapter 2 **Working with Menus and Dialog Boxes** 11

Reviewing the Desktop Menus 12
Choosing a Menu Command 16
 Identifying Special Commands in Menus 18
 Using a Keyboard Shortcut To Choose a Command 19
Using a Contextual Menu 20
Responding to a Dialog Box 22

Chapter 3 **Working with Finder (and Other) Windows** 25

Understanding the Parts of a Window 26
Opening Another Finder Window 27
Choosing a Window 29

Using the Finder Window Toolbar 30

Changing a Finder Window View 33

Manipulating Windows 36

Moving a Window 36

Resizing a Window 37

Scrolling a Window 38

Minimizing and Expanding a Window............................. 39

Closing a Window 41

Chapter 4   Working with Folders and Files 43

Understanding Home Folders 44

Using Folders 46

Navigating to a Disk or Folder 46

Creating a Folder 50

Moving a Folder 51

Using Files 54

Opening a File 54

Duplicating and Moving a File 55

Working with the Trash 58

Trashing a File or Folder 58

Retrieving a File or Folder 59

Emptying the Trash 61

Showing Disk, File, or Folder Information 62

Renaming a File or Folder 66

Using Aliases 68

Creating an Alias for a File or Folder 68

Adding a File or Folder to Your Favorites 70

Chapter 5   Getting Help When You Need It 73

Starting Help Viewer 74

Starting Help Viewer from the Desktop 74

Starting Help Viewer from an Application 75

Starting Help Viewer from a Dialog Box or Dialog.......... 75

Browsing Help 76

Searching Help 78

Quitting Help Viewer 80

Part I Review Questions *82*

PART II
WORKING WITH APPLICATIONS 83

Chapter 6   **Using the Dock and Applications 85**

Starting an Application from the Dock 86

Switching to an Application Using the Dock 87

Saving a File in an Application 88

Setting Application Preferences 91

Hiding and Redisplaying an Application 92

Minimizing and Expanding Documents and Finder Windows 94

Quitting an Application 95

Forcing an Application to Quit 96

Redisplaying the Desktop 98

Chapter 7   **Working in the Classic (Mac OS 9) Environment 99**

Starting the Classic Environment 100

Starting and Quitting a Classic Application 102

Adjusting Classic Preferences (Advanced Settings) 104

Closing the Classic Environment 107

Part II Review Questions 109

PART III
CUSTOMIZING MAC OS X 111

Chapter 8   **Setting up the Desktop 113**

Changing Disk and Finder Settings 114

Changing Dock Settings 117

Adding and Removing Dock Icons 120

     Adding a Folder Icon and Viewing Its Contents 122

     Adding Dock Extras to the Dock 123

Changing the Clock Appearance 125

Chapter 9   **Changing Essential System Preferences 127**

Displaying System Preferences 128

     Displaying a Preferences Pane 128

     Unlocking and Locking a Preferences Pane 130

     Redisplaying All the Preferences 132

Reviewing Key System Preferences 133

Setting Date & Time Preferences 133
Setting Displays Preferences 135
Setting Energy Saver Preferences 137
Setting General Preferences 138
Setting International Preferences 140
Setting Keyboard Preferences 142
Setting Mouse Preferences 143
Setting Screen Saver Preferences 145
Setting Software Update Preferences 147
Setting Sound Preferences 148
Setting Speech Preferences 149

Chapter 10 Working with Printers 151
Setting up a Printer from the Print Center 153
Selecting a Printer and Printing 157
Choosing the Default Printer 162
Removing a Printer 164
Part III Review Questions *167*

**PART IV
JUMPING ONLINE 169**

Chapter 11 Setting up the Connection 171
Setting Internet Preferences 172
Creating a Connection with Internet Connect 175
Connecting to and Disconnecting from the Internet 179

Chapter 12 Corresponding with Mail 183
Starting and Exiting Mail 184
Changing Mail Settings 186
Sending Mail 191
Checking Mail 195
Reading and Responding
to a Message 197
Working with Address Book 199
  Starting and Quitting Address Book 199
  Adding a Contact 201
  Addressing a Message to a Contact 204

Chapter 13 **Traveling the Web** **205**

Starting and Exiting Internet Explorer 206

Navigating Online 209

Following a Link 210

Entering a URL 212

Backing up and Going Forward 213

Working with Favorites 214

Marking a Page as a Favorite 214

Organizing Your Favorites 215

Going to a Favorite Page 218

Performing a Basic Web Search 220

Downloading Files 221

Chapter 14 **Snooping for Content with Sherlock** **225**

Starting and Exiting Sherlock 226

Finding a File on Your System 227

Finding Web Pages about a Topic 230

Locating a Person Online 232

Searching for News 233

Chapter 15 **Downloading and Installing Software** **235**

Downloading Applications 236

Unstuffing Files 238

Running an Install Program 239

Using Software Update 242

Part IV Review Questions 247

PART V
BECOMING A MULTIMEDIA MASTER 249

Chapter 16 **Jamming with iTunes** **251**

Downloading and Installing iTunes 252

Starting and Exiting iTunes 257

Playing a CD 259

Making MP3s and Adding Them to Your Library 261

Building and Playing an MP3 Playlist 263

Playing an Internet Radio Stream 265

Pausing and Muting Playback 267

Chapter 17 Using QuickTime Player **269**

Starting and Exiting QuickTime 270

Opening and Closing a Movie File 271

Controlling Movie File Playback 274

Viewing a Movie from the Web 275

Viewing a QTV Channel 277

Adding a Favorite QTV Channel 279

Setting QuickTime Preferences 282

Chapter 18 Working with Other Features **287**

Creating and Deleting a Stickie 288

Starting and Quitting a Chess Game 291

Performing a Calculation 293

Creating an RTF (Text) File 295

Shooting a Picture of Your Screen 300

Viewing a Graphic or PDF File 303

Adding a Picture to a Text File 305

Creating a Basic PDF File 308

Working with Speakable Items 311

Part V Review Questions *314*

PART VI
BASIC MAINTENANCE
AND TROUBLESHOOTING 315

Chapter 19 Emergency Startup Measures **317**

Restarting the System 318

Starting up from a CD-ROM 319

Changing the Startup Disk 320

Changing to a Mac OS 9.1 Disk 320

Changing Back to a Mac OS X Disk 322

Rebuilding the Classic Desktop 325

Chapter 20 Tackling Disk Issues **327**

Starting and Exiting Disk Utility 328

Verifying a Disk 331

Repairing a Disk 333

Erasing a Disk 334

Chapter 21   **Managing Users** **337**

Setting up Multiple Users 338

Adding a User 339

Deleting a User 341

Updating a Password or Administration Privileges 343

Working with Keychain Access 344

Setting up Automatic Login 347

Part VI Review Questions *350*

Appendix   **Installation Notes** **351**

Considering Installation Options 352

Completing the Mac OS Setup Assistant 353

Glossary **355**

Index **361**

Introduction

This *Fast & Easy* guide from Prima Tech will introduce you to the new and innovative operating system from Apple—Mac OS X. This book will show you how to master the many and diverse features built into the Mac OS X operating system, so you can work effectively with your Macintosh.

Mac OS X Fast & Easy teaches the steps that will enable you to navigate the Mac OS X interface (called the Aqua interface), manage your files and disks, customize your Mac, surf the Web, handle your e-mail, and more. You also will learn how to work with multimedia features, enjoy your music files, and recover from common emergencies.

If you want to get the most from your Macintosh, Mac OS X and this book provide everything you need.

Who Should Read This Book?

This book is geared for novices who are new to Mac OS X, including first-time Macintosh users. Mac OS X is a brand new, next-generation operating system, offering hundreds of features users must learn to work effectively. Because nearly every step in this book includes a clear illustration, you won't have to struggle to learn a process or find the right tool. The non-technical language also helps smooth the transition from newbie to comfortable user.

Special Features of This Book

Besides the detailed descriptions of useful tasks, this book also includes:

- **Tips**. These give shortcuts or hints so you learn more about the ins and outs of Mac OS X.

- **Notes**. These offer more detailed information about a feature.

- **Cautions**. These keep you on your toes by alerting you of potential pitfalls.

An Appendix at the end of the book covers issues to consider before installing Mac OS X. Finally, the Glossary explains key terms that you need to understand to work effectively in Mac OS X.

Whether you have used a Macintosh before or not, you'll have fun as you dive into *Mac OS X Fast & Easy*!

P A R T   I

Meet Aqua

Chapter 1
Getting Started with Mac OS X 3

Chapter 2
Working with Menus and Dialog Boxes 11

Chapter 3
**Working with Finder
(and Other) Windows** 25

Chapter 4
Working with Folders and Files 43

Chapter 5
Getting Help When You Need It 73

1

Getting Started with Mac OS X

Apple developed Mac OS X as a brand new OS (*Operating System*). Because the OS uses completely original programming code, Apple took the opportunity to also implement a complete redesign of the user interface. As a result, when you start Mac OS X you are greeted with the Aqua interface, which you use to work with programs, files, and other functions and content. In this chapter, you will learn how to:

- Start up your Macintosh.
- Recognize the parts of the Aqua interface.
- Start using the programs, utilities, and features included in Mac OS X.
- Work with the sleep feature.
- Shut the system down.

Starting up

Macintosh systems have historically offered an easy startup process. Press a button on the keyboard or system; the happy Mac makes its appearance; and then the OS finishes loading. With Mac OS X, the process works just about the same.

1. **Press** the **Power button** (sometimes found near the upper-right corner of the keyboard) to start up the Macintosh. The system will power up, and the Aqua desktop will appear.

Looking at the New Desktop

Aqua provides a new look and feel with functionality similar to previous Macintosh operating systems. Later chapters will review the specifics of working with various features of the Aqua interface. Here, take a first glimpse at the new features:

- **Desktop**. The entire screen area, which holds the features of the OS, is the *desktop*. The program and file windows with which you will work appear on the desktop. You also can store files, post notes called *Stickies*, and even add a custom picture to change the appearance of the desktop.

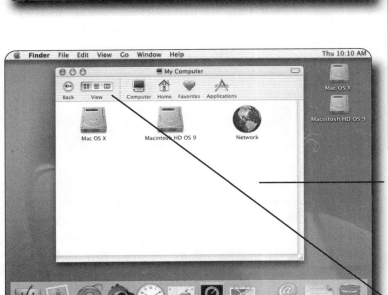

- **Menu bar**. The *menu bar* at the top of the screen holds pull-down menus. When you're working with the desktop, the menu bar shows the Finder application menus. When you later open or switch to another application (program), the menu bar changes to display the menus for that application.

NOTE

Many menu commands have keyboard shortcuts. Chapter 2, "Working with Menus and Dialog Boxes" will teach you more about using both the mouse and the keyboard to work with menus.

- **Finder window**. The *Finder* enables you to work with the folders and files on the system's hard disk and any other disks connected to the system.

- **Finder window toolbar**. The buttons at the top of the Finder window form a *toolbar* that you can use to navigate quickly to key folders and locations on the system's hard disk, and change the way you view files and folders in the Finder.

- **Dock**. Perhaps the most significant new feature of Aqua is the *Dock* along the bottom of the screen. You can use the icons on the left section of the Dock (to the left of the dividing line) to start programs and switch between running programs. The icons on the right section of the Dock represent minimized document files; document or server shortcuts that you can click to open or go to the document or server; and the Trash, which you use to delete files and eject disks.

Reviewing Mac OS X Features

Mac OS X offers a wide variety of programs, utilities, and features that you can use to perform tasks and set up the system as you prefer. Again, you'll learn more about many of these features in later chapters throughout the book. The following table summarizes the basic programs, utilities, and features you're most likely to use for now. (As you work further in Mac OS X, you'll discover even more!)

NOTE

Mac OS X is the default name for the system's hard disk. (The following table references disk locations.) In earlier OS versions, the hard disk was generally named Macintosh HD by default.

Name	Location	Description
Finder	Dock	Use this icon to open a new Finder window.
Mail	Dock or Mac OS X> Applications folder	This brand new application enables you to manage your e-mail.
Internet Explorer	Dock or Mac OS X> Applications> Internet Explorer folder	You can use the latest version of this leading Web browser to view pages of information from the World Wide Web.
Sherlock	Dock or Mac OS X> Applications folder	Sherlock enables you to search for files on your system or to find information from the World Wide Web.
System Preferences	Dock or Mac OS X> Applications folder	System Preferences enables you to choose many aspects of how Mac OS X looks and works.
QuickTime Player	Dock or Mac OS X> Applications folder	Use this application to view QuickTime movies (digital video) and to work with still images.
Address Book	Mac OS X> Applications folder	Track and update your list of contacts in the Address Book.
Calculator	Mac OS X> Applications folder	Check your math with this application.
Internet Connect	Mac OS X> Applications folder	This application enables you to set up a dial-up connection to use for the Internet.
Preview	Mac OS X> Applications folder	You can use this viewer to open and print graphics and .PDF (Adobe Acrobat) files.
Stickies	Mac OS X> Applications folder	Use this application to create electronic "sticky notes" that you can place on your desktop to remind yourself of important tasks or items.
TextEdit	Mac OS X> Applications folder	This basic word processing program enables you to create, save, and edit .RTF (text) files.
Chess	Mac OS X> Applications folder	Play chess against your Mac using the Chess application.
Image Capture	Mac OS X> Applications folder	You can use Image Capture to download images from a compatible digital camera to your Mac.
Disk Utility	Mac OS X> Applications> Utilities folder	This utility helps you to format and repair disks.
Grab	Mac OS X> Applications> Utilities folder	If you need take picture of your screen , you can use this utility to do so.
Keychain Access	Mac OS X> Applications> Utilities folder	Enhance system security using this utility.
Multiple Users	Mac OS X> Applications> Utilities folder	Manage user access to the system with this utility.
Print Center	Mac OS X> Applications> Utilities folder	Use this utility to set up and manage printers to work with Mac OS X.
Stuffit Expander	Mac OS X> Applications> Utilities folder	Use this utility to expand a compressed file.

Putting the Mac to Sleep and Waking It up

The *sleep* feature enables your Mac to conserve power when it's not in use. After a designated time of inactivity (5 minutes at a minimum in Mac OS X), the hard disk and monitor will go into the power-conserving sleep mode. You also can put the system to sleep at will, such as when you need to be away from your desk for a designated period of time. Using sleep mode creates less wear and tear on the system than repetitively turning the system off and on. That's because sleep mode keeps a small supply of power flowing to system components, so that they stay warm and can ramp up more smoothly when the system leaves sleep mode. In contrast, starting the system zaps a higher amount of electricity to the system all at once, taxing the components.

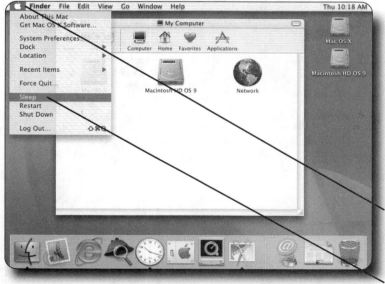

NOTE

To *click* with the mouse, move the mouse on your desk until the mouse pointer moves over the desired item on-screen. Then press and release the button on the mouse.

1. **Click** on the **Apple icon** on the menu bar. The Apple menu will appear.

2. **Click** on **Sleep**. The screen will turn black as the system goes to sleep.

3. Press any **key**. The Mac will wake up, and the desktop will reappear.

Shutting Down

When you have finished working with your Mac, you need to close any open applications and the OS and then power down the system. This ensures a safe shutdown that won't in any way damage the system hardware.

Using a Menu to Shut Down

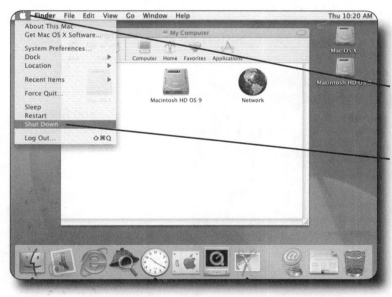

You can use a menu command to shut down your Macintosh.

1. Click on the **Apple icon** on the menu bar. The Apple menu will appear.

2. Click on **Shut Down**. The desktop will disappear from the screen and the system will shut down.

NOTE

If you forgot to save any document or file on which you were working before choosing the Shut Down command, a dialog box appears to remind you to save your work. You can click on Save to display a Save As dialog box (if needed) so that you can save the file or click on Don't Save to continue shutting down without saving your work.

Using the Power Button to Shut Down

If you prefer a single button approach to shutting down the system, you can use the Power button on your Macintosh.

1. **Press** the **Power button**. An alert box will open that prompts you to verify the system shut down.

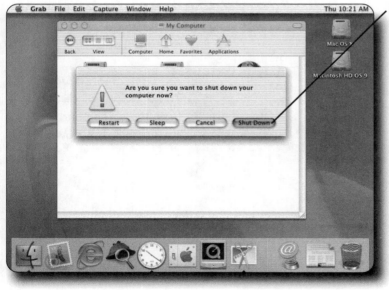

2. **Click** on **Shut Down**. The desktop will disappear from the screen and the system will shut down.

2

Working with Menus and Dialog Boxes

Early Apple computers shook up the computer industry by adding a new input device called a mouse. With the mouse and the graphical user interface created for the Apple systems, users no longer had to remember arcane commands or tricky keyboard combinations. The mouse made selecting a command almost as easy as moving a finger. In this chapter, you will learn how to:

- Recognize the Finder pull-down menus.
- Choose a menu command.
- Use a contextual menu when you need it.
- Work with dialog box choices.

Reviewing the Desktop Menus

Virtually every current computer program accepts your instructions via pull-down menus. Like other programs, the Finder offers a series of pull-down menus which are found on the menu bar that spans the top of the desktop. When you click on the name of a pull-down menu on the menu bar, the menu appears, listing its commands.

NOTE

If you've used a prior Macintosh operating system, you may be tempted to skip over this introduction to the Mac OS X menus. However, the menus have changed substantially in Mac OS X, so you should pause to review this section.

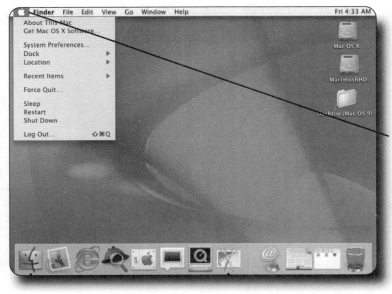

Learning the menus available via the Finder menu bar in Mac OS X is a good starting point for learning your way around Mac OS X.

- The **Apple menu** enables you to review basic information about your Mac, log out, shut down, restart, and put your Macintosh to sleep. The Apple menu remains the same regardless of which application you are using.

• The **Finder menu** enables you to hide the any open Finder windows or hide any other windows that may be open. You can also change the picture on your desktop and empty your Trash using the commands available on the Finder menu.

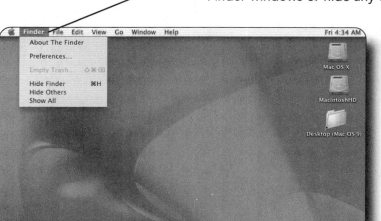

• The **File menu** enables you to work with files and includes file management tools. For example, you can open another Finder window, create a folder, open a selected file or folder, close the current window, view file information, trash and duplicate files, mark a favorite file, or find files.

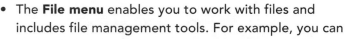

• The **Edit menu** enables you to work with the contents of a folder. You can cut, copy, and paste file and folder name information; select all the icons in a folder; and even undo your mistakes!

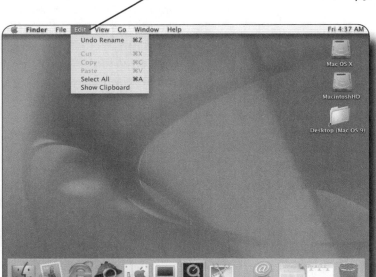

• The **View menu** enables you to change the way files and folders are listed in a window. In addition, you can arrange window contents, show and hide a Finder window toolbar, or even display the options for changing overall view settings.

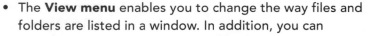

● The **Go menu** helps you navigate more quickly in Mac OS X. You can open a specific folder in a Finder window, display a default Finder window such as your Home folder, jump to a favorite or recently used folder, or connect to a network server.

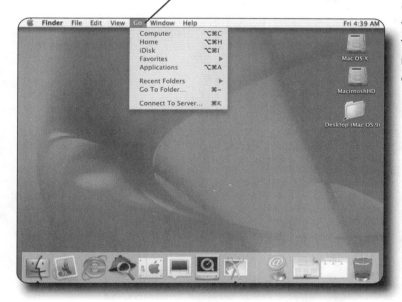

● The **Window menu** enables you to reduce a window to an icon on the Dock or switch to a particular window.

• Use the **Help menu** to launch Help Viewer and get Mac OS X help.

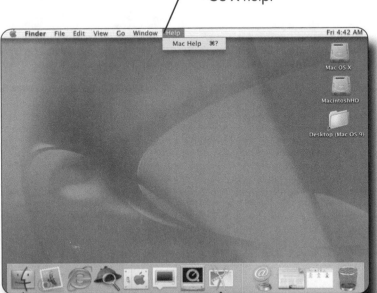

Choosing a Menu Command

Using the mouse to choose a command is a rather simple operation. Further, knowing the ins and outs of working with menus makes you much more efficient in working with Mac OS X. The techniques described in this section apply not only to menus in Mac OS X, but also to Mac applications with which you'll be working.

1. Click on the **menu name** on the menu bar. The menu will open.

TIP

With a menu already open, press the left or right arrow keys to move to and open another menu instead.

2. **Drag** the **mouse pointer down** the menu to the command you wish. The command will be highlighted. To *drag* with the mouse, press and hold the mouse button, then move the mouse on your desk until the mouse pointer moves over the desired item or the desired items are selected.

3. **Click** on the **command** to select it. The command will be activated.

TIP

If you press and hold the Option key while the File or Window menu is open, a command on the menu changes. On the File menu, the Close Window command changes to the Close All command. On the Window menu, the Bring All to Front command changes to the Arrange in Front command. Once you display an alternate command by pressing Option, you can click on that command to choose it.

Identifying Special Commands in Menus

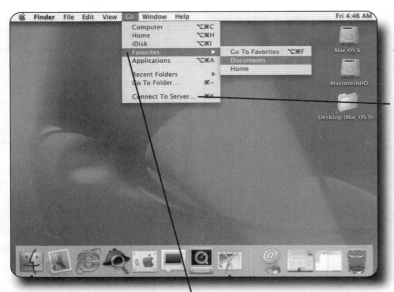

Mac OS X makes it easy to recognize special commands that are available from pull-down menus.

- A command that has an ellipsis (...) following its name, will open a dialog box to ask you for more information. See the section "Responding to a Dialog Box" later in this chapter to learn more about working with dialog boxes.

- A command that has an arrow to the far right of its name will display a submenu with additional commands when you highlight it. Drag the mouse pointer down the submenu to highlight the desired command, then click on the command name.

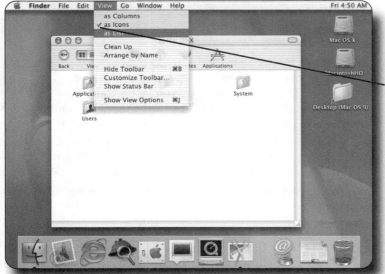

- A command that has a check to the left of its name is the currently selected choice among a group of related choices. Click on another choice in the group to choose it instead.

> ### NOTE
> Click away from the menu on the desktop or press the Escape (Esc) key to close or cancel a menu without making a selection.

Using a Keyboard Shortcut To Choose a Command

Using a keyboard shortcut saves time because you don't have to complete multiple steps—clicking on a menu and then clicking on a command. Plus, if you're typing in a document, it's generally faster to keep your hands on the keyboard and use a shortcut key combination rather than taking a hand off the keyboard to grab the mouse.

To learn a shortcut key for a particular command, look at the command on its menu. If a shortcut key combination is available for a command, "shorthand" characters to the right of the command name tell you what keys to press as the shortcut. For a command to work, you need to press all the keys together. Usually, it's easier to press and hold the first key, or press and hold any others, and then release them all.(This book uses a + symbol between the keys to press when it presents a shortcut key combination.) Following are the characters you'll see on the menu to represent special keyboard keys:

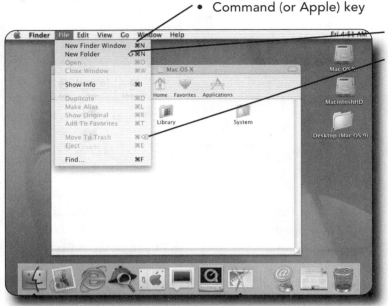

• Command (or Apple) key

• Shift key

• Delete key

You also may need to choose the tilde (~) key by pressing Shift+' on the keyboard. Finally, some keyboard combinations may call for the Control key or Option key.

Using a Contextual Menu

A *contextual menu* offers commands for dealing with a particular selection or item. Because the contextual menu applies to only the selected command or location, it displays a more limited range of commands that pertain specifically to that selection or location. This means you can more quickly identify and choose the appropriate command to use. In Mac OS X, you'll use contextual menus often for working with files and folders in a Finder window, or for working with items on the desktop. (You also can display a contextual menu within an application or file to see commands for working with the current selection.)

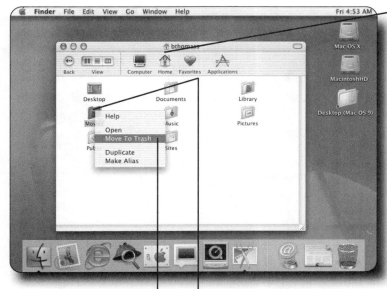

1. Click on the **Home button** on the Finder window toolbar. The Finder window will display the contents of your Home folder—the folder set up for your files in Mac OS X. This folder already contains a number of predefined folders for you.

2. Press and hold the **Control key**. The mouse pointer will change to include a small menu icon.

3. Click on the **Movies folder**. The contextual menu will appear.

NOTE

Of course, when you're displaying a contextual menu on your own, you'd Control+click on the appropriate location or selection, such as the desktop.

---

4. Move the **mouse pointer down** the contextual menu to highlight the command you wish to perform.

You can click on the Computer button on the toolbar to return to the original contents of the Finder window.

Responding to a Dialog Box

Remember that if a command on a menu includes an ellipsis (...), selecting the command opens a dialog box so that you can provide further information about how the command should work. Dialog boxes include a number of different types of options.

- **Text box**. A text box or entry box enables you to type in and edit an entry, such as a file name. Click in the text box and type an entry as needed. Or, select the contents of the text box by dragging over the existing entry, and type a new entry to replace the previous entry.

- **Pop-up menu**. Click on the double-arrow button to display a pop-up menu, then click on the desired choice in the menu.

- **Check box**. Click on a check box to check (enable) it or uncheck (disable) it.

- **Slider control**. Drag the slider on the slider control to change a setting.

- **Option button**. Option buttons appear in groups. Only one button in the group can be selected at any time. To choose another option button in the group, click on it.

- **Command button**. Click on a command button to display another dialog box (if an ellipsis follows the button name) or to continue with the dialog box choices. Many dialog boxes include Cancel and OK command buttons. Click on Cancel to close the dialog box without applying its choices or executing the command. Click on OK to finish the command, apply the dialog box choices, and close the dialog box.

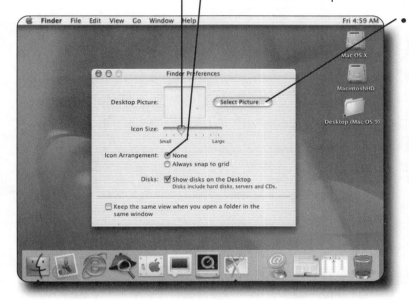

NOTE

Some dialog boxes in Mac OS X actually work as windows that you can resize and close. If this is the case, you'll see special red, yellow, and green buttons in the upper-left corner of the window. Chapter 3, "Working with Finder Windows," describes the techniques for using these buttons. Also note that some dialog boxes include a question mark or Help button on which you can click to display help about the dialog box choices.

3

Working with Finder (and Other) Windows

As in prior Macintosh operating systems, *windows* on the Mac OS X desktop hold applications, files (documents), and folders. You perform all your work within windows. The use of windows also provides an elegant solution to the need to work on multiple tasks at (nearly) the same time. You can move seamlessly between windows and tasks to handle your work in the order you prefer. This chapter builds your Mac OS X skills by leading you through a number of window management tasks. In this chapter, you will learn to:

- Identify the parts of a window.
- Display another Finder window when needed.
- Choose the window in which you want to work.
- Navigate in a Finder window and change the view.
- Move, resize, minimize, or close a window.

Understanding the Parts of a Window

As you learned in Chapter 1, the Finder enables you to work with the folders and files on the system's hard disk and any other disks connected to the system. To understand how to work with a Finder window, you need to understand the parts of a window in Mac OS X.

Many of the features described here appear in Finder windows only. However, some of the features in this list also appear in application and file (document) windows.

- **Title bar**. The title bar displays the name of the folder, application or document in the window. You also can use the title bar to position the window.

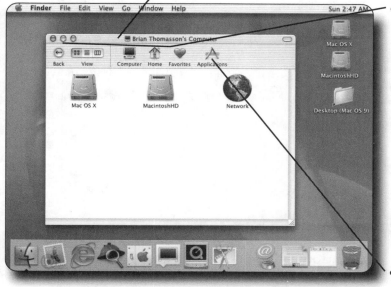

- **Close, minimize, and zoom buttons**. These buttons appear in the upper-left corner of Finder windows, application windows, document windows, and some dialog boxes. You can click on the buttons to manipulate the window, such as reducing the window to an icon on the Dock. Later sections of this chapter cover these buttons in more detail.

- **Finder toolbar buttons**. The buttons that form the Finder toolbar enable you to more quickly navigate to particular folders in Mac OS X. The section later in this chapter called "Using the Finder Window Toolbar" explains the destination for each of these buttons.

• **Back button**. Once you've used a Finder toolbar button or another method to display the contents of a particular folder in the Finder window, you can click on this button to return to a previous location or folder with which you were working.

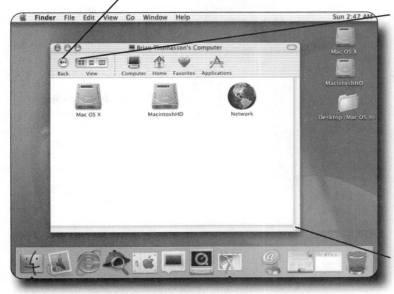

• **View buttons**. By default, the Finder window contents appear in a large icon format. You can click on one of these buttons to change to another of the new views available in Mac OS X. See the section called "Changing a Finder Window View" later in this chapter to learn how the view buttons work.

• **Size box**. You can use the size box to change the size of the window, as described in the later section "Resizing a Window."

Opening Another Finder Window

In older Macintosh operating systems, each folder appeared in its own window. By contrast, Mac OS X enables you to navigate to a particular location within a single Finder window. As you make your way through various folders, the contents of the current Finder window simply change. This streamlined approach helps reduce clutter on the desktop, making it easier for you to select a particular window.

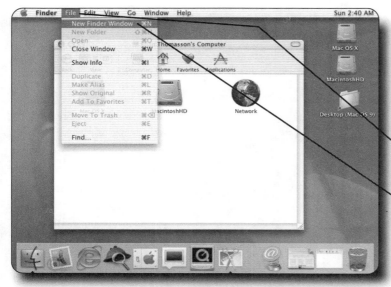

On the other hand, there will be instances where you need to see multiple Finder windows, such as when you want to move a file from one folder to another.

1. **Click** on **File**. The File menu will appear.

2. **Click** on **New Finder Window**.

An additional Finder window will open.

NOTE

When the toolbar is visible, Command+ double-click on an icon to open a new window for the disk or folder. When the toolbar does not appear, simply double-click on the icon.

Choosing a Window

Before you can work with the files or folders in a window, you must make it the active window on your desktop. An *active window* is the frontmost window among all the windows on your desktop. Any command or action you next take will apply to the contents of the active window. There are several ways to move between open windows.

1. **Click** on **Window**. The Window menu will appear.

2a. **Click** on the **name of the window** to display. The window will move in front of (on top of) other open windows.

OR

2b. **Click** on a **visible portion** of the **window** you want to choose.

The window will move in front of (on top of) other open windows.

TIP

Most application menu bars also include a Window menu that you can use to choose the window for an open document (file).

Using the Finder Window Toolbar

Mac OS X organizes a great deal of information for you in specific folders. For example, for each user (user name) set up for the system, Mac OS X creates a Home folder to hold that user's working files. Clicking on one of the buttons on a Finder window toolbar displays the contents of one of those specially-designated folders or locations.

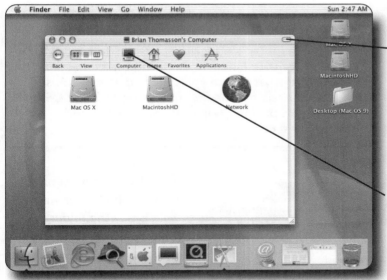

TIP

If you don't see the Finder window toolbar, choose View, Show Toolbar or click on the oblong button in the upper-right corner of the Finder window.

1. Click on the **Computer button**. The Finder window will display the disk drives (both internal and removable) connected to your system, as well as a Network choice you can use to view and connect with network servers.

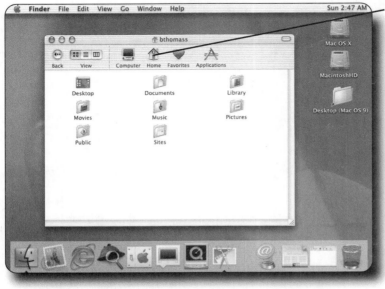

2. Click on the **Home button**. The Finder window will display the contents of the Home folder set up for your user name. By default, the Home folder contains additional folders for your documents, pictures, movies, and more.

TIP

Your Home folder is not called "Home." Instead, Mac OS X names your Home folder using the first eight letters of the user name you specified when you used the Setup Assistant the first time you used Mac OS X or the Users pane of System Preferences to add yourself as a user.

3. Click on the **Favorites button**. The Finder window will display the folder holding *aliases* you can use to jump quickly to additional folders that you often use. Chapter 4 includes a section called "Adding a File or Folder to Your Favorites" to show you how to work with your Favorites.

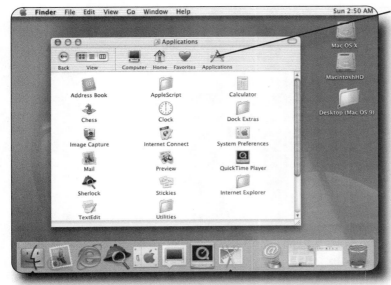

4. Click on the **Applicatons button**. The Finder window will display the Applications folder contents. The Applications folder holds the applications that come with Mac OS X, as well as folders containing additional utilities and tools.

TIP

You can add an icon for a particular folder to the Finder window toolbar by dragging the folder icon onto the toolbar. Drag the icon back off the toolbar to remove it at any later time.

Changing a Finder Window View

Like its predecessor Macintosh operating systems, Mac OS X by default represents disks, files, and folders as large icons within a Finder window. This default view is called the *icon view*. You can change the way a Finder window lists its contents so that you can work in the view that offers the most convenience. In addition to the icon view, you can choose the *list view*, which presents a single list of file and folder names along with brief information about the file; or the column view, which illustrates the *path* or various folders within which the currently-selected file or folder is located.

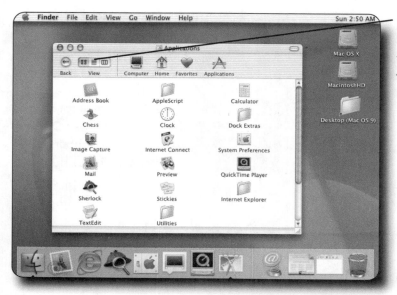

1. **Click** on the **list view button**. The Finder window will display the contents of the folder (or disk) in the list view.

2. **Click** on the **column view button**.

The Finder window displays the contents of the folder (or disk) in the column view.

3. Click on **View**. The View menu will appear.

4. Click on the **desired view**. The Finder window will display the contents of the folder (or disk) in the view you specified.

NOTE

If the commands for the various views are disabled (dimmed) on the View menu, it means that you haven't selected a Finder window. In such a case, click on the desktop to close the View menu, click on a Finder window to make it active, then choose the appropriate View menu command.

Manipulating Windows

We all like a nice, large desk so that we can organize our files and printouts into neat piles and still have a large workspace for the current task. As you switch from one task to another, typically you'll set aside one stack of paper, grab another stack, and carry on with your business. Similarly, you can work with the windows on the Mac OS X desktop to arrange them as your work needs dictate. (This is why many computer users love a large monitor, which provides a great deal of room for arranging various windows.) The remainder of this chapter reviews the various techniques you can use to work with the Finder, disk, and file windows on your Mac OS X desktop.

Moving a Window

When you move a window, you change its location. The following steps illustrate how to "make your move" with a Finder window, but the technique applies to any type of window or dialog box.

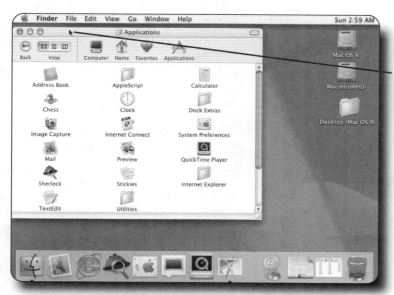

1. Point to the **window title bar**. The mouse pointer will appear on the title bar.

2. Drag the **window and release** the **mouse button** when the window reaches the desired location. The window will appear in its new location.

Resizing a Window

If you want to fit a number of windows on-screen and perhaps view their contents simultaneously, you'll probably need to resize one or more of the windows to facilitate the fit.

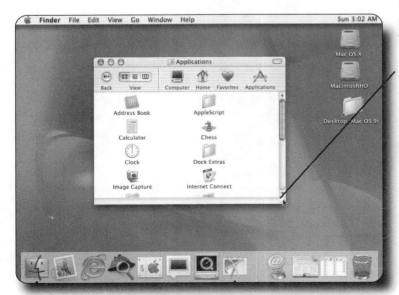

1. Drag the **size box** in any direction **and release** the **mouse button** when the window reaches the desired size and shape. The window will appear in its new shape.

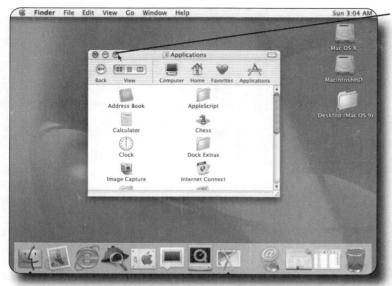

2. Click on the **maximize button** near the upper-left corner of the window. The window will snap back to its previous, larger size.

NOTE

If you're working in an application and want to have quick access to all your open Finder windows, click on the desktop to display the Finder's menus. Then click on Window and choose Bring All To Front.

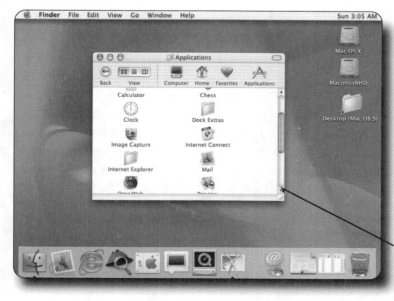

Scrolling a Window

When you make a window too small to display all of its contents, a *scroll bar* appears at the bottom, and sometimes the right side, of the window. You can use a scroll bar to view additional folder contents.

1. Click on the **scroll arrow** at either end of the scroll bar. The window contents will scroll slightly in the direction of the arrow each time you click.

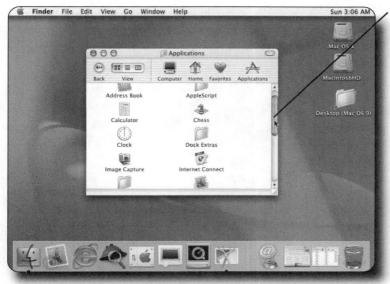

2. Drag the **scroller** on a scroll bar in the desired direction. The window contents will scroll more quickly in the direction in which you drag.

TIP

You can press and hold the Option button then drag within a window with the mouse to scroll the window's contents. When you use this technique, a gray bar appears to the left of the mouse pointer.

Minimizing and Expanding a Window

Rather than leaving multiple Finder or document windows on-screen and sizing and dragging them around, you can use the Dock as a convenient parking place for files and folders that you're not currently using but may need during the current work session. It is simple to reduce a window to an icon on the Dock (also called *minimizing* the window) and then reopen it from the Dock.

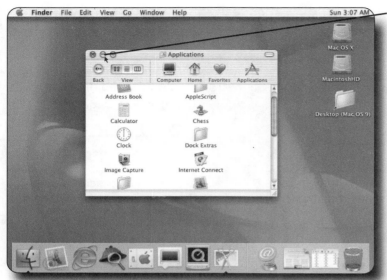

1. Click on the **minimize button** near the upper-left corner of the window. The window will reduce immediately to an icon near the right end of the Dock, to the right of the vertical dividing line on the Dock.

TIP

You also can double-click on a window's title bar or choose Minimize Window from the Window menu to reduce the active window to an icon on the Dock.

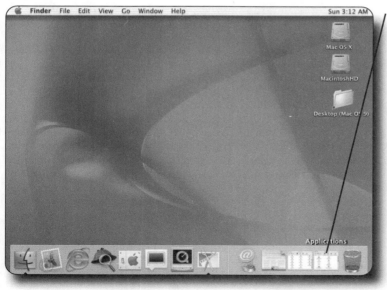

2. Double-click on the **window's icon** on the Dock. The window will reopen immediately.

TIP

Alternately, open the Window menu and click on the window name to reopen the window.

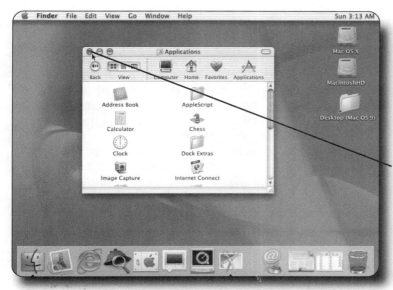

Closing a Window

Closing a window removes it from the screen altogether. There are two easy ways to close the active window on your screen.

1a. **Click** on the **close button** near the upper-left corner of the window. The window will close immediately.

OR

1b. **Click** on **File**. The File menu will appear.

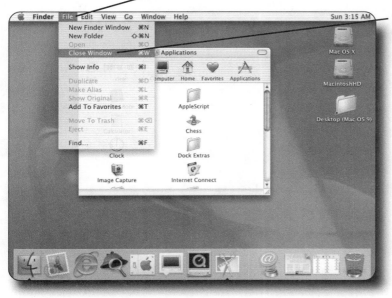

2. **Click** on **Close Window**. The active window will close immediately.

NOTE

If you're working in an application, closing a window closes the file (document) in the window. If you haven't saved any work or changes in the document, a dialog box will prompt you to do so. You can click on Save to save the file or click on Don't Save to close the document without saving it or Cancel to return to working in the document window. Closing the documents in an application does not close the application itself, however. Chapter 6, "Using the Dock and Applications," provides more details about working with applications.

4

Working with Folders and Files

Files and folders flesh out the framework of your computing organization. You must store your work in each program as a file on a disk. (Programs or applications also run from files that are stored on the Mac's hard disk.) To enable you to find files more easily when you need them, you organize the files in folders. Mac OS X conveniently sets up a few storage folders for you. If you're a beginner, you'll find this chapter particularly useful. If you have a little Mac time under your belt, this chapter will help you identify where Mac OS X differs from its predecessor operating systems in terms of file management—and there are differences. In this chapter, you'll learn how to:

- Open, make, or move a folder.
- Copy or duplicate a file.
- Throw a file in the Trash and retrieve it.
- Review file information.
- Change a file or folder name.
- Create an alias or favorite.

Understanding Home Folders

In older Macintosh operating systems, you could save your files in virtually any location on the hard disk. This made for a great deal of flexibility in organizing your files, but also created a housekeeping issue—having files and folders scattered about made it more difficult to find a file or folder when needed.

Mac OS X takes a different approach toward user files and folders, which was touched on in earlier chapters. For each user name set up under Mac OS X (and there is always at least one user by default—you), Mac OS X creates a Home folder. The Home folder, in turn, contains several folders that are organized to hold your personal files and data.

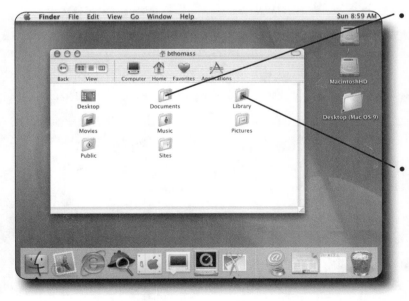

- **Documents**. Store all the documents (files) you create in this folder so that they can be found when you need them. You can create additional folders within this folder to further organize your work.

- **Library**. This folder holds several predefined folders for special uses. For example, the Desktop folder holds items you've saved to the Mac OS X desktop. The Addresses folder holds your e-mail address book information. And you'll use the Favorites folder to mark favorite files and folders that you use frequently.

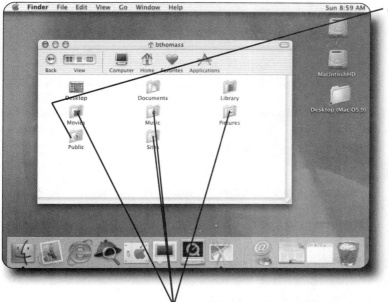

- **Public**. If your Mac is connected to a network and you enable the file sharing feature in Mac OS X, other users can copy files into this folder. This technique helps you more clearly identify files you need to handle in the near future and helps prevent others from tampering with your more vital files in the Documents folder that resides within your Home folder.

- **Movies, Music, Pictures, and Sites**. These other folders enable you to store various types of content you create, view online, or download to your Mac. Later chapters will cover these folders as they apply.

NOTE

This book doesn't cover the networking features in Mac OS X, but you can connect your Macintosh to a network rather easily. Consult the Help Viewer or the Apple Web site (http://www.apple.com) to get more help with networking your system.

Mac OS X doesn't just create your Home Folder to be your organizational helper. It actually forces you to use the Home folder. If you try to save a file or create a folder in another location on your system, such as in the root (base location) of the hard disk, an alert box appears. The error message reads "An error occurred while trying to save." What that message really means is that you don't have permission to save information in the specified location. Instead, use your Home folder or one of the folders it contains.

NOTE

Your Home folder is actually a subfolder of the Users folder in the root of the hard disk.

Using Folders

NOTE

For most of the procedures in this chapter (and the rest of the book, for that matter), you must be working at the desktop or in a Finder window. If a command doesn't work or you hear a beep and nothing happens, click on the desktop or the appropriate Finder window title bar, then try again.

Computer disks, especially hard disks and CD-ROMs, can hold thousands of files. Folders serve as containers for related files. This helps keep files organized. For example, a folder might hold all the files for a program, as well as subfolders with additional files for the program. An install routine usually sets up the folders for a program and places the program files in those folders. You can use and create other folders to hold your document files and data, separating them from the program file information.

The rest of this section describes how to manage your folders in Mac OS X. This new operating system incorporates some changes in how you work with folders, so even more experienced Mac users should take care to spin through the next few topics.

Navigating to a Disk or Folder

Every disk has a *root*, which is its base location or folder that holds all other folders on the disk. In Mac OS X, you can display the root of the hard disk by clicking on the Computer button on a Finder window toolbar, then double-clicking on the Mac OS X hard disk icon. As was noted earlier in the section titled "Understanding Home Folders," you generally cannot save information or create new folders in any location except your Home folder and its subfolders. However, you can navigate to any folder, starting from the

NOTE

You can change a preference to have the Finder open a new Finder window for each disk or folder you open. To do so, click on Finder, then click on Preferences. Click on the Keep the Same View When You Open a Folder in the Same Window check box.

root, as described here. Navigating to a folder means moving to a folder and displaying the contents in a Finder window on the desktop.

In general, double-clicking a disk icon will open the disk; double-clicking a folder icon will open the folder. In previous Mac operating system versions, a new window opened each time you double-clicked on a disk or folder icon. In Mac OS X, the process works a bit differently. After you double-click on a disk or folder icon, the current Finder window changes to display the contents of that disk or folder. In addition, you can navigate to some folders using the Go menu and back button on the Finder window, as well as the toolbar buttons, which display a particular folder when clicked.

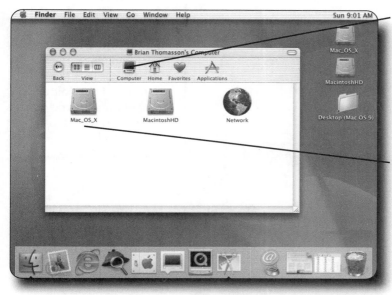

1. **Click** on the **Computer button**, if needed. The icons for your hard disk, network locations, and any other connected disk drives or inserted disks will appear in the Finder window.

2. **Double-click** on **Mac OS X**. The contents of the root of the hard disk will appear in the Finder window.

NOTE

By default, Mac OS X names your hard disk "Mac OS X." Earlier Macintosh operating systems called the hard disk "Macintosh HD" by default. If you format your hard disk in the UFS format, it will be named "/" by default.

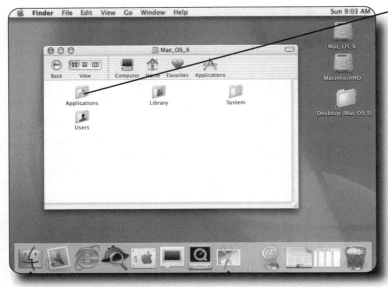

3. Double-click on the **Applications folder**. The contents of the Applications folder will appear in the Finder window. This folder holds the applications (programs) and utilities that come with Mac OS X.

NOTE

If you're working in list view, double-click on the folder in the list at the far left. If you're working in column view, double-click on the folder in the column at the far right. In column view, each column displays the contents of the folder or location selected in the column to the immediate left.

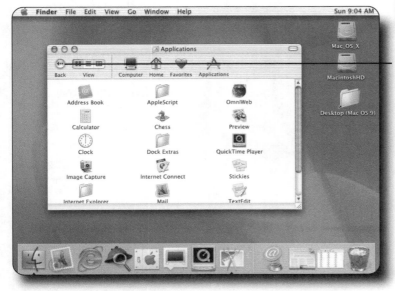

4. Click on the **back button**. The Finder window will redisplay the contents of the base location (root) of the hard disk.

TIP

You can click on the back button multiple times to continue backing up to prior folders or locations that you've displayed in the Finder window.

5. **Click** on the **Applications button**. The contents of the Applications folder will appear in the Finder window.

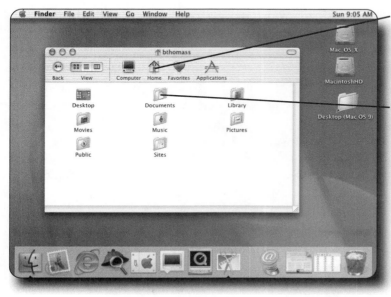

6. **Click** on the **Home button**. The contents of your Home folder will appear in the Finder window.

7. **Double-click** on the **Documents folder**. The contents of your Documents folder will appear in the Finder window.

8. Click on **Go**. The Go menu will appear that displays a list of locations to which you can navigate.

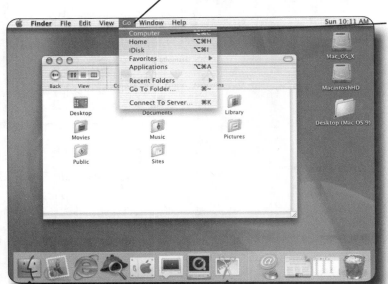

9. Click on a **folder or location** in the menu. The contents of the selected location will appear in the Finder window.

Creating a Folder

If needed, you can create your own folder within your Home folder or one of its subfolders to further organize your work. (Remember that the Mac OS X only enables you to create new folders or store files within your Home folder.) For example, you could create a folder within the Documents folder to hold the files related to each of your projects or clients.

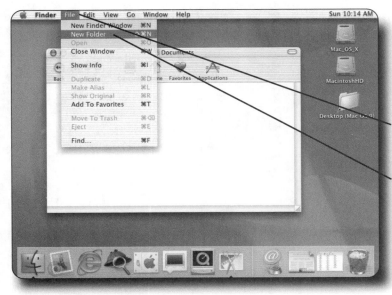

1. Open the **folder** in which you want to create a new folder. The contents of the folder will appear in the Finder window.

2. Click on **File**. The File menu will appear.

3. Click on **New Folder**. A new folder will appear, and its name will be selected so that you can enter the name of your choice.

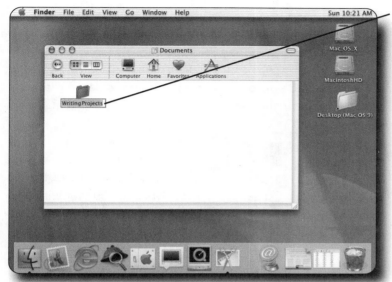

4. **Type** a **name** for the new folder **and press Return**. The name for the new folder will appear below it.

NOTE

Folder names can use spaces and capitalization, and can be more than 100 characters long even though you probably won't see the full name listed below the icon. Do not start a folder name with a period or the # sign, as doing so can create problems. In addition, it's best to avoid including a / (slash) character because some programs may have problems recognizing a folder name that includes a / character. Note that the full folder name may not display in the Finder window, which can display only a limited number of characters for folder and file names.

Moving a Folder

You may need to change a folder's location from time to time as part of maintaining your system. For example, you may want to organize several folders with information pertaining to a particular client into a new folder that is clearly identified by the client's name. Mac OS X enables you to drag a folder and its contents to a new location.

The steps used to move a folder from one location to another differ slightly depending on where the original folder and the destination folder exist.

To move a folder into another folder that resides in the same location is the easiest.

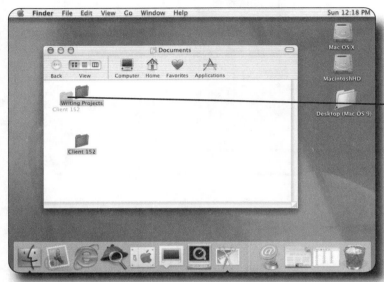

1. **Open** the **folder** containing both of the folders. You will see both folders in the Finder window.

2. **Drag** the **folder** to be moved over the destination folder, **then release** the **mouse button**. The icon for the moved folder will disappear from the current Finder display, since it is now within the destination folder.

Moving a Folder to a New Location

If the folder to be moved and the destination folder are in different locations it gets a little more complicated.

1. **Open** the **folder** in which the folder to be moved resides. You will see the subfolder displayed in the Finder window.

2. Click on **File**. The File menu will appear.

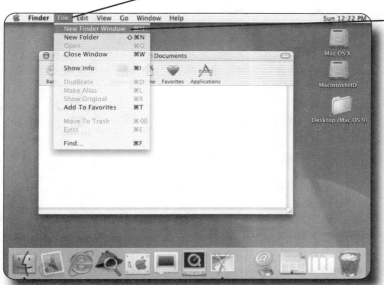

3. Click on **New Finder Window**. Another Finder window will appear.

4. Open the **folder** into which you want to move the original folder in the new Finder window.

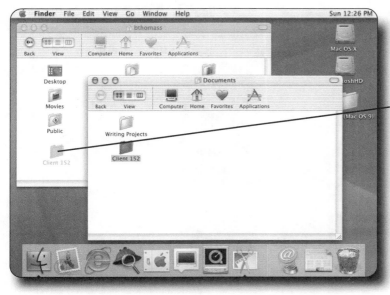

5. Move the **Finder windows** so that you can see both the folder to be moved and the destination folder.

6. Drag the **folder** over the Finder window, **then release** the **mouse button**. The moved folder will disappear from its original location and reappear in the Finder window for the destination folder.

Using Files

A *file* holds a particular document or set of data. Some files are also program files (or data files used by program files). This section covers the basics of managing your files in the Finder.

Opening a File

Mac OS X tracks the program used to create each document file. When you open a file, Mac OS X knows what application or program to launch to display the file. The program files that come with Mac OS X reside in the Applications and Utilities folders.

1. Open the **folder** in which the file you want to open exists. The folder contents will appear in the Finder window.

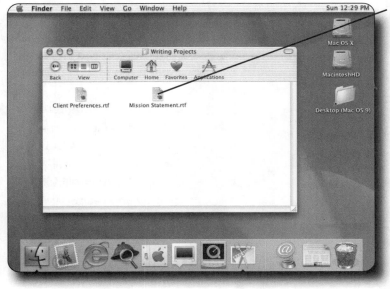

2. Double-click on the **file**. The file will open in the correct program.

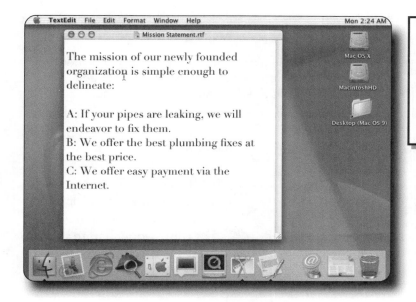

NOTE

Once the file is open, you can press Command+Q to quit the program and close the file.

Duplicating and Moving a File

Moving a file uses the same process as moving a folder. Creating a copy of a file and moving it involves only an extra step or two.

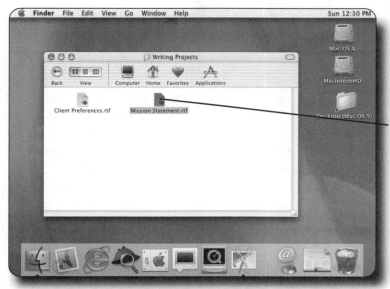

1. Open the **folder** that holds the file to be duplicated. The folder's contents will appear in the Finder window.

2. Click on the **file** to copy. The file will be selected (or highlighted).

NOTE

To select multiple files, drag over the files in a Finder window. If you want to select files that are not adjacent to one another in a list, Command+click on them.

3. Click on **File**. The File menu will appear.

4. Click on **Duplicate**. A copy of the file will appear in the folder, with the word "copy" appended to the file name. (See the later section called "Renaming a File or Folder" to learn how to rename a file copy.)

TIP

If the Duplicate command isn't active, close the menu, click on the Finder window title bar to reselect the window, then try selecting the command again.

5. Click on **File**. The File menu will appear.

6. Click on **New Finder Window**. Another Finder window will open.

7. In the new Finder window, **open** the **folder** into which you want to place the file you copied.

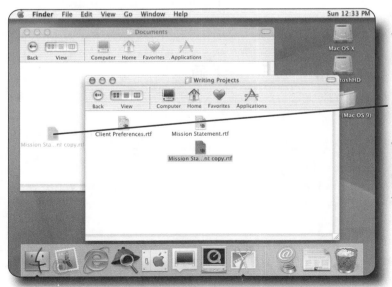

8. Move the **Finder windows** so that you can see both the file to move and its destination.

9. Drag the **copied file** over the destination folder, **then release** the **mouse button**. The copied file will appear in the Finder window for the destination folder.

> **NOTE**
>
> If you press and hold the Option key while dragging a file to a new location on the same disk, Mac OS X will create the file copy automatically and move the file copy to the destination location. If the destination location or folder is on a different disk (such as a removable disk like a Zip disk rather than the system hard disk), Mac OS X will copy any file that you drag automatically, so that you don't have to duplicate it first.

Working with the Trash

Today's computer hard disks—and even other removable types of disks—store many more files than was possible on disks even a few years ago. A Zip disk, for example, has ten times the space of the hard disks first offered in computers in the late 1980s. That being said, you should get rid of files and folders that you no longer need in order to keep your Home folder well organized. As in previous Mac operating systems, Mac OS X includes the *Trash*, which is used to delete files temporarily or permanently.

Trashing a File or Folder

> **NOTE**
>
> To eject a CD-ROM or floppy disk from the drive, drag it from the desktop to the Trash.

When you no longer need a document in your office, you wad it up and drop it in the round file. Throwing a whole folder into the wastebasket removes both the folder and its contents from your desk or filing cabinet. Similarly, dropping a computer file or folder from a Finder window into the Trash icon on the Dock removes it from action.

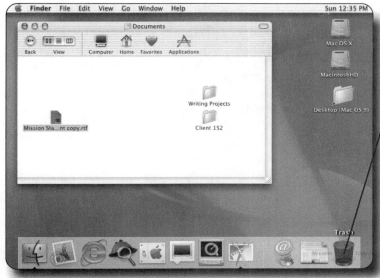

1. Open the **folder** that holds the file or folder to delete. You will see the folder's contents in the Finder window.

2. Drag the **file or folder** over the Trash icon, **then release** the **mouse button**. The file or folder will disappear from the Finder window and an image of wadded up paper will appear in the Trash icon.

NOTE

You also can press Command+Delete to delete a selected file or folder.

CAUTION

If you move a program file into the Trash, Mac OS X does not warn you in any way. Press Command+Z to undo the move immediately. If you mistakenly trash a program file and don't immediately undo the move or retrieve the file later and replace it in the correct folder, the program may not run and you may have to reinstall it.

Retrieving a File or Folder

Just as you can reach into a wastebasket and pull a file or folder back out if you've mistakenly thrown it away, you can retrieve a file or folder unless you've permanently deleted it.

1. Open the **folder** into which you want to place the deleted file. The folder's contents will appear in the Finder window.

2. Double-click on the **Trash icon**. A Finder window for the Trash will open.

3. Drag the **deleted file or folder** from the Trash Finder window to the folder you opened, **then release** the **mouse button**. The file or folder will move into the Finder window of the specified folder.

4. Click on the **close button** of the Trash Finder window. The Trash Finder window will close.

Emptying the Trash

Emptying the Trash in Mac OS X is akin to having the garbage man haul your bags away from the curb: you pass the point of no return and can no longer retrieve your files and folders. However, you do want to empty the Trash on your Mac from time to time because it does consume storage space.

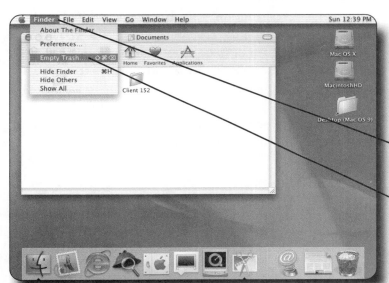

1. **Click** on **Finder**. The Finder menu will appear.

2. **Click** on **Empty Trash**. A dialog box will open to prompt you to confirm the deletion.

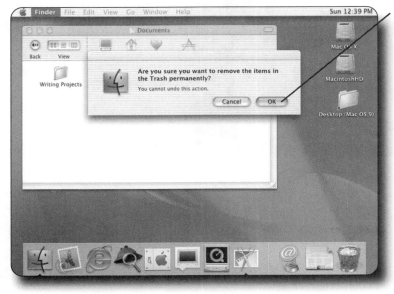

3. **Click** on **OK**. Mac OS X will empty the Trash, and the wadded up paper will disappear from the Trash icon on the Dock.

Showing Disk, File, or Folder Information

The Show Info command in Mac OS X enables you to view and change certain information about files and folders. For example, you can see the storage space occupied by the file or folder (the file or folder size). You can lock a file or folder to prevent others from making changes to it, add a comment, and more.

1. **Open** the **folder** that holds the file or folder you want to examine. You will see the folder's contents in the Finder window.

2. **Click** on the **file or folder**. The file or folder will be selected.

3. Click on **File**. The File menu will appear.

4. Click on **Show Info**. The Info dialog box showing the file information will open.

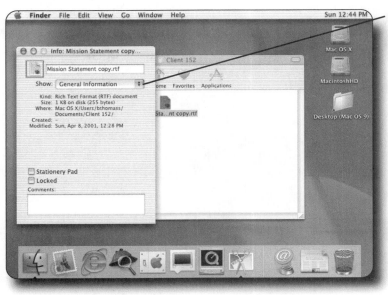

5. Click on the **Show pop-up menu**. The pop-up menu will open.

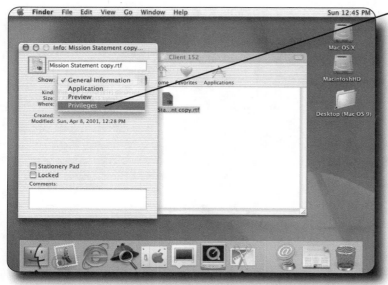

6. Click on **Privileges**. The sharing settings for the selected file or folder will appear in the Info dialog box. These settings apply if your system is connected to a network and you've enabled file sharing on your system. You can determine whether other users can make changes to the file.

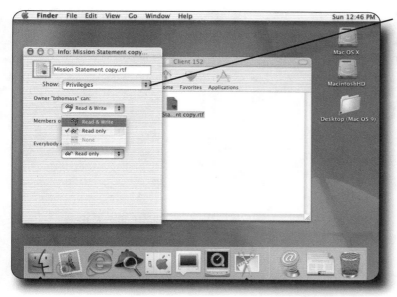

7. Click on the **Show pop-up menu**. The pop-up menu will open.

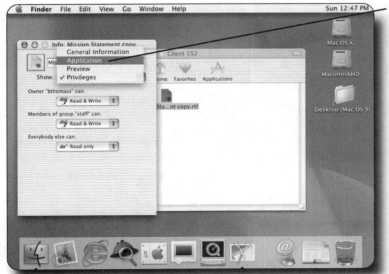

8. Click on **Application**. The application settings for the selected file will appear in the Info dialog box. These settings control which application the file will open when you double-click a file of this type in a Finder window.

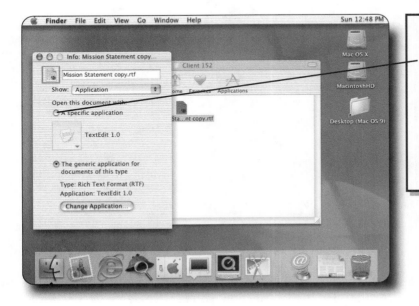

NOTE

If you select the A specific application option button, a pop-up menu appears from which you can click on the application you want to use to open files of the same type.

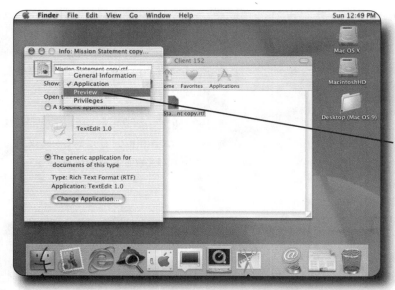

The last settings apply to files, but not folders.

9. Click on the **Show pop-up menu**. The pop-up menu will open.

10. Click on **Preview**. A preview image of the selected file will appear in the Info dialog box.

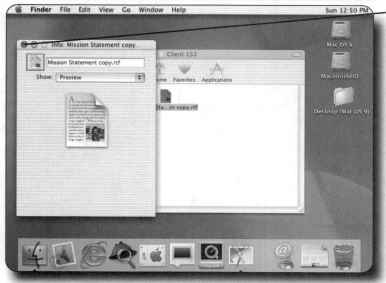

11. After you view the preview, **click** on the **close button**. The Info dialog box will close.

Renaming a File or Folder

As noted in the last section, you can type a new name for a file or folder using the Info dialog box. However, it's handier to rename a file or folder right in a Finder window.

1. Open the **folder** that holds the file or folder you want to rename. The folder's contents will appear in the Finder window.

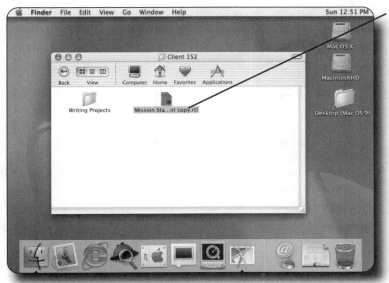

2. Click on the **file or folder name** you want to change. The file or folder name will appear highlighted in gray and a gray border will appear around it.

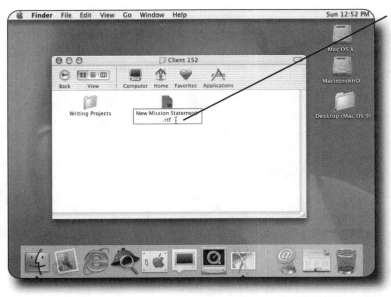

3. Type a **new name, then press Return**. The new file or folder name will appear immediately in the window.

Using Aliases

In Mac lingo, an *alias* is a shortcut link to a file or folder that you can double-click to open the file or folder. By creating and moving aliases to different folders (within your Home folder), you can set up numerous ways to access your files and folders.

Creating an Alias for a File or Folder

You can move an alias to a variety of locations, but you have to create it first.

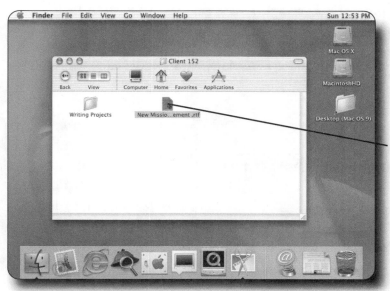

1. Open the **folder** that holds the file or folder for which you want to create an alias. You will see the folder's contents in the Finder window.

2. Click on the **file or folder**. The file or folder will be selected.

3. Click on **File**. The File menu will appear.

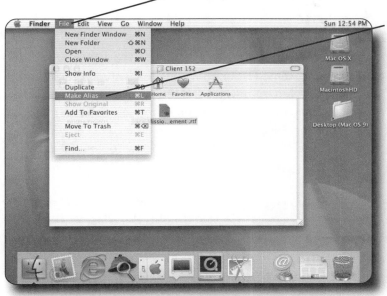

4. Click on **Make Alias**. The alias will appear immediately, with the file or folder name selected for renaming.

NOTE

You also can Control+click on the file or folder, then click on Make Alias in the contextual menu that appears.

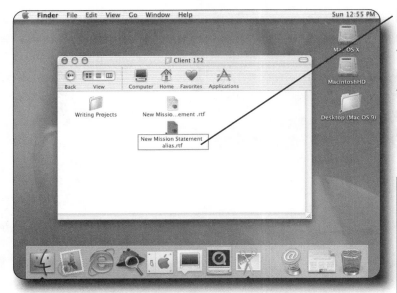

5. Type a **new name** if needed, **then press Return**. The new alias name will appear immediately below the alias icon. You can then move the alias to the desired location, just as you would any other file or folder.

TIP

The icon for an alias includes a small, angled, black arrow in the lower-left corner, so that you can distinguish the alias from the original file or folder.

Adding a File or Folder to Your Favorites

While you can move an alias to the desktop or to any folder within your Home folder, that still means that you may sometimes have to navigate to the appropriate location to use the alias. For added convenience, you also can move an alias into the Favorites folder. Then, you can simply click on the Favorites button in a Finder window toolbar to access the alias.

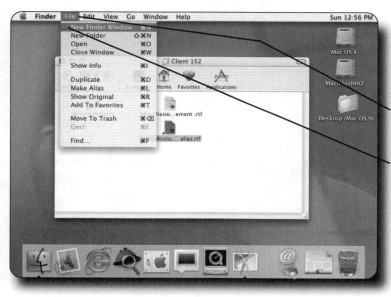

1. **Open** the **folder** that holds the alias. You will see the folder's contents in the Finder window.

2. **Click** on **File**. The File menu will appear.

3. **Click** on **New Finder Window**. Another Finder window will open.

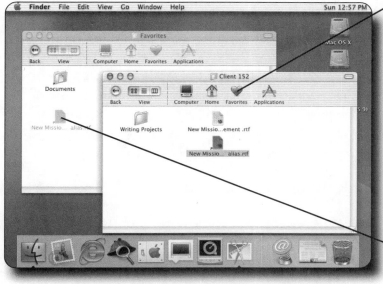

4. Click on the **Favorites button** in the toolbar of the new Finder window. The current contents of the Favorites folder will appear.

5. Move the **Finder windows** so that you can see both the alias and its destination. The folders will appear in the positions you indicate.

6. Drag the **alias** from its current location to the new Finder window, **then release** the **mouse button**. The alias will move into the Favorites folder.

5

Getting Help When You Need It

Macintosh systems and software have long had a reputation of being virtually idiot-proof. Computer novices, users making a shift from another type of system to a Mac, and even grade school children could always jump right in and click and peck their way through nearly any operation. That being said however, today's Macintoshes are more sophisticated than ever, accommodating a wide variety of hardware add-ons, communications connections, and more. Given the wide variety of features in Mac OS X and the fact that it's a departure from previous Mac operating systems, even experienced Macintosh users may need to review some helpful information now and then. In this chapter, you'll learn how to:

- Start Help Viewer when you need it.
- Follow links to find the help you need.
- Find a topic in Help Viewer.

Starting Help Viewer

Mac OS X offers help via the Help Viewer application. Mac OS X and its applications and tools actually offer a variety of methods for starting Help Viewer.

Starting Help Viewer from the Desktop

In many cases, you will start Help Viewer from the menu bar.

1. Click on **Help**. The Help menu will appear.

2. Click on **Mac Help**. Help Viewer will open.

Starting Help Viewer from an Application

Most applications in Mac OS X offer specific help from their Help menu.

1. While using an application, **click** on **Help**. The Help menu will appear.

2. Click on **(Application Name) Help**. Help Viewer will open and show the Help topics for the application.

NOTE

The (Application Name) notation in step 2 refers to the fact that the Help command name will be different in each application. The Help command changes to include the name of the current application.

Starting Help Viewer from a Dialog Box or Dialog

Many dialog boxes and *dialogs* (dialogs which drop down from the title bar of a window like a sheet) include a help button to quickly access Help Viewer.

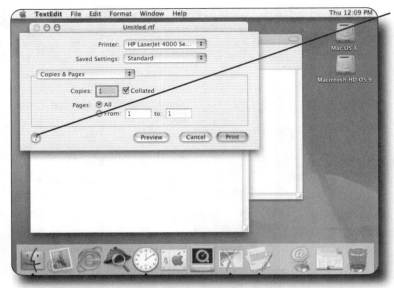

1. Click on the **? button**. Help Viewer will open and show the Help topics regarding the dialog box or dialog options.

Browsing Help

Apple designed Help Viewer to make it easy for you to find the information you need. Basically, Help Viewer works like a Web browser. You simply click on topic links (formatted in blue and underlined by default) to navigate to the Help topic you need.

1. Click on a **help topic link** on the initial Help Viewer page. Another page of help information will appear.

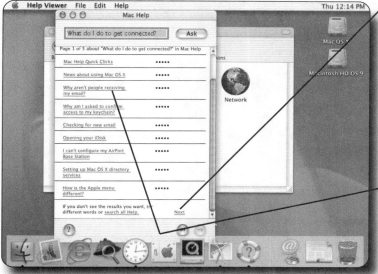

2. **Click** on the **Next link** after scrolling down the list, if available, if you don't see the topic of interest. Help Viewer will display a page listing additional topics. (You can click on Next repeatedly if there are more than two pages of topics.)

3. **Click** on the **link** for the topic of interest. If needed, Help Viewer will download the needed help page from a help Web site maintained by Apple. Then the topic will appear in the Help Viewer window.

NOTE

For the download to work, Mac OS X must be set up to connect to the Internet. Otherwise, you will see a message that the needed HTML page cannot be found. See Chapter 11, "Setting up the Connection," to learn how to set up a dial-up Internet connection and specify Internet connection settings in Mac OS X.

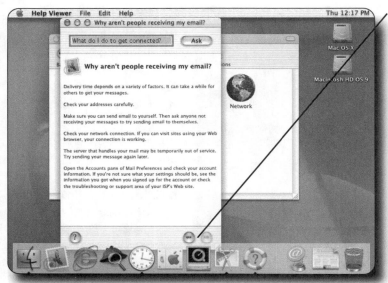

4. Click on the **back or forward buttons** as needed to move between pages of information in Help. The Help Viewer will navigate to the appropriate page. You also can click on additional links as needed.

NOTE

Once you've displayed a Help topic of interest and have set up a printer under Mac OS X as described in Chapter 10, "Working with Printers," you can print the current Help page by choosing File, Print in Help Viewer and completing the Print dialog.

Searching Help

Help Viewer's search feature offers an even speedier way to get the help you need. Simply type in the topic of interest and start the search. Help Viewer will display a list of possible matching topics.

1. **Click** in the **text box** at the top of any Help Viewer page, then **type** the **word or phrase** that you want to research.

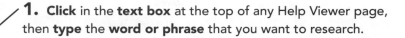

NOTE

If a word or phrase already appears in the text box, drag over it to highlight it, then type the new word or phrase for which you want to search.

2. **Click** on **Ask**. Another page or screen listing specific help topics will appear in the Help Viewer window.

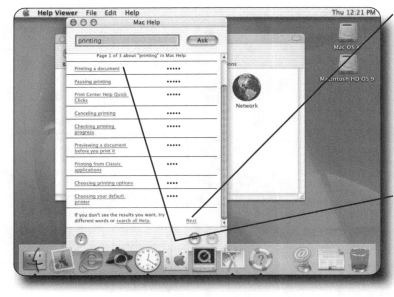

3. **Click** on the **Next link** after scrolling down the list, if available, if you don't see the topic of interest. Help Viewer will display a page listing additional topics. (You can click on Next repeatedly if there are more than two pages of topics.)

4. **Click** on the **link** for the topic of interest. If needed, Help Viewer will download the needed help page from a help Web site maintained by Apple. Then the topic will appear in the Help Viewer window.

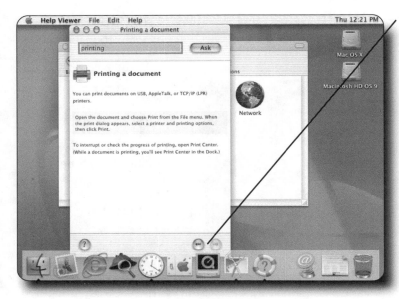

5. Click on the **back or forward buttons** as needed to move between pages of information in Help. Help Viewer will navigate to the appropriate page. You also can click on additional links as needed.

Quitting Help Viewer

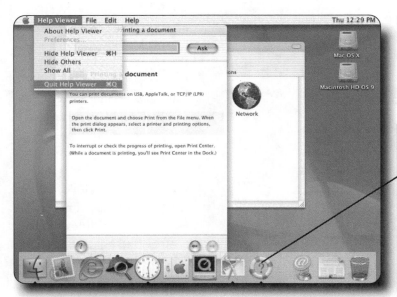

Similar to quitting any other application, you should quit or close the Help Viewer once you've finished searching for help.

TIP

If you don't see the Help Viewer choice on the menu bar, click on the Help Viewer icon (it looks like a life ring with a question mark in it) on the Dock. Then you can close Help Viewer as explained.

1. Click on **Help Viewer**. The Help Viewer menu will appear.

2. Click on **Quit Help Viewer**. Help Viewer will close.

Part I Review Questions

1. How do I start up my Mac? *See "Starting up" in Chapter 1.*

2. How do I shut down my Mac? *See "Shutting Down" in Chapter 1.*

3. How do I choose a command? *See "Choosing a Menu Command" in Chapter 2.*

4. How do I work with a dialog box? *See "Responding to a Dialog Box" in Chapter 2.*

5. What is a Finder window? *See "Understanding the Parts of a Window" in Chapter 3.*

6. Where did my window go? *See "Minimizing and Expanding a Window" in Chapter 3.*

7. What's my Home folder? *See "Understanding Home Folders" in Chapter 4.*

8. How do I open a file? *See "Opening a File" in Chapter 4.*

9. How do I use the trash? *See "Working with the Trash" in Chapter 4.*

10. What's the fastest way to get the help I need? *See "Searching Help" in Chapter 5.*

Working with Applications

Chapter 6
   Using the Dock and Applications 85

Chapter 7
   **Working in the Classic
       (Mac OS 9) Environment 99**

6

Using the Dock and Applications

The Dock stands out as one of the most important new features of the Aqua interface in Mac OS X. You can use the Dock to start applications. You also can temporarily "park" open files and windows on the Dock. In this chapter, you'll learn how to:

- Start a program and select the current program.
- Save a file on disk.
- Find preference settings in an application.
- Hide and redisplay an application.
- Use the Dock as a parking place for files and folders.
- Quit an application.
- Go back to the desktop when needed.

Starting an Application from the Dock

The icons to the left of the vertical dividing line on the Dock represent applications, utilities, and key features of Mac OS X. The Dock icons provide easy access for starting a program or utility.

> ### NOTE
> You can customize the Dock to include icons for other programs, as described in Chapter 8 "Setting up the Desktop."

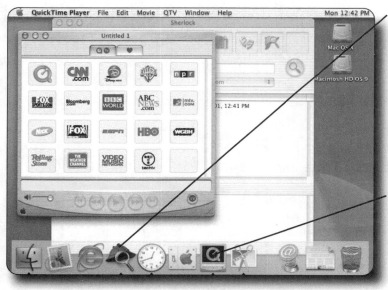

1. Click on the **icon** on the dock for the application or utility you want to start. The application will launch and its window will open. A small, black triangle will appear below the Dock icon to tell you that the application or utility is running.

2. Click on **another icon**. The next application or utility will start and its window will open.

> ### NOTE
> You can start as many applications or utilities as the amount of memory in your Mac allows.

Switching to an Application Using the Dock

Once you start an application or utility an icon for the application or utility appears on the Dock (if it is not already there). You can use Dock icons to switch between running applications and utilities.

1. Click on the **icon** for the application or utility to which you want to switch. The application or utility window will jump to the front of other open windows, meaning that it has become the active application.

2. Click on **another icon.** The next application or utility will become the active application.

Saving a File in an Application

For utilities and features of Mac OS X, you generally change settings in a window or dialog box, then close the window to apply your changes. In other types of programs, such as the TextEdit word processor, you need to save your work to a particular file before closing your work or the application.

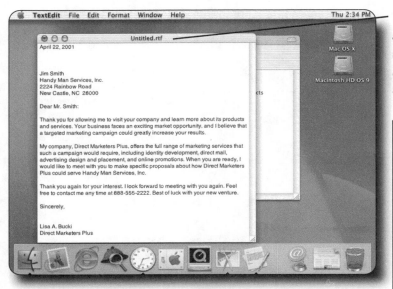

1. Start the **application and create** your **file**, if needed. Your work will appear in a window for the application.

2. **Click** on **File**. The File menu will appear.

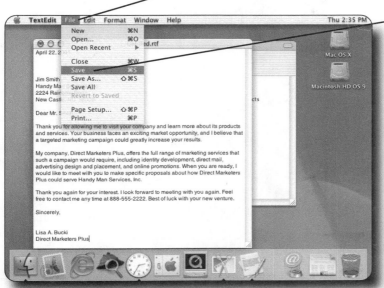

3. **Click** on **Save**. (In some applications, you may need to click on Save As.) The Save as dialog will open. By default, it will suggest that you save the file in the Documents folder within your Home folder

TIP

If you've already saved a file once but want to save a copy under a new name, choose File, Save As instead.

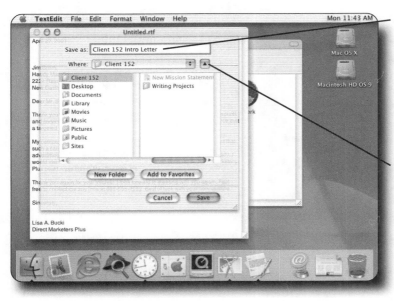

4. **Type** a **name** for the file in the Save as text box. Do not start a file name with the # sign or a period and avoid the / (slash) character, although you can use capitalization and spaces.

5. **Skip** to **Step 7** if you want to save the file in the Documents folder. Otherwise, **click** on the **arrow button** to the right of the Where pop-up menu. The dialog will expand to show a list of folders, so you can navigate to the folder where you want to save the file.

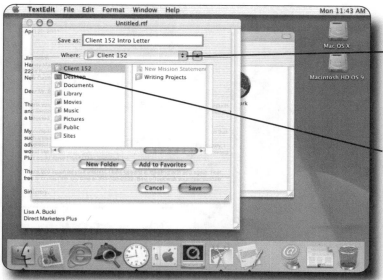

NOTE

You also can simply click on the Where pop-up menu and click on a folder.

6. Double-click on a **folder** in the left-most column until you have opened the folder where you want to place the saved the file. Its contents will appear in the column at the right.

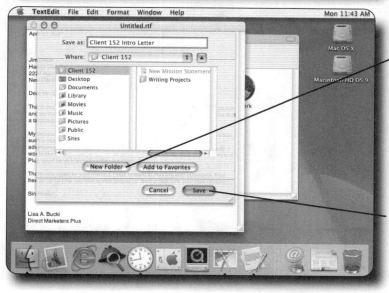

TIP

Click on the New Folder button to create a new folder for the file you're saving. In the New Folder dialog box that opens, type a name for the new folder and then click on Create.

7. Click on **Save**. Mac OS X will save the file in the location you specified.

TIP

Choose File, Close or click on the close button in the upper-left corner of the file window to close your document.

Setting Application Preferences

In Chapter 9,"Changing Essential System Preferences," you'll learn about a number of the preferences that you can set to control how Mac OS X operates. Similarly, each application offers a number of preferences that enable you to set basic parameters about how the application works.

1. Start the **application**, if needed. Its window will open, and its menus will appear on the menu bar.

TIP

To start TextEdit, for example, click on the Applications toolbar button in a Finder window, locate the TextEdit icon, and then double-click on it.

---

2. Click on the **application menu**. The application menu will appear.

3. Click on **Preferences**. The Preferences dialog box will open. The Preferences dialog box includes settings appropriate to the application or utility.

4a. **Make changes** to the settings as needed.

OR

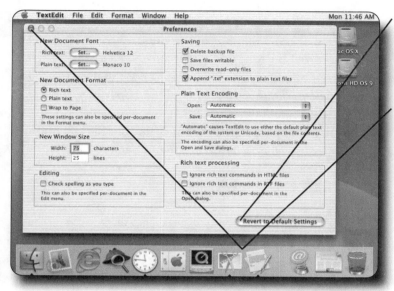

4b. **Click** on **Revert to Default Settings**. All the settings will return to their original state.

5. **Click** on the **close button**. The dialog box will close, and the new preference settings will take effect.

Hiding and Redisplaying an Application

Hiding an application or utility removes its windows and menu from view without closing (quitting) it. The icon for the application or utility remains on the Dock, still displaying the black triangle that indicates that it's running. Hiding an application merely provides a way to reduce the number of open windows so that you have an easier time choosing the one you want to use.

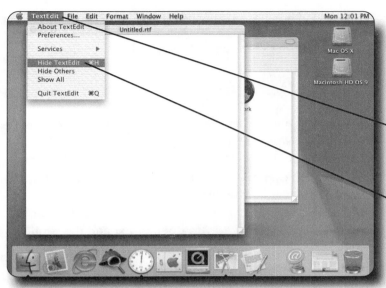

1. Switch to the **application**, if needed. Its window will appear and its menus will appear on the menu bar.

2. Click on the **application menu**. The application menu will appear.

3. Click on **Hide (Application Name)**. The application and its windows and menus will disappear from the desktop.

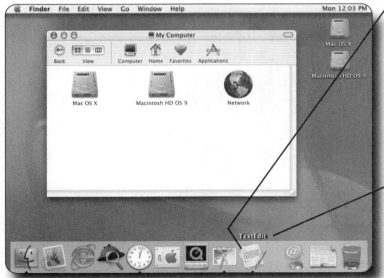

4. Click on the **icon** for the application to redisplay on the Dock. The application window will reopen and it will become the current application.

TIP

When you move the mouse pointer over any icon on the Dock, the name of the application, utility, file, or folder (for a Finder window) appears above the icon. If you've minimized multiple files or Finder windows, the pop-up name can help you make sure you're clicking on the right icon.

Minimizing and Expanding Documents and Finder Windows

The icons for applications and utilities appear to the left of the vertical divider line on the Dock. If you're working with a Finder window or a file window within an application, you can reduce the window to an icon on the Dock. In such an instance, the icon for the Finder window or file window appears to the right of the vertical divider line on the Dock, so that you can find it easily to open or expand the window.

1. **Switch to** the **window** to minimize, if needed. The window will come forward as the active window.

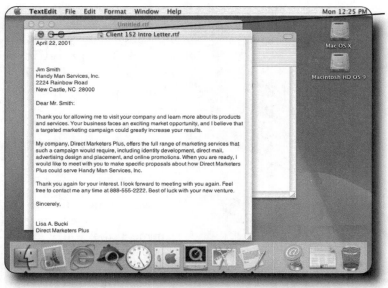

2. **Click** on the **minimize button**. The window will minimize to an icon on the Dock.

3. Click on the **icon** on the Dock. The window will expand becoming the current window. If you opened a file window, its application also becomes the current application.

Quitting an Application

When you've finished working with an application or utility, it's a good practice to quit the application or utility. This frees up the system memory that the application or utility was using, enabling the system to apply that memory to another function. For example, playing video in QuickTime Player requires a lot of memory, so you'll want to close any other open programs or utilities to ensure the best video playback, especially if your Mac system is a bit low on memory. Fortunately, quitting an application is a quick process.

1. Switch to the **application**, if needed. Its window will appear, and its menus will appear on the menu bar.

2. Click on the **application menu** The application menu will appear.

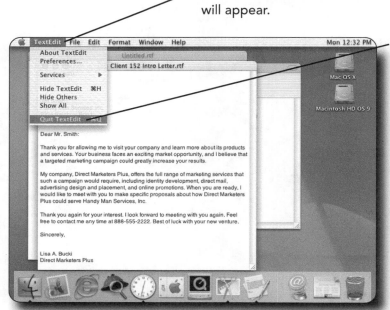

3. Click on **Quit (Application Name)**. The application will close.

NOTE

If you made changes to a file that's open in the application and you didn't save the changes before quitting the application, a Close dialog appears to ask whether you want to save the file. You can click on Don't Save to quit the application without saving the file, or Save to display the Save as dialog so that you can use it to save the file.

Forcing an Application to Quit

If you encounter a situation where an application has "locked up" so that you cannot switch to it or use its menu to quit the program, Mac OS X offers an alternate way to force a program to quit.

1. Press Command+Option+Escape. The Force Quit Applications window will open, listing the running applications and utilities.

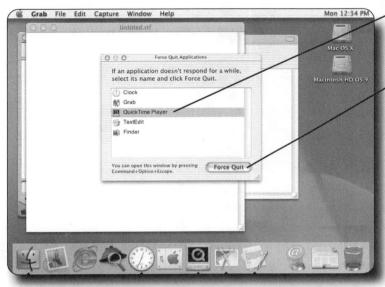

2. Click on the **application or utility name** in the list. The name will be selected.

3. Click on **Force Quit**. An Alert dialog will appear, asking you to confirm that you want to force the application to quit and noting that you will lose any unsaved work in the selected application.

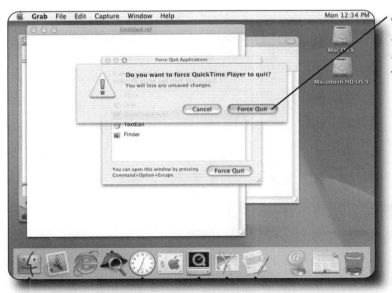

4. Click on **Force Quit**. The application or utility will quit and its icon will be removed from the Dock, if applicable.

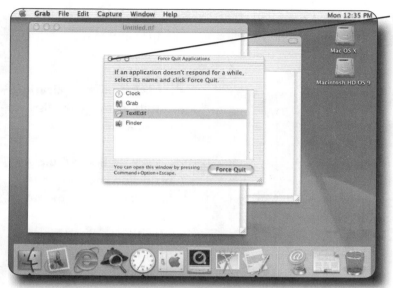

5. Click on the **close button**. The Force Quit Applications window will close.

Redisplaying the Desktop

If you have been working with many applications, you may want to quickly return to the desktop and display only Finder windows and the Finder menu bar.

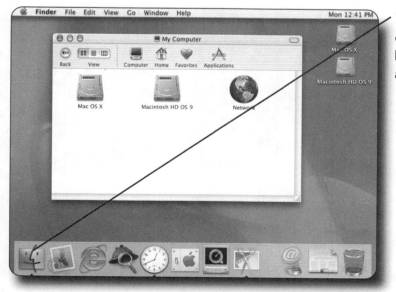

1. Click on the **Finder icon** on the Dock. The Finder will become the active application.

7

Working in the Classic (Mac OS 9) Environment

Apple started with a relatively clean slate when developing Mac OS X. It developed all new software code based on Unix rather than simply updating the existing Mac OS 9 code. While this departure enabled the Mac OS X system to be as sleek, fast, and reliable as it is, adopting the radically different code also created a challenge. How would Mac OS X be able to run applications developed for the Mac OS 9 (or older) operating systems? Apple's answer is the Classic environment, allowing you to seamlessly use older software while working in Mac OS X. In this chapter, you'll learn how to:

- Enter and exit the Classic environment.
- Start a Classic application.
- Move between Mac OS X applications and Classic applications.

Starting the Classic Environment

Mac OS X has built-in software that enables it to run applications designed for the older Mac OS 9 (referred to as *Classic applications*). The *Classic environment* in Mac OS X offers this capability. This important feature enables you to continue using your favorite Mac applications until upgraded versions designed for Mac OS X become available.

The Classic environment starts automatically when required. However, you also can start the Classic environment at any time.

1. **Click** on the **System Preferences icon** on the Dock. System Preferences will launch.

NOTE

Read more about using System Preferences in Chapter 9, "Changing Essential System Preferences."

---

2. **Click** on the **Classic icon**. The Classic pane will appear in the System Preferences window.

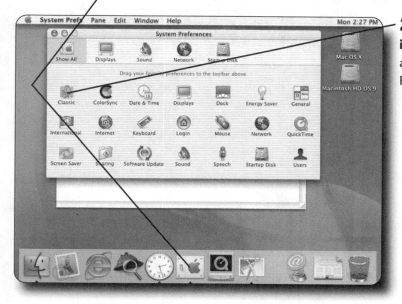

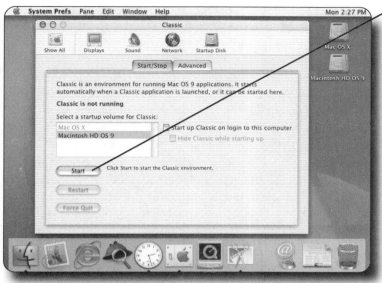

3. Click on **Start**. A progress bar will appear as Classic starts up. The Classic icon will appear briefly on the Dock, and the other choices for working with Classic will be enabled on the Start/Stop tab of the Classic pane in the System Preferences window.

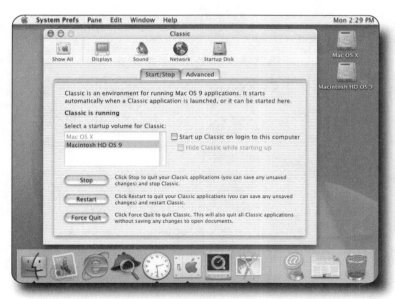

Now you can start Classic applications as needed.

NOTE

The first time you start the Classic environment, a dialog box will open asking if it is OK to update your Mac OS 9.1 System Folder. Click on OK to continue.

Starting and Quitting a Classic Application

As noted earlier, the Classic environment enables you to run an application designed for older Mac operating systems. To start a Classic application, you use the same method as you would to start an application designed for Mac OS X. Once you start a Classic application, the desktop changes a bit to include the Mac OS 9 menu bar. You can then use that menu bar to work in the application, just as you would have in Mac OS 9. The following example illustrates how this works with the SimpleText application, while any Classic application is started in the same manner.

1. Open the **Applications (Mac OS 9) folder** in the Finder. The folder's contents will appear in the Finder window.

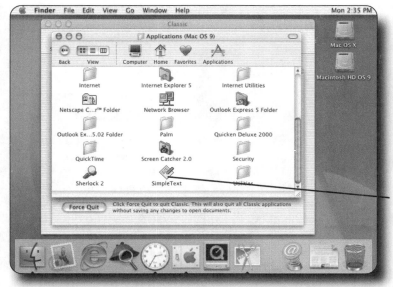

NOTE

The Applications (Mac OS 9) folder may appear on a separate disk volume if you installed Mac OS X to a new partition on the system's hard disk.

2. Double-click on **SimpleText**. The application will launch and its icon will appear on the Dock.

TIP

If you didn't start the Classic environment prior to starting a Classic application, the Classic environment will launch automatically.

3. Review the **menu bar**. It will change to look like a Mac OS 9 menu bar, and it will offer the menus for SimpleText. Dialog boxes for the application also will look and work just as they did in Mac OS 9.

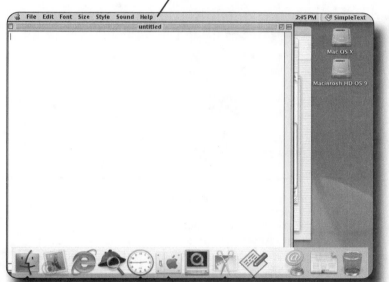

NOTE

When you're using a Mac OS X application, the Mac OS X menu bar appears. When you're using a Classic application, its Classic menu bar appears. This visual clue helps you ensure that you've made the correct application active. You can use the Dock to switch between Classic applications and Mac OS X applications.

4. When you're ready to close a Classic application like SimpleText, **click** on **File**. The File menu will appear.

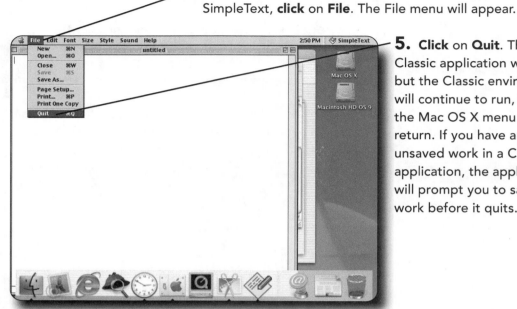

5. Click on **Quit**. The Classic application will quit, but the Classic environment will continue to run, while the Mac OS X menu bar will return. If you have any unsaved work in a Classic application, the application will prompt you to save that work before it quits.

NOTE

Not all older applications will run in the Classic environment. Any applications which require access to the Internet will not be able to make the connection. If you need to use all your Classic applications, then you should have Mac OS 9.1 installed on another partition on your system. The Appendix, "Installation Notes," gives you pointers about how you can set up your system for both Mac operating systems.

Adjusting Classic Preferences (Advanced Settings)

You can control just a few aspects of how the Classic environment behaves. You do this in the Classic pane of

System Preferences you used earlier to start the Classic environment. The following section show you how to find the Classic preferences, also called the Advanced settings.

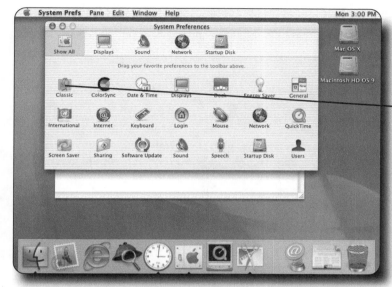

1. **Click** on the **System Preferences icon** on the Dock. System Preferences will launch.

2. **Click** on the **Classic icon**. The Classic pane will appear in the System Preferences window.

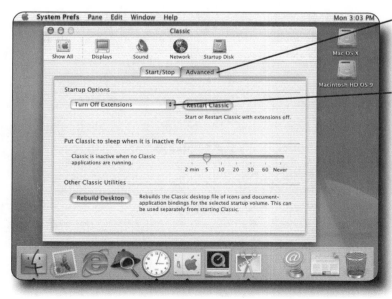

3. **Click** on the **Advanced tab**. The Advanced tab will come forward.

4. **Click** on the **Startup Options pop-up menu**. The pop-up menu will open.

5. **Click** on a **startup option**. The option will appear in the pop-up menu.

The options in the Startup options pop-up menu designate which system extensions load when the

Classic environment starts under Mac OS X. Use these options to troubleshoot Classic applications and improve overall Classic environment performance.

6. If you want to activate the startup option you selected, **click** on **Restart Classic**. Classic will restart with the newly-designated setting.

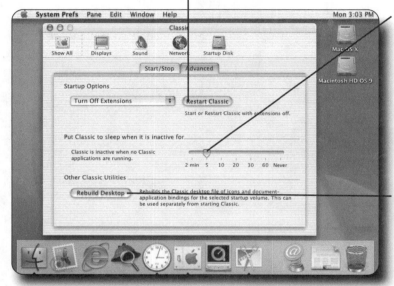

7. Drag the **Put Classic to sleep when it is inactive for slider** to control how long Classic applications will remain active before Classic sleeps. Your system performance will improve when the Classic environment is in sleep mode.

8. Click on **Rebuild Desktop** if you are having trouble with files opening with the incorrect application in Classic. A dialog box will appear that you can use to update the application *bindings* (the application associated with files of a particular type) on a disk volume.

CAUTION

After clicking on the Rebuild Desktop button, you may end up with application/file bindings that you don't prefer.

9. Click on **System Prefs**. The System Prefs menu will appear.

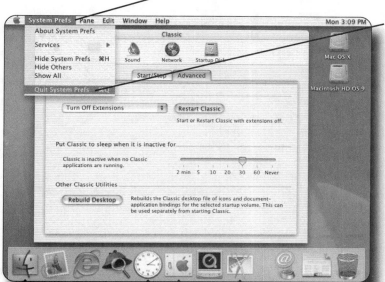

10. Click on **Quit System Prefs**. System Preferences will close and the settings will be applied.

NOTE

Closing the System Preferences window while the Classic environment is running does not shut down or exit the Classic environment.

Closing the Classic Environment

If you've finished working in your Classic applications for the current work session and have quit those applications, it's a good idea to quit the Classic environment, as well. Like any other application or utility, the Classic environment consumes system memory. Quitting the Classic environment releases that memory so that your Mac can use it for other applications.

1. Click on the **System Preferences icon** on the Dock. System Preferences will launch.

2. Click on the **Classic icon**. The Classic pane will appear in the System Preferences window.

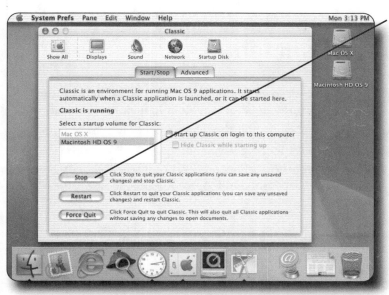

3. Click on **Stop**. The Classic environment will shut down. If any Classic applications were still running, they will also close when the Classic environment shuts down.

Part II Review Questions

1. How do I start a Dock application? *See "Starting an Application from the Dock" in Chapter 6.*

2. How do I move between running applications? *See "Switching to an Application Using the Dock" in Chapter 6.*

3. How do I save a file? *See "Saving a File in an Application" in Chapter 6.*

4. How do I work with preferences in an application? *See "Setting Application Preferences" in Chapter 6.*

5. How do I dock a file or Finder window? *See "Minimizing and Expanding Documents and Finder Windows" in Chapter 6.*

6. How do I start a Classic application? *See "Starting and Quitting a Classic Application" in Chapter 7*

7. How do I get back to Mac OS X? *See "Starting and Quitting a Classic Application" in Chapter 7.*

PART III

Customizing Mac OS X

Chapter 8
    Setting up the Desktop **113**

Chapter 9
    Changing Essential
        System Preferences **127**

Chapter 10
    Working with Printers **151**

Setting up
the Desktop

It's more fun to use a computer when you can personalize the desktop or customize a few settings to meet your needs. You can control a number of settings affecting how Mac OS X works and appears. This chapter focuses only on those settings pertaining to the appearance and function of the Dock and desktop. In this chapter, you'll learn how to:

- Change the way disks and Finder windows appear.
- Choose a desktop picture.
- Adjust how the Dock looks.
- Control which icons appear on the Dock.
- Set up the Clock to work the way you want.

TIP

You can download graphics files from any number of locations on the Web. Start with http://www.macaddict. com/community/ artgallery, then click on the Desktop Pictures link. Just be sure that you observe the fair use provision of copyright law and only use downloaded images for personal purpose.

Changing Disk and Finder Settings

By default, Mac OS X places an icon on the desktop whenever you insert a new disk into a CD-ROM, DVD-ROM, or removable disk drive. It also, by default, displays the contents of a folder in the same Finder window when you double-click on a folder (rather than opening a new window). Both of these settings can be customized.

In addition to adjusting disk and window behavior, you can fine-tune the appearance of your desktop and any icons on it. Mac OS X enables you to use a graphic file in one of a variety of formats (such as .gif and .jpg images) as a new desktop picture.

1. Click on the **Finder icon** on the Dock. The Finder will become active and its menus will appear on the menu bar.

2. Click on **Finder**. The Finder menu will appear.

3. Click on **Preferences**. The Finder Preferences dialog box will open.

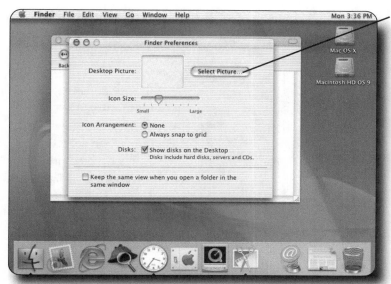

4. To begin choosing a new desktop picture, **click** on **Select Picture**. The Choose A Picture dialog box will open, and the pre-installed image files in the Desktop Pictures folder will appear in the right column of the folder list.

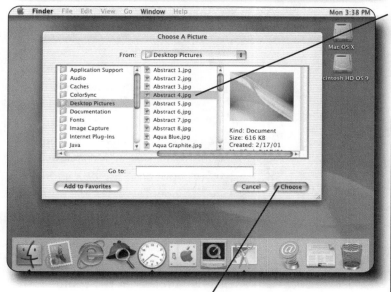

5. **Click** on the **image file** that you wish to use as a desktop picture. A new column will appear displaying a preview of the image.

NOTE

The default desktop picture in Mac OS X is the Aqua Blue.jpg file. You can reopen the Choose A Picture dialog box and reselect this graphic file at any time to return the desktop to its original appearance.

6. **Click** on **Choose**. The Choose A Picture dialog box will close, and the selected picture will appear in the Finder Preferences dialog box and on your desktop.

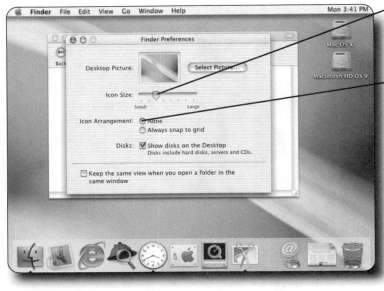

7. **Drag** the **Icon Size slider** to adjust the size of any desktop icons.

8. **Click** on an **Icon Arrangement option button**. The option will be selected. When selected, the Always snap to grid option will cause all icons on the desktop to line up according to a neat, invisible grid on the desktop.

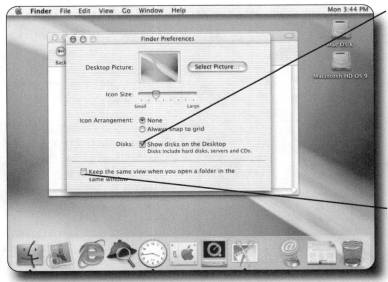

9. **Click** on the **Show disks on the Desktop check box** if you want Mac OS X to display a desktop icon for an inserted disk, connected network server, or mounted disk image. A check will appear in the box and any mounted disks will appear immediately.

10. **Click** on the **Keep the same view when you open a folder in the same window check box** if you want to display a folder opened from a Finder window using the same view. A check will appear in the box and Finder windows will maintain view settings when opening folders.

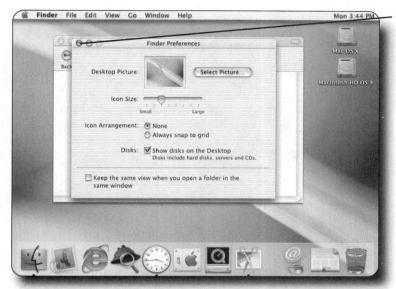

11. **Click** on the **close button**. The dialog box will close and Mac OS X will apply the settings you specified.

Changing Dock Settings

If you're not quite satisfied with how the Dock looks, you can make a few cosmetic changes, as well as some functional ones. For example, you can:

- Alter the size (height) of the Dock.

- Add *magnification* (which causes a Dock icon to zoom to a larger size when you position the mouse pointer over the icon).

- Turn on the *auto hide* feature (which hides the Dock until you move the mouse pointer to the bottom of the screen).

- Turn off the animation effect when you open an application or expand a window from the Dock.

Making these changes to the Dock is simple.

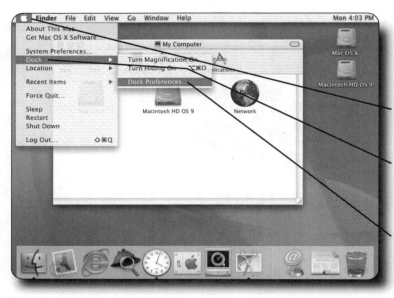

1. **Click** on the **Finder icon** on the Dock. The Finder will become active and its menus will appear on the menu bar.

2. **Click** on the **Apple icon**. The Apple menu will appear.

3. **Move** the **mouse pointer down** to Dock. The Dock submenu will appear.

4. **Click** on **Dock Preferences**. System Preferences will launch and display the Dock pane.

NOTE

Alternately, you can click on the System Preferences icon on the Dock, and then click on the Dock icon.

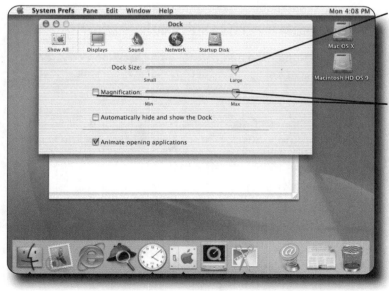

5. **Drag** the **Dock Size slider**. The Dock will appear smaller or larger, as you move the slider.

6. **Click** on the **Magnification check box and drag** the **slider**. A check will appear in the box and icons on the Dock will enlarge as you move the mouse pointer over them.

NOTE

If you display the Dock submenu of the Apple menu, note that it also offers the Turn Magnification On/Off and Turn Hiding On/Off commands. You can use these commands as a faster way to turn Dock magnification and auto-hiding on or off.

7. Click on the **Automatically hide and show the Dock check box** if you don't want to see the Dock unless you move the mouse pointer down to the bottom of the desktop. A check will appear in the box and the Dock will hide immediately.

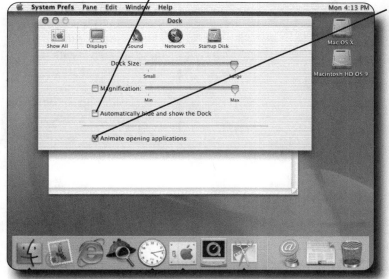

8. Click on the **Animate opening applications check box** if you want application icons to bounce on the Dock while launching. A check will appear in the box and application icons will not bounce on the Dock.

9. Click on **System Prefs**. The System Prefs menu will appear.

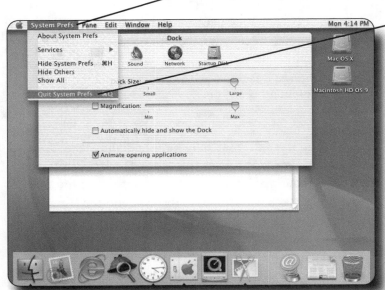

10. Click on **Quit System Prefs**. System Preferences will close and the settings will be applied.

NOTE

You also can use the mouse to resize the Dock. Move the mouse pointer over the vertical divider line on the Dock until the resizing pointer appears. (The pointer is a vertical double-headed arrow with a horizontal bar through it.) Then drag the divider line up or down to adjust the Dock size.

Adding and Removing Dock Icons

The Dock offers a great deal of convenience, but you can make it even more convenient by adding Dock icons for your favorite programs and files.

1. Open the **folder** that holds the application or file that you want to place on the Dock. The folder's contents will appear in the Finder window.

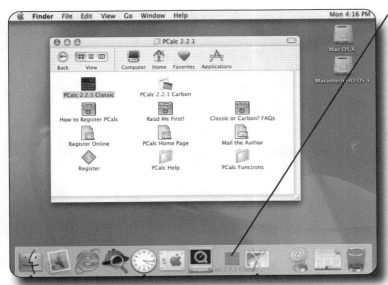

2. Drag the **icon** from the folder to the desired Dock location, **then release** the **mouse button**. The icon will appear in the specified location on the Dock.

NOTE

You can only place application icons to the left of the vertical divider line.

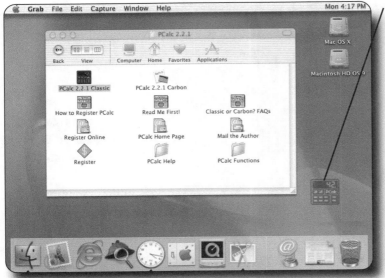

3. To remove a Dock icon, **drag** the **icon** from the Dock to the desktop, **then release** the **mouse button**. The icon will disappear from the Dock.

CAUTION

You can remove the default Dock icons by dragging them off the Dock as well. If you do so mistakenly, click on the Applications toolbar button in a Finder window, then look in the resulting folder (and its subfolders) for the desired application or utility. Then drag its icon back onto the Dock.

Adding a Folder Icon and Viewing Its Contents

If you add a folder icon to the right section of the Dock, you can then use a shortcut to open the folder's contents in a Finder window. This setup can be even more handy than adding a folder icon to the Finder window toolbar. Creating and using a Dock folder icon is simple.

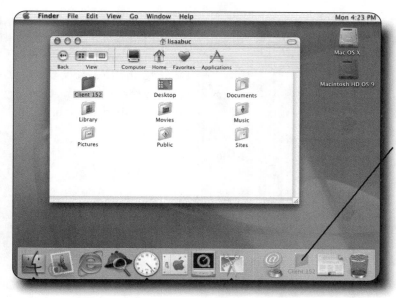

1. Navigate to the **disk** or **folder** that holds the folder that you want to place on the Dock. The folder's contents will appear in the Finder window.

2. Drag the **icon** from the folder to the desired Dock location, **then release** the **mouse button**. The icon will appear in the specified location on the Dock.

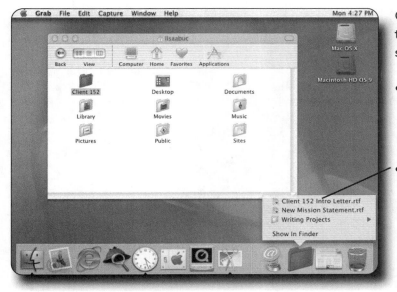

Once the folder icon is on the Dock, you can use it as a shortcut in one of two ways:

- Click on the folder icon and a Finder window showing the folder's contents will appear.

- Control+click on the folder icon and a contextual menu listing the folder's contents will appear. You can click on any file or application listed in the menu.

Adding Dock Extras to the Dock

Mac OS X includes a few different extra features that you can add to the Dock. These include:

- **Battery Monitor.dock**. Useful for PowerBooks, this utility enables you to monitor remaining battery power from the Dock.

- **Displays.dock**. This utility enables you to change display resolutions right from the Dock.

- **Signal Strength.dock**. If you have an AirPort card installed on your system, add this utility to the Dock so that you can check how well your system's communicating with the AirPort.

Use the following steps to add a Dock extra to the Dock:

1. **Click** on **Applications** on a Finder window toolbar. The contents of the Applications folder will appear in the window.

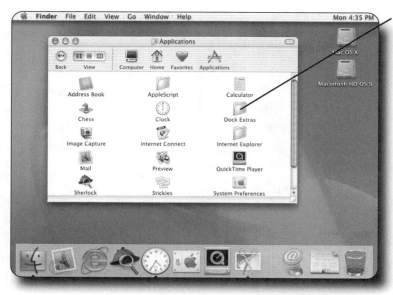

2. Double-click on the **Dock Extras folder**. The contents of the folder will appear in the Finder window.

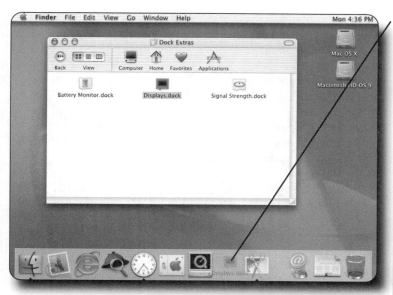

3. Drag a **Dock extra icon** from the folder to the desired Dock location, **then release** the **mouse button**. The icon will appear in the specified location on the Dock.

TIP

In some cases, the Dock extra icon displays information for you. In other instances, such as with the Displays.dock extra, click on the Dock icon and then click on a setting in the menu that appears.

Changing the Clock Appearance

The Clock application supplements the clock on the Finder menu bar. You can launch Clock by clicking on its icon in the Applications folder. You can change the Clock application so that it displays as a digital clock or appears in its own floating window instead of on the Dock.

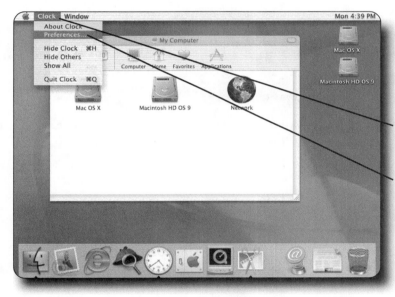

1. Click on the **Clock icon** on the Dock. The Clock will become active, and its menus will appear on the menu bar.

2. Click on **Clock**. The Clock menu will appear.

3. Click on **Preferences**. The Clock Preferences dialog box will open.

TIP

The "Setting Date & Time Preferences" section in Chapter 9 "Changing Essential System Preferences" explains how to change the system time.

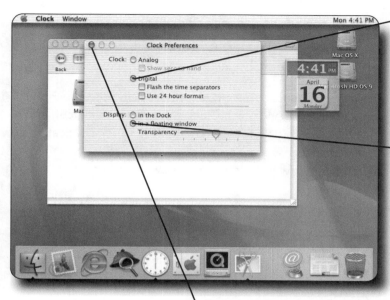

4. Click on the **Analog or Digital option button**, **then click** on the **check boxes** as needed. The settings you select will immediately adjust Clock's appearance.

5. Click on a **Display option button**, **then drag** the **Transparency slider** if you opted to place the Clock in a floating window. The settings you select will immediately adjust Clock's appearance.

6. Click on the **close button**. The dialog box will close, and Mac OS will apply the settings you specified.

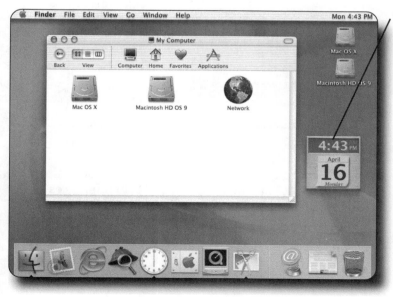

7. Drag the **Clock** to a new location on the desktop as needed. The Clock will move immediately.

9

Changing Essential System Preferences

Early computers from Apple had a killer selling point: they were easy to set up and adjust. You didn't have to be a programmer to change important settings. The new Mac OS X continues the tradition, organizing its numerous preference settings in a central location. Anyone can easily find and change system preferences. This chapter serves as a reference to the most commonly used preferences in Mac OS X. In this chapter, you'll learn how to:

- Launch System Preferences.
- Display a pane of preferences.
- Unlock and re-lock a pane of preferences.
- Set the most important preferences.

Displaying System Preferences

Mac OS X includes System Preferences, which organizes the settings that control how the system operates. System Preferences replaces the control panels found in previous Mac operating systems. When you start System Preferences, its menu appears and the System Preferences window opens. The window holds an icon for each pane of settings and has a toolbar at the top that you can use to navigate in System Preferences. This section explains how to find the settings pane that you need and how to lock and unlock a pane of preferences.

Displaying a Preferences Pane

To change a particular preference setting, you need to start System Preferences. After you do so, display the particular pane (group of preferences) in which you want to make changes by clicking on the icon for that pane.

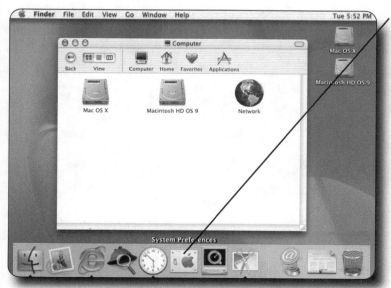

1. **Click** on the **System Preferences icon** on the Dock. The System Preferences window will open and its menus will appear.

TIP

You also can click on the Apple menu icon and then click on System Preferences to start System Preferences.

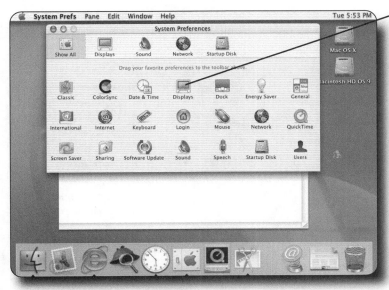

2. Click on the **icon** for the preferences pane of your choice. The pane will appear in the System Preferences window. Some panes contain a collection of settings that appear immediately. Others offer multiple tabs of settings.

TIP

You also can click on Pane in the menu bar and then click on the name of the desired pane

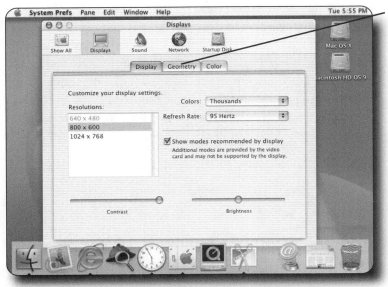

3. Click on the **tab** that you want to display.

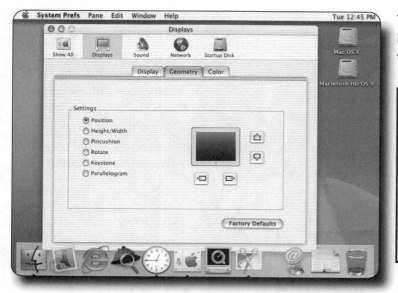

The tab comes forward and its settings appear in the pane.

Unlocking and Locking a Preferences Pane

Mac OS X really makes it easy for multiple users to share a system. When you log in with your user name, you can work on your files without disrupting the work of any other user. However, sharing a system can create a problem if one user changes a preference without the knowledge and consent of other system users. To prevent this problem, some of the System Preferences panes can be locked and unlocked—but only by an administrator of the system.

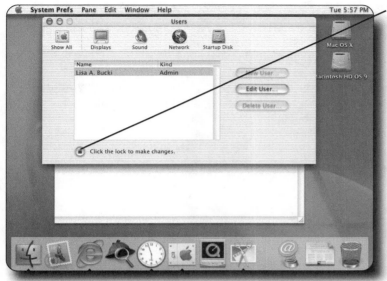

1. Click on the **small locked lock icon**. A dialog box will open that prompts you to enter the administrator password.

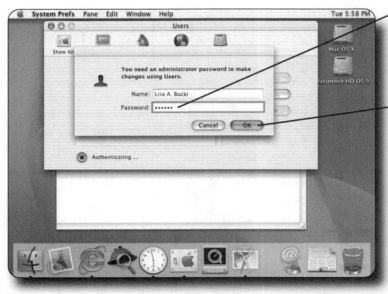

2. Type the **password** into the Password text box. A dot appears in the text box for each letter you type.

3. Click on **OK**. Mac OS X will verify that you have administrator privileges and will then unlock the pane. The locked lock icon will change to an unlocked lock icon and you can then change settings on the pane.

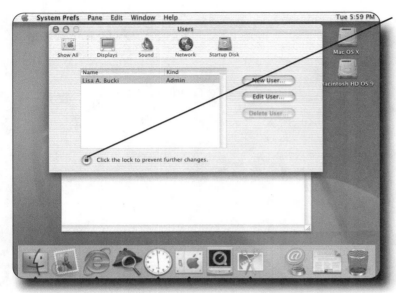

4. **Click** on the **unlocked lock icon**. The icon will change to a locked lock and changes will be prevented until you unlock the pane again.

Redisplaying All the Preferences

Once you display a particular pane of preferences, you may notice there's no back button to redisplay all the icons. Redisplaying all the icons is simple.

1. **Click** on the **Show All icon**. All of the icons will appear in the System Preferences window.

TIP

If you use a particular preferences pane often, you can drag its icon onto the System Preferences window toolbar for easier access.

Reviewing Key System Preferences

Now that you've learned how to find the settings that you need in System Preferences, you can take a little time to familiarize yourself with what's available. This section reviews some of the more general panes in System Preferences. (Other, more specific, preferences panes such as the Internet pane, are covered in the chapters where they apply.) Once you've read this section, you can keep it in mind to use as a reference.

Now that you understand how to open the preferences panes and navigate among them, making your settings should be a snap. The controls on a System Preferences pane work just like those in dialog boxes. You can click on option buttons and check boxes, drag sliders, and so on to make the changes you want. For the most part, your changes take effect immediately.

NOTE

The descriptions in this section assume that you've unlocked preferences panes as needed to change settings.

Setting Date & Time Preferences

The Date & Time pane includes four tabs of settings that you use to adjust how your Mac displays the time and date.

1. Click on the **Date & Time icon**. The Date & Time pane will appear in the System Preferences window.

2. Click on the **correct date** on the calendar. The correct date will be highlighted.

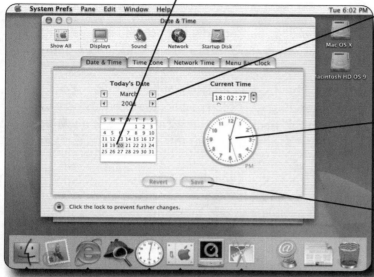

3. Click on the **arrow buttons** on either side of the month and year. The month and year will be updated.

4. Drag the **hands** on the clock. The hands will move to the correct time and your system clock will be set.

5. Click on **Save**. Your changes will be saved.

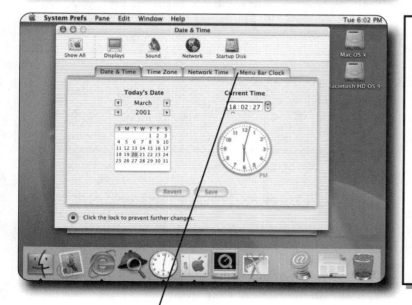

NOTE

If you have the Network Time Synchronization feature on the Network Time tab of the Date & Time pane enabled, then you can't reset the system time on the Date & Time tab. Go to the Network Time tab and click the Stop button, then return to the Date & Time tab to make your changes.

6. Click on the **Menu Bar Clock tab**. The Menu Bar Clock tab will come forward.

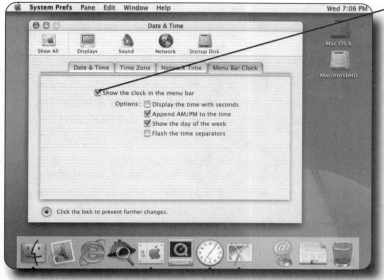

7. **Click** on the **Show the clock in the menu bar check box** if you want the system time to appear at the far right of the menu bar. A check will appear in the box and the time will display on the menu bar.

Use the four Options check boxes to control how the time appears. You can choose to Display the time with seconds, Append AM/PM to the time, Show the day of the week, and Flash the time separators.

Setting Displays Preferences

Most Mac models (except iMacs, iBooks, and PowerBooks) can use a variety of displays (monitor models). The Displays pane offers two tabs used to specify the proper display and the settings you prefer.

NOTE

Depending on the monitor connected to your Macintosh, additional tabs may appear in the Displays pane.

---

1. **Click** on the **Displays icon**. The Displays pane will appear in the System Preferences window.

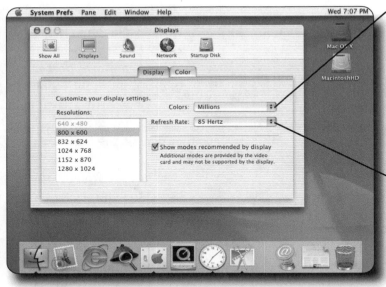

2. **Click** on the **Colors pop-up menu**. The pop-up menu will open.

3. **Click** on the **number of colors** to display. The screen will flash and the colors will change.

4. **Click** on the **Refresh Rate pop-up menu**. The pop-up menu will open. The *refresh rate* is the speed at which the monitor redraws its image—a higher value reduces any flicker you may perceive.

5. **Click** on the **refresh rate**. The screen will flash and the refresh rate will change.

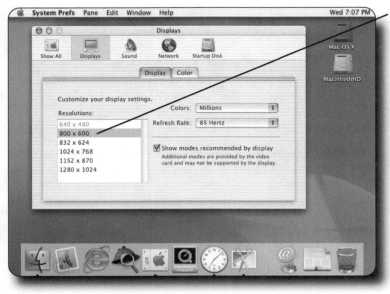

6. **Click** on a **resolution** in the Resolutions list. The *resolution* is the number of pixels displayed on the screen. The screen will flash and the resolution will change.

7. **Click** on the **Color tab**. The Color tab will come forward.

CAUTION

You can clear the Show modes recommended by display check box to enable more choices, but choosing one of the enabled settings can cause your monitor to behave in unreliable or unexpected ways. Consult any documentation that came with your monitor.

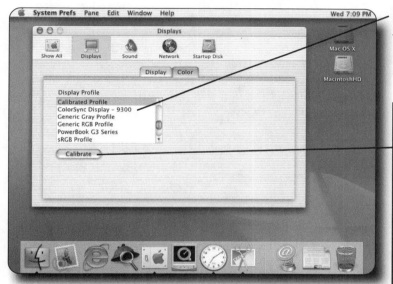

8. Click on your **Monitor** in the Display Profile list. Your monitor's color, contrast, and brightness will change.

TIP

If you would like to fine tune your monitor's color, click on the Calibrate button to start the Display Calibration Assistant, which will help you create a ColorSync profile for that display.

Setting Energy Saver Preferences

The Energy Saver pane provides settings to take full advantage of your Mac's power-saving capabilities. (Given the rolling blackouts occurring in California as I write this, we all should do everything possible to conserve power.) The settings enable you to control the timing for when the system automatically enters the power-conserving sleep mode.

1. **Click** on the **Energy Saver icon**. The Energy Saver pane will appear in the System Preferences window.

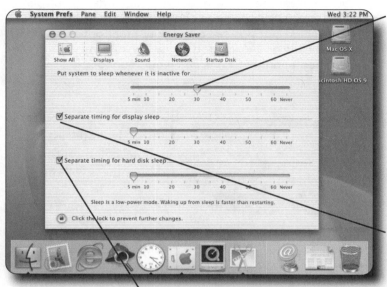

2. **Drag** the **Put system to sleep whenever it is inactive for slider** to adjust the specified period of inactivity. When the system has been inactive for the period, both the display and hard disk will sleep unless you override this setting by enabling one of the other two settings.

3. **Click** on the **Separate timing for Display sleep check box and drag** the **slider** to adjust the specified period of inactivity triggering when the display or monitor should sleep. When this feature is enabled, it overrides the general Sleep setting.

4. **Click** on the **Separate timing for hard disk sleep check box and drag** the **slider** to adjust the specified period of inactivity triggering when the hard disk should sleep. When this feature is enabled, it overrides the general Sleep setting.

Setting General Preferences

The General pane offers settings to control the colors used for screen elements like menus. It also has an option to adjust how scroll bars function in Finder and application windows.

1. **Click** on the **General Preferences icon**. The General Preferences pane will appear in the System Preferences window.

2. Click on the **Appearance pop-up menu**. The pop-up menu will open.

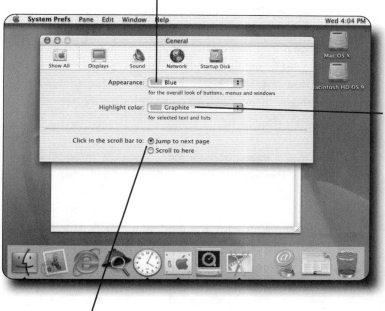

3. Click on a **color** to change the color used for buttons, menus, and windows.

4. Click on the **Highlight color pop-up menu**. The pop-up menu will open.

5. Click on a **color** to be used for items that you highlight or select in documents and lists. This is the color that appears when you drag over text in a document or click an item in a list or window.

6. Click on the **option buttons** to control how far window (or list) contents scroll when you click on the scroll bar above or below the scroll box. A dot will appear in the option button when it is selected.

NOTE

When the Jump to next page option button is selected, each click scrolls the window contents a full page. When the Scroll to here option button is selected, the window contents scroll a distance that's proportionate to the location where you click above or below the box.

Setting International Preferences

If you create or work with documents not written in English, then you can change a variety of settings in the International pane. You can control how the menus appear, how dates and times appear, how numbers and currency values appear, and whether or not Mac OS X displays a keyboard menu to enable you to switch quickly between keyboard layouts.

1. Click on the **International icon**. The International pane will appear in the System Preferences window.

2. Drag an **entry** in the Languages list to the top of the list to make it the primary language used in OS X. The language you place at the top of the list will be used in application menus and dialogs.

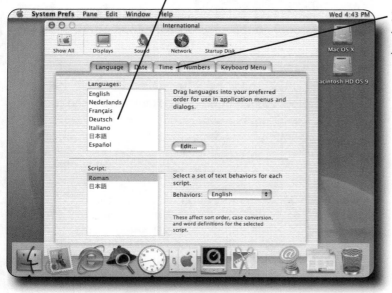

3. Click on the **Time tab**. The Time tab will come forward.

4. **Click** on the **Region pop-up menu**. The pop-up menu will open.

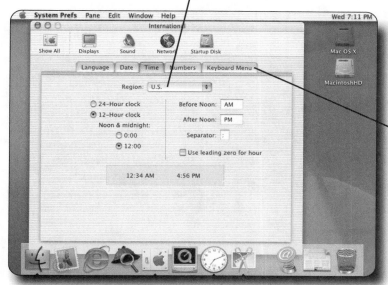

5. **Click** on your **time region**. The region will appear in the pop-up menu and Mac OS will handle time display accordingly.

6. **Click** on the **Keyboard Menu tab**. The Keyboard Menu tab will come forward.

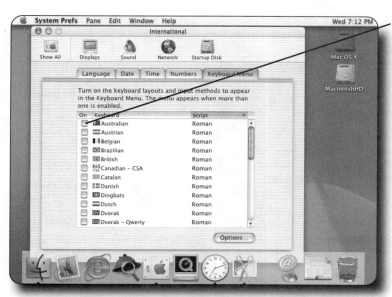

7. **Click** on the **check boxes** beside the languages that you may need to switch your keyboard layout too using the Keyboard menu (identified by a small flag icon on the menu bar). The corresponding keyboard layouts will be available from the Keyboard menu.

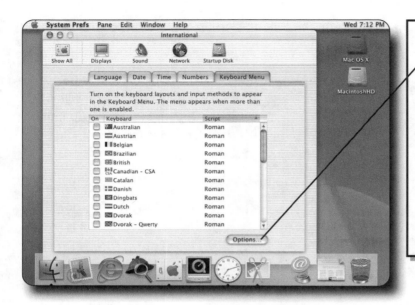

TIP

If you click on the Options button, you can specify whether the Command+Option+Space keyboard combination also cycles through the specified keyboard layouts and whether or not the font script on screen always changes to match the selected keyboard layout.

Setting Keyboard Preferences

We all type at different speeds and have varying levels of dexterity. As such, you may want to adjust how the keyboard responds as you press a key.

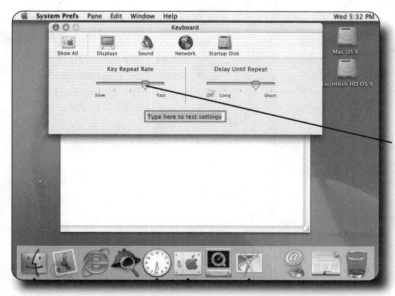

1. **Click** on the **Keyboard icon**. The Keyboard pane will appear in the System Preferences window.

2. **Drag** the **Key Repeat Rate slider**. The speed at which Mac OS X repeats a character when you press and hold the key will be adjusted.

TIP

Less experienced typists or folks whose fingers may have been slowed down by arthritis or other illness may be more comfortable using a slower Key Repeat Rate setting.

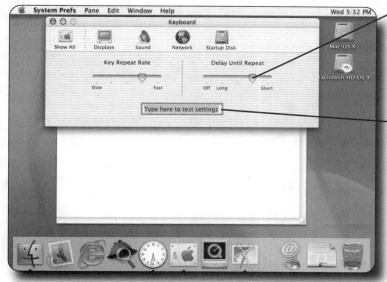

3. **Drag** the **Delay Until Repeat slider**. The delay before Mac OS X repeats a character once you press and hold a key will be set.

4. **Type** some **text** into the text box. This allows you to test the changes you made to one or both of the settings.

Setting Mouse Preferences

Like the Keyboard preferences, the preferences on the Mouse pane enable you to change settings that affect your mouse's responsiveness when you drag and click.

1. **Click** on the **Mouse icon**. The Mouse pane will appear in the System Preferences window.

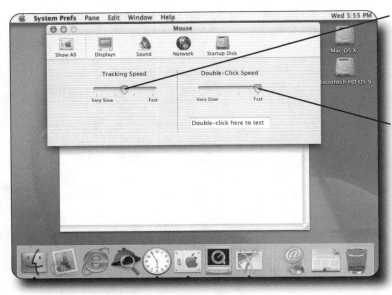

2. Drag the **Tracking Speed slider**. The speed at which the mouse pointer moves on the screen will increase or decrease.

3. Drag the **Double-Click Speed slider**. The rate at which you must double-click the mouse button in order for Mac OS X to recognize the double-click will be set.

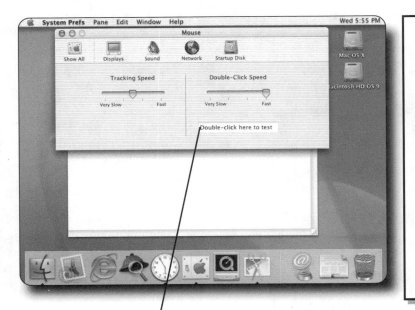

TIP

If you're less experienced with your Mac and using a mouse, slower Tracking Speed and Double-Click Speed settings can help you have greater control. On the other hand, a faster Tracking Speed setting coupled with a slower Double-Click Speed setting can be useful if your physical range of motion is limited.

4. Type some **text** into the text box. You will see if the settings you made are comfortable for you. If double-clicking highlights part of the text box entry, then Mac OS X has recognized the double-click.

Setting Screen Saver Preferences

Years ago, screen savers protected your screen because their motion prevented an image from permanently burning into the phosphors. Today's displays are much heartier, so screen savers mostly serve to entertain. However, screen savers also can function as a privacy measure to hide sensitive data displayed on screen. To deactivate a screen saver once it displays, wiggle your mouse or press a key.

1. Click on the **Screen Saver icon**. The Screen Saver pane will appear in the System Preferences window.

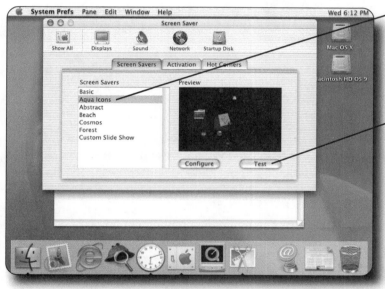

2. Click on the **screen saver** that you want Mac OS X to use in the Screen Savers list. Your selection will appear in the Preview screen.

3. If you would like to preview the screen saver at full-size, **click** on **Test**. The screen saver will run until you interrupt it.

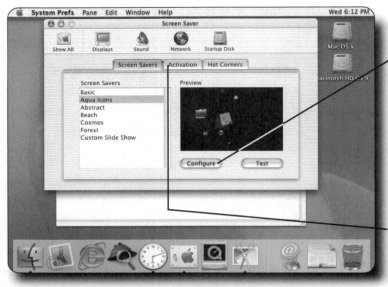

TIP
Click on the Configure button if you would like to display the available options for the selected screen saver (these vary). A dialog box will appear allowing you to configure the settings.

4. **Click** on the **Activation tab**. The Activation tab will come forward.

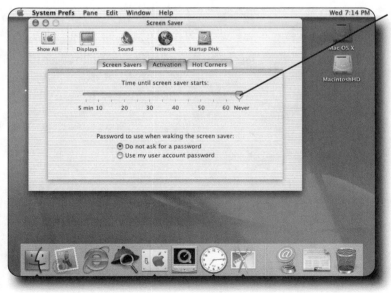

5. **Drag** the **Time until screen saver starts slider** to specify how much idle time should elapse before the screen saver activates.

NOTE

The screen saver does not appear when your Mac goes to sleep based on the preferences you've chosen on the Energy Saver pane (nor is the screen saver an energy-saving feature). The time you select using the Time until screen saver starts slider on the Activation tab should be shorter than the inactivity periods you specify on the Energy Saver pane of System Preferences. Otherwise, your computer will always go to sleep before it displays the screen saver.

Setting Software Update Preferences

Software Update enables Mac OS X to connect to the Internet periodically, check for updates to the system software, and download and install those updates. You can use the choices on the Software Update pane to control when you want Software Update to run.

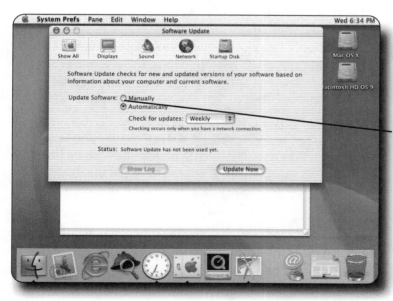

1. **Click** on the **Software Update icon**. The Software Update pane will appear in the System Preferences window.

2a. **Click** on the **Manually option button** if you want to use Software Update only when you click on the Update Now button in this pane. The option button will be selected.

OR

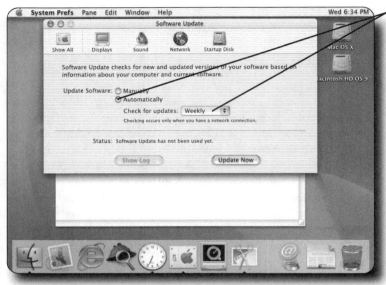

2b. **Click** on the **Automatically option button and choose** a **frequency setting** from the Check for updates pop-up menu to have Software Update run at the specified interval. The option button will be selected.

Setting Sound Preferences

Newer Macs have pretty slick sound capabilities, and the settings on the Sound pane enable Mac OS X to take full advantage of those capabilities.

1. **Click** on the **Sound icon**. The Sound pane will appear in the System Preferences window.

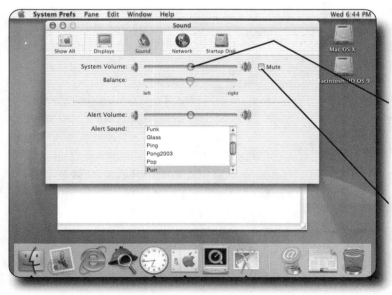

The System Volume slider controls the volume for music and other audio as opposed to system alerts.

2a. **Drag** the **System Volume slider** to increase or decrease the volume.

OR

2b. **Click** on the **Mute check box** to turn the system volume off altogether. A check will appear in the box.

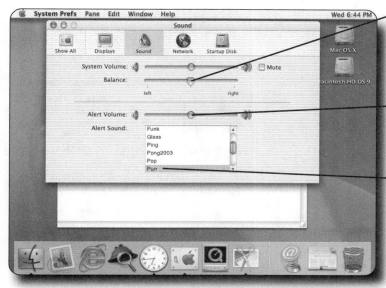

3. Drag the **Balance slider** to adjust the relative volume levels for the left and right speakers on your system.

4. Drag the **Alert Volume slider** to decrease or increase the alert volume.

5. Click on the **alert sound** you prefer to use for system alerts in the Alert Sound list. The sound will be selected and you will hear it immediately.

Setting Speech Preferences

Mac OS X enables you to take advantage of recent improvements in speech recognition technology. When you turn on the Speakable Items feature, you can use voice commands to have Mac OS X perform certain actions. You also can use this pane to control how the Text-to-Speech capability sounds when it speaks text back to you.

1. Click on the **Speech icon**. The Speech pane will appear in the System Preferences window.

NOTE

See Chapter 18 "Working with Other Features," for more on using Speakable Items in Mac OS X.

2. Click on the **On option button** to enable Speakable Items. You will now be able to activate certain commands with your voice!

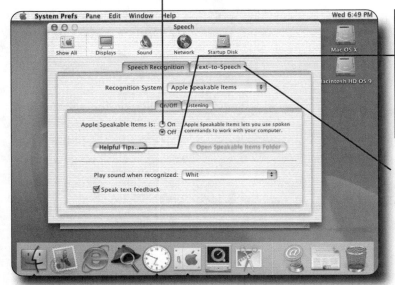

TIP

If you want to learn more about using speech recognition, click on the Helpful Tips button.

3. Click on the **Text-to-Speech tab**. The Text-to-Speech tab will move forward.

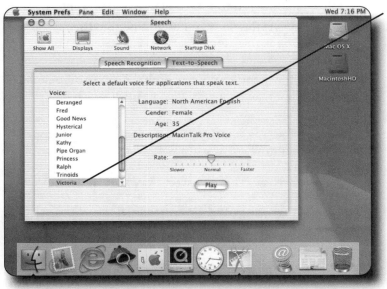

4. Click on a **voice** in the Voice list. The voice will be selected and Mac OS X will use it when you're running any application that speaks text back to you.

10

Working with Printers

Despite its capabilities for play, chances are that your Macintosh will serve as a working tool for you during a significant portion of its life. While technology has made great strides in sharing digital content in recent months, most of us still need to generate a fair amount of printed matter for both our jobs and our personal lives. In this chapter, you'll learn how to:

- Install a printer to work with Mac OS X.
- Choose which printer to use and print from an application.
- Specify a default printer.
- Remove a printer that you've set up.

Mac OS X supports a number of inkjet printers directly. All you have to do is connect such a printer to your system and turn it on (many of them are USB printers), and Mac OS X automatically sets up the printer. The following list identifies printers directly supported by the initial Mac OS X release in this way (other printers may be added later via updates to Mac OS X):

Canon	Epson	Hewlett-Packard
BJF360	Stylus COLOR 680	Deskjet 810
BJF660	Stylus COLOR 740	Deskjet 812
BJF870	Stylus COLOR 760	Deskjet 816
BJS600	Stylus COLOR 777	Deskjet 830
S400	Stylus COLOR 860	Deskjet 832
S450	Stylus COLOR 880	Deskjet 840
S600	PM-720C	Deskjet 842
S800	PM-780C	Deskjet 880
	PM-880C	Deskjet 882
	PM-900C	Deskjet 895
	PM-3500C	Deskjet 930
		Deskjet 932
		Deskjet 935
		Deskjet 950
		Deskjet 952
		Deskjet 955
		Deskjet 957
		Deskjet 960
		Deskjet 970
		Deskjet 990

> ### NOTE
>
> Some printers aren't yet supported by Mac OS X. In other cases, even when Mac OS X supports a particular printer model, it may not support all features of that model, such as custom paper sizes. Using the Software Update feature regularly can help you check for printer support improvements for Mac OS X. See the section called "Setting Software Update Preferences" in Chapter 9 "Changing Essential System Preferences" to learn more about downloading Mac OS X updates.

Setting up a Printer from Print Center

Print Center serves as the printer management utility for Mac OS X. It enables you to set up other printers that don't set up automatically, select a default printer, and control printing. The steps presented here are a generalization showing you how to set up a printer using Print Center. Be sure to read the documentation for your printer prior to installation and follow its directions if they differ from the steps presented here.

1. **Connect** your **printer** to its power source and to the Mac (via the appropriate cable) **and turn on** the **printer**. The printer will start up and be ready for set up.

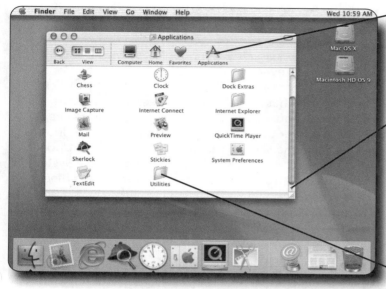

2. Click on the **Applications toolbar button** in a Finder window. The contents of the folder will appear in the Finder window.

3. If needed, **click** on the **down arrow** of the vertical scroll bar as many times as needed to scroll down to the bottom of the window. The Utilities folder will scroll into view.

4. Double-click on the **Utilities folder**. The contents of the folder will appear in the Finder window.

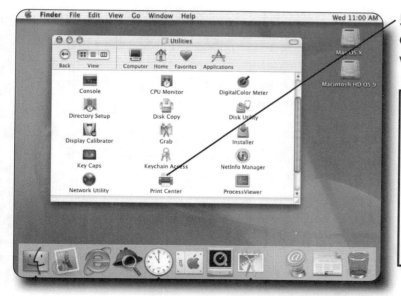

5. Double-click on **Print Center**. Print Center will start.

NOTE

The first time you set up a printer, a dialog box will inform you that you have no printers available. In this instance, click on the Add button, and then skip to Step 7.

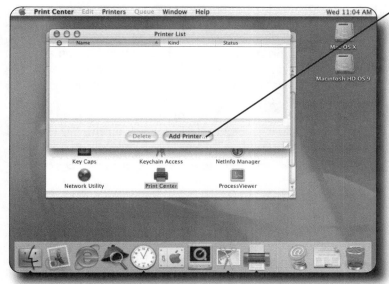

6. Click on **Add Printer**. A dialog for adding printers will appear.

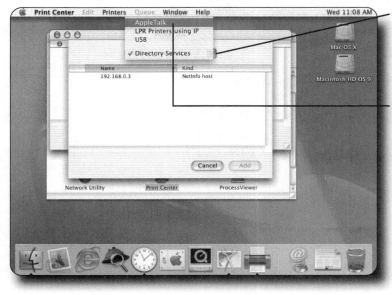

7. Click on the **pop-up menu** near the top of the dialog. The pop-up menu will open.

8. Click on the **type of connection** your printer uses. A list of printers available via that connection type will appear in the dialog.

NOTE

To choose a printer connected to a network or on an older Mac system that uses AppleTalk connections, AppleTalk must be enabled. Click on the System Preferences icon on the Dock, then click on the Network icon. Click on the Configure pop-up menu and select Built-in Ethernet. Then click on the AppleTalk tab and use it to enable AppleTalk.

9. **Click** on the **desired printer** in the list. The printer will be selected.

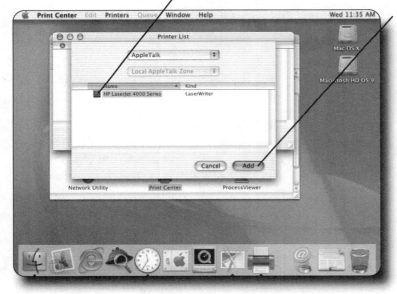

10. **Click** on **Add**. The dialog will close and the printer will appear in Print Center and be available for printing from your applications.

11. **Click** on **Print Center**. The Print Center menu will appear.

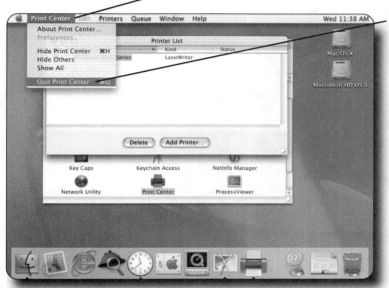

12. **Click** on **Quit Print Center**. Print Center will close.

Now you can resume your work in other applications, as you're ready to print. You can repeat this procedure to add new printers at any time.

Selecting a Printer and Printing

You do not need to open Print Center every time that you want to print a document. Any application you're using provides the capability for you to select a printer and choose settings for the printout. You should note, however, that the settings will vary depending on your printer model, its driver software, and the capabilities of the application from which you're printing.

1. **Open** a **document or create** a new **document** in the preferred application. You will see an approximation of how your printout will look.

2. **Click** on **File**. The File menu will open.

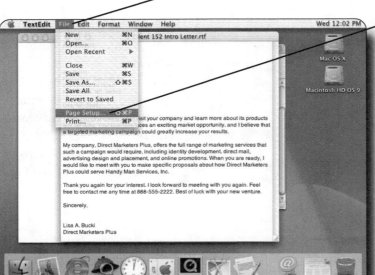

3. **Click** on **Page Setup**. A dialog will appear.

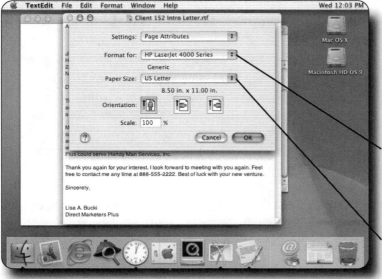

Here you can make changes to the overall layout of your document for printing. The available settings may vary depending on your application and the selected printer.

4. If needed, **click** on the **Format for pop-up menu and click** on the **printer** to use for the print job.

5. **Click** on the **Paper Size pop-up menu**. The pop-up menu will open.

6. **Click** on the **paper size** that wish to print on **and load** the **paper** in your printer

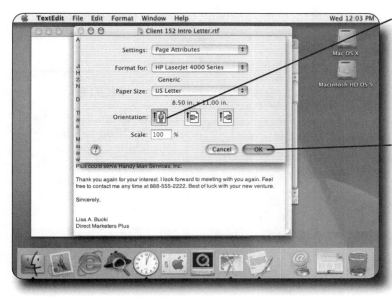

7. Click on an **orientation button**. The button will be selected. This setting determines what direction the printer will print your document on the paper.

8. Click on **OK**. The dialog will close and the settings will be applied.

9. Click on **File**. The File menu will open.

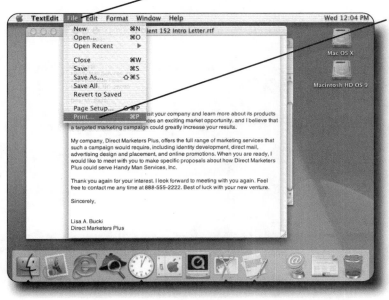

10. Click on **Print**. A dialog will appear. The available settings will vary depending on your application and the selected printer.

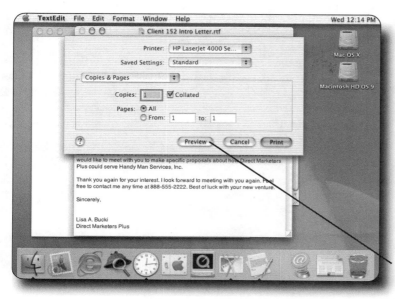

11. **Verify** the **settings** as needed.

NOTE

In this example using the TextEdit application, you can view additional printing options by clicking on the Copies & Pages pop-up menu.

12. **Click** on **Preview**. Preview will open and display your document.

13. **Click** on **Preview**. The Preview menu will appear.

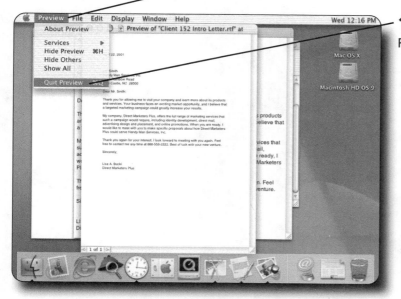

14. **Click** on **Quit Preview**. Preview will close.

15. **Click** on **File**. The File menu will appear.

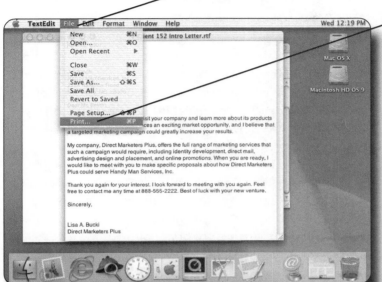

16. **Click** on **Print**. A dialog will open. The settings you selected earlier will still be active.

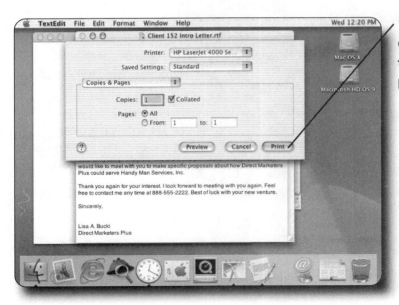

17. **Click** on **Print**. Print Center will open temporarily to send the document to the printer, and then close.

Choosing the Default Printer

Printers today offer a wide range of benefits and features; therefore, you can install multiple printers for use with your Macintosh. For example, you may have a color inkjet printer for printing family photos, cards, or business promotional materials. But because the inkjet ink can be a little pricey and the printer itself is slow, you may also have an inexpensive laser printer for a speedier and less-costly method of printing. Use Print Center to designate which printer to use as the default printer—the printer that is first suggested in your applications. Choosing the proper default printer reduces how often you need to change the printer selection and settings before printing.

1. **Click** on the **Applications toolbar button** in a Finder window. The contents of the folder will appear in the Finder window.

2. If needed, **click** on the **down arrow** of the vertical scroll bar. The Utilities folder will scroll into view.

3. **Double-click** on the **Utilities folder**. The contents of the folder will appear in the Finder window.

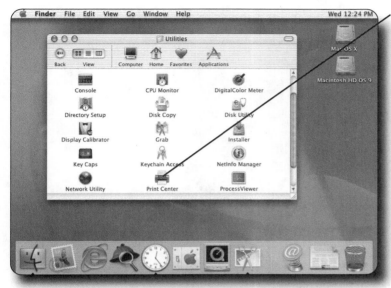

4. Double-click on **Print Center**. Print Center will start.

5. Click on the **desired printer** in Print Center. The printer will be selected in the list.

6. Click on **Printers**. The Printers menu will appear.

7. Click on **Make Default**. The selected printer will be immediately designated as the default printer.

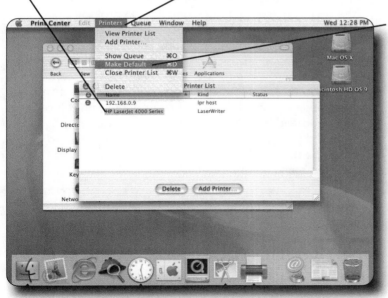

8. Click on **Print Center**. The Print Center menu will appear.

9. Click on **Quit Print Center**. Print Center will close.

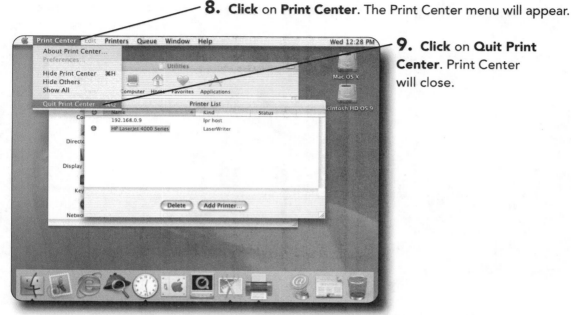

NOTE

If you've started a number of lengthy printouts, notice that you can use the Print Center to control the *print queue*—the list of documents sent to the printer. Select a printer in Print Center, then choose Printers, Show Queue. Click on a print job in the list that appears, and then click on the menu and use its various commands. The Stop Queue command stops printing to the printer, but does not cancel the remaining pending print jobs. Hold Job and Resume Job pause and restart the selected print job. Delete Job removes the selected job from the queue. Click on the close button when you've finished manipulating print jobs.

Removing a Printer

You may need to remove a printer that's been set up for your system if you no longer plan to use it. Pruning out old

printers is part of a good practice of keeping your system
streamlined and working well.

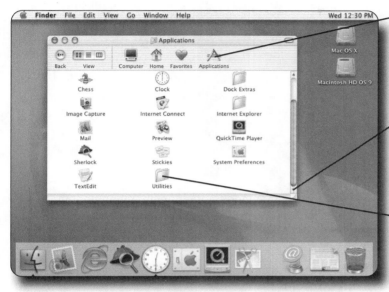

1. Click on the **Applications toolbar button** in a Finder window. The contents of the folder will appear in the Finder window.

2. If needed, **click** on the **down arrow** of the vertical scroll bar. The Utilities folder will scroll into view.

3. Double-click on the **Utilities folder**. The contents of the folder will appear in the Finder window.

4. Double-click on **Print Center**. Print Center will start.

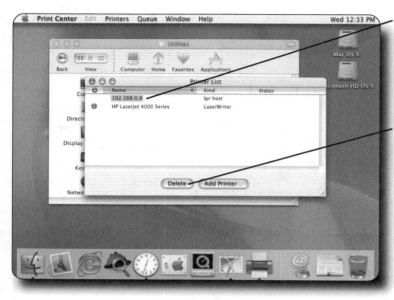

5. **Click** on the **printer name** to be deleted in the Print Center window. The printer will be selected in the list.

6. **Click** on **Delete**. The printer will be removed from the list.

7. **Click** on **Print Center**. The Print Center menu will appear.

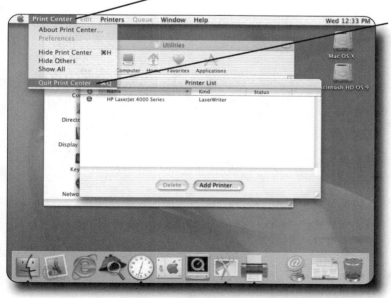

8. **Click** on **Quit Print Center**. Print Center will close.

Part III Review Questions

1. How do I change Finder settings? *See "Changing Disk and Finder Settings" in Chapter 8.*

2. How do I use another graphic on my desktop? *See "Changing Disk and Finder Settings" in Chapter 8.*

3. Can I customize the Dock? *See "Changing Dock Settings" in Chapter 8.*

4. Where are the System Preferences? *See "Displaying System Preferences" in Chapter 9.*

5. The Preferences are asking me for an administrator password. What gives? *See "Unlocking and Locking Preferences Pane" in Chapter 9.*

6. How do I get back to the full list of preferences? *See "Redisplaying All the Preferences" in Chapter 9.*

7. How do I reset the time? *See "Setting Date & Time Preferences" in Chapter 9.*

8. My system keeps going black. What is that? *See "Setting Energy Saver Preferences" in Chapter 9.*

9. I try to print but there's no printer. How do I add one? *See "Setting up a Printer from Print Center" in Chapter 10.*

10. How do I print my file? *See "Selecting a Printer and Printing" in Chapter 10.*

PART IV

Jumping Online

Chapter 11
   Setting up the Connection **171**

Chapter 12
   Corresponding with Mail **183**

Chapter 13
   Traveling the Web **205**

Chapter 14
   Snooping for Content with Sherlock **225**

Chapter 15
   Downloading and Installing Software **235**

11

Setting up the Connection

If your Mac connects to the Internet via a dial-up modem connection rather than through a network, you may need to take some preparatory action to ensure that the connection works correctly. In this chapter, you'll learn how to:

● Enter or adjust Internet preferences for Mac OS X.

● Use Internet Connect to specify a connection phone number and other connection details.

Setting Internet Preferences

If you used the Setup Assistant the first time Mac OS X was started on the system, you provided Mac OS X with some basic information about the account you have with your ISP *(Internet Service Provider)*. If you change ISPs or if your ISP makes some changes to the way you must log in to your account, you may need to alter the Internet settings used by your system. Your ISP should provide any additional account information that you need. You need to set up for your ISP connection or make changes in two places. First, you need to add or change the Internet account information in System Preferences as described in this section. Then, you need to enter or alter the specific dial-up information using Internet Connect, as described in the next section.

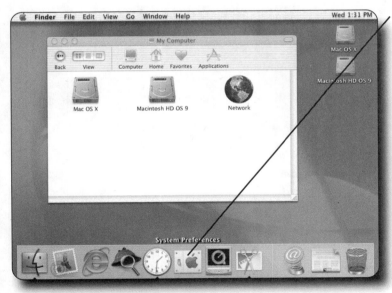

1. Click on the **System Preferences icon** on the Dock. The System Preferences window will open.

TIP

Alternately, you can choose System Preferences from the Apple menu to launch System Preferences.

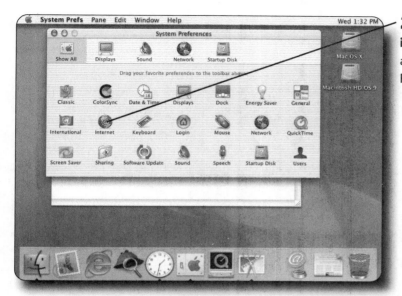

2. Click on the **Internet icon**. The Internet pane will appear in the System Preferences window.

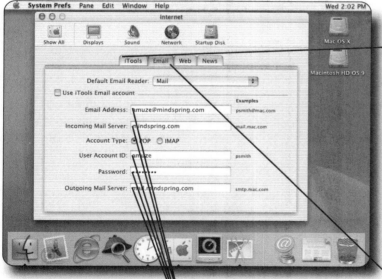

NOTE

You can use the iTools tab to enter your iTools account information or to sign up for an iTools account if you wish. With iTools, you can get email service via Mac.com, take advantage of your iDisk online storage space, create iCards to share online, or even set up your own Web site.

3. Click on the **Email tab**. The Email tab will come forward.

4. Type your **Email Address**, **Incoming Mail Server**, **User Account ID**, **Password**, and **Outgoing Mail Server** in the text boxes. These settings are provided by your ISP.

5. **Click** on an **Account Type option button**. The option will be selected.

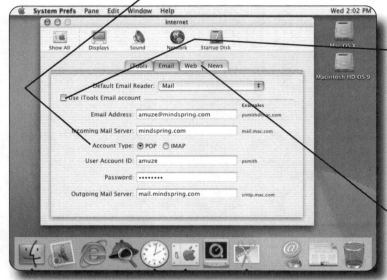

NOTE

If you entered account information on the iTools tab, you can click on the Use iTools Email account check box to automatically enter the account information on the Email tab.

6. **Click** on the **Web tab**. The Web tab will move forward.

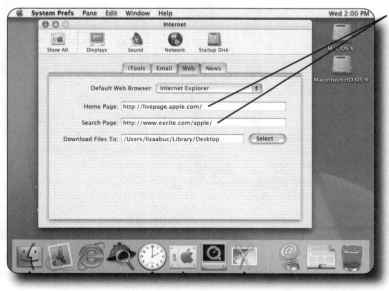

7. **Type** a **Home Page** (the page that displays first when you start your Web browser), **and** a **Search Page** (the page that you'll use to search the Web) in the text boxes.

8. **Click** on **System Prefs**. The System Prefs menu will appear.

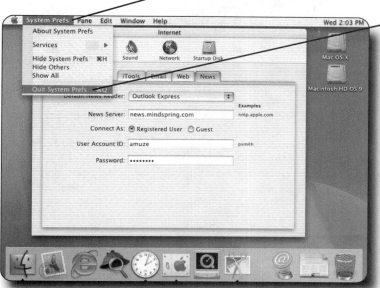

9. **Click** on **Quit System Prefs**. Mac OS X will apply your new settings and close System Preferences immediately.

Creating a Connection with Internet Connect

Changing the Internet settings for your system completes half of the preparation for going online. Next, you must specify what phone number your modem should dial to connect with your ISP. (Again, the ISP should provide all information needed for the connection.) To make or edit the actual connection, you use a Mac OS X application called Internet Connect, which works with the System Preferences settings for your modem (on the Network pane).

1. Click on the **Applications button** on the toolbar in a Finder window. The contents of the folder will appear in the Finder window.

2. Double-click on **Internet Connect**. Internet Connect will open.

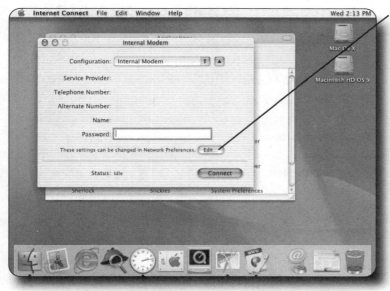

3. Click on **Edit**. System Preferences will open and display the Network pane.

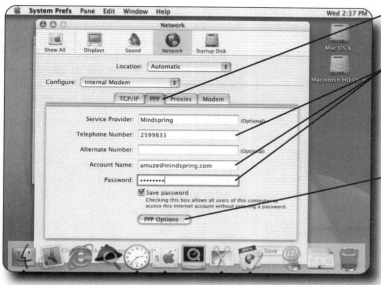

4. **Click** on the **PPP tab.**The PPP tab will move forward.

5. **Type** the **Telephone Number**, **Account Name** (user name), **and Password** provided by your ISP in the text boxes.

6. **Click** on **PPP Options**. The Session Options dialog will appear with options for further adjusting how your dial-up connection behaves.

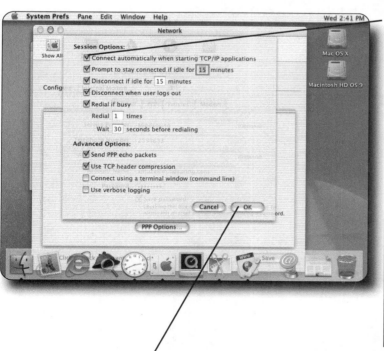

7. **Click** on the **Connect automatically when starting TCP/IP applications check box**. a check will appear in the box and Internet Connect will automatically dial your Internet connection whenever you start an application or activity that requires it.

NOTE

There is no setting that automatically disconnects when you quit an Internet activity or application.

8. **Click** on **OK**. The Session Options dialog will close.

9. Click on **System Prefs**. The System Prefs menu will appear.

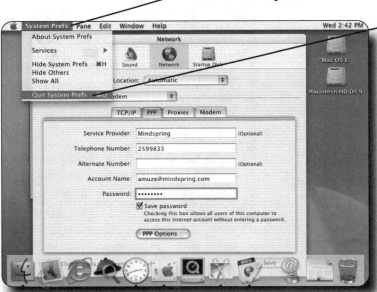

10. Click on **Quit System Prefs**. A dialog will prompt you to save your configuration changes.

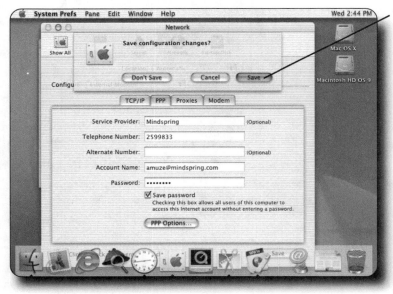

11. Click on **Save**. Your changes will be saved and System Preferences will close, returning you to Internet Connect. Internet Connect will immediately dial the specified Internet connection.

NOTE

The next time you start Internet Connect, it will display the connection settings you've most recently entered.

Connecting to and Disconnecting from the Internet

Even if you configured Internet Connect to dial your Internet connection automatically (via the Network pane in System Preferences as described in the last section), you still may encounter times when you want to connect manually. Further, since Internet Connect won't automatically disconnect, it's a good practice to always check for an active connection and disconnect it if needed.

1. Click on the **Applications button** on the toolbar in a Finder window. The contents of the folder will appear in the Finder window.

2. Double-click on **Internet Connect**. Internet Connect will open.

TIP

For easy access to Internet Connect, drag its icon from the Applications folder onto the Dock.

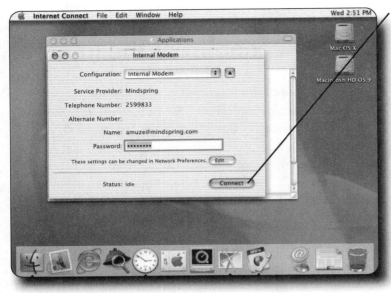

3. Click on **Connect**. Internet Connect will dial the ISP and use the settings you've entered to log in. (You may not hear sounds from your modem during the process.) After the connection is made, Internet Connect will display the connection status.

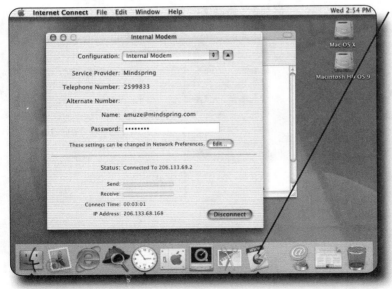

4. When you are ready to disconnect, **click** on the **Internet Connect icon** on the Dock. The Internet Connect window will become the active window.

NOTE

When you use some Internet applications, Internet Connect makes the connection without displaying a Dock icon. In such a case, repeat Steps 1 and 2 to redisplay Internet Connect, then use Step 5 to disconnect.

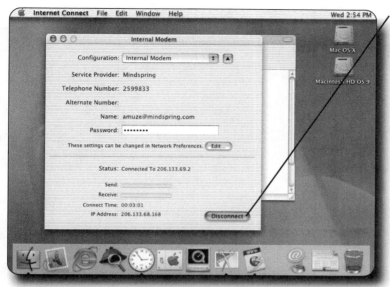

5. Click on **Disconnect**. Your system will hang up the Internet connection.

6. Click on **Internet Connect**. The Internet Connect menu will open.

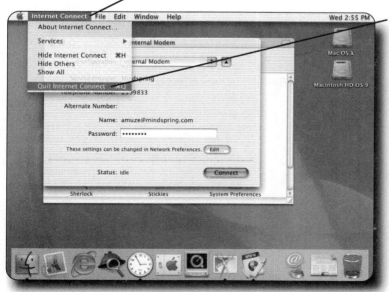

7. Click on **Quit Internet Connect**. Internet Connect will close.

NOTE

You can quit Internet Connect without clicking on the Disconnect button. This will improve your system performance without hanging up the connection.

12

Corresponding with Mail

E-mail has become an important tool in both home and business settings. In the home, e-mail enables you to share information more easily with multiple friends and relatives and economize on long distance charges. In an office, e-mail not only enables fast, responsive communication but also enables you to maintain a record of your correspondence. Mac OS X provides the Mail application to enable you to send, receive, and store e-mail messages. This chapter introduces you to using the key features in Mail. In this chapter, you'll learn how to:

- Launch and close Mail as needed.
- Control how Mail works by changing settings.
- Write and send e-mail messages.
- Receive, respond to, and file e-mail.
- Organize your e-mail addresses in Address Book.

Starting and Exiting Mail

Mac OS X offers easy access to the Mail program via the Dock.

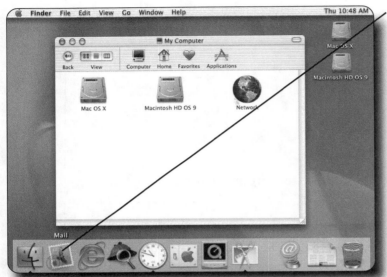

1. **Click** on the **Mail icon** on the Dock. The Mail application window will open and its menus will appear. You will see a main Viewer window that displays the list of messages as well as a Mailboxes window.

NOTE

If your system connects to the Internet via a dial-up connection, and you have configured the system to connect automatically as explained in Chapter 11, "Setting up the Connection," Internet Connect will launch and your modem will dial your ISP when you start Mail.

2. Click on **Mail**. The Mail menu will appear.

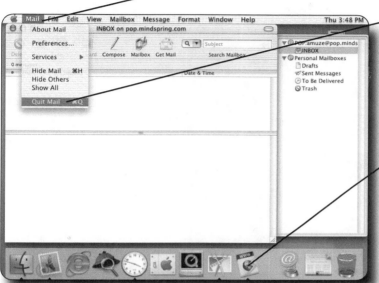

3. Click on **Quit Mail**. The Mail application window will close.

Now you will need to manually disconnect from the Internet.

4. Click on the **Internet Connect icon** on the Dock. Internet Connect will become the active application.

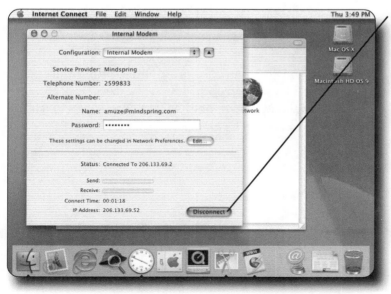

5. Click on **Disconnect**. Internet Connect will hang up the Internet connection.

6. Click on **Internet Connect**. The Internet Connect menu will appear.

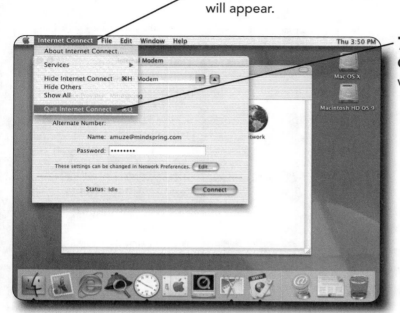

7. Click on **Quit Internet Connect**. Internet Connect will close.

Changing Mail Settings

You can personalize some of the settings used in Mail.

1. Click on the **Mail icon** on the Dock. The Mail application window will open and its menus will appear.

2. Click on **Mail**. The Mail menu will appear.

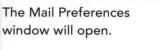

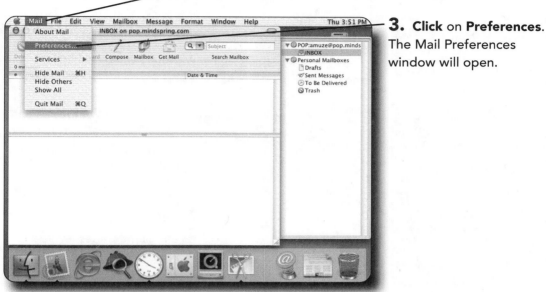

3. Click on **Preferences**. The Mail Preferences window will open.

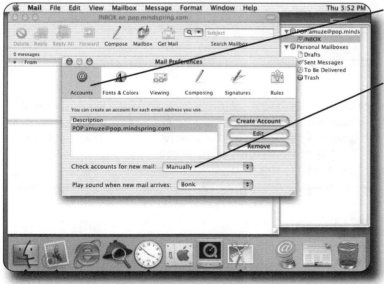

4. Click on the **Accounts icon**. The Accounts pane will appear in the window.

5. Click on the **Check accounts for new mail pop-up menu**. The pop-up menu will open.

6. Click on a **setting** to specify how often Mail should check for new messages. Choose Manually to check mail only when you specify.

TIP

If you have a dial-up connection, it's best to use the Manually or Every Hour choices so your modem isn't continuously going online without your knowledge.

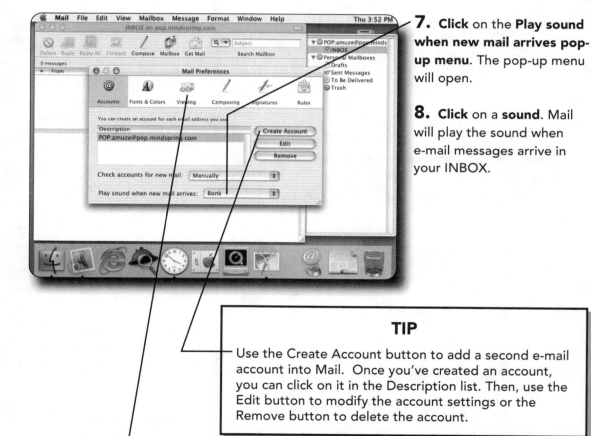

7. Click on the **Play sound when new mail arrives pop-up menu**. The pop-up menu will open.

8. Click on a **sound**. Mail will play the sound when e-mail messages arrive in your INBOX.

TIP

Use the Create Account button to add a second e-mail account into Mail. Once you've created an account, you can click on it in the Description list. Then, use the Edit button to modify the account settings or the Remove button to delete the account.

9. Click on the **Viewing icon**. The Viewing pane will appear.

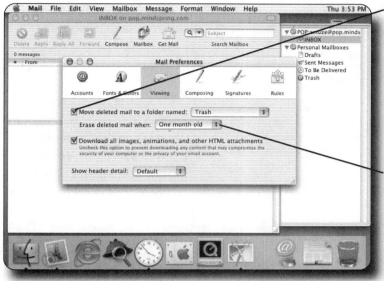

10. Click on the **Move deleted mail to a folder named check box and choose** the **folder** you want to use to store deleted messages from the pop-up menu. Mail will create the folder for you when needed.

11. Click on the **Erase deleted mail when pop-up menu**. The pop-up menu will open.

12. Click on a **setting** to control how long a message will remain in the deleted messages folder before Mail permanently erases it.

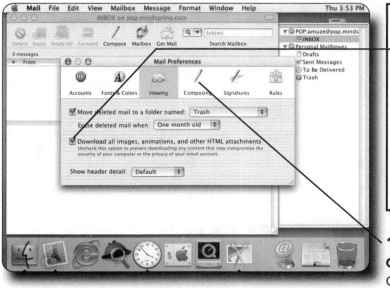

TIP

Normally, Mail downloads all attachments with your incoming messages. If you're concerned about system security, clear the Download all images, animations, and other HTML Attachments check box.

13. Click on the **Composing icon**. The Composing pane will appear in the window.

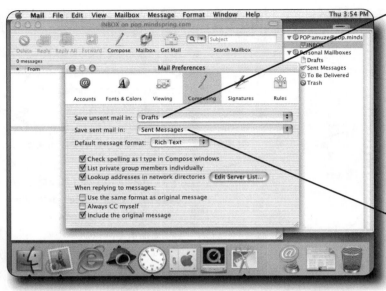

14. **Click** on the **Save unsent mail in pop-up menu**. The pop-up menu will open.

15. **Click** on the **folder** in which you want Mail to store messages that you've composed but haven't sent. The folder will be selected.

16. **Click** on the **Save sent mail in pop-up menu**. The pop-up menu will open.

17. **Click** on the **folder** in which you want Mail to store messages that you have sent. The folder will be selected.

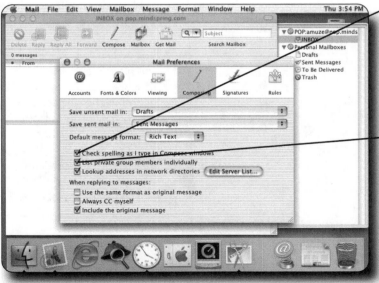

18. **Leave** the **Check spelling as I type in Compose windows check box** checked if you want to have your messages spell-checked automatically.

19. **Leave** the **List private group members individually check box** checked If you've organized e-mail addresses into groups in the Address Book and want to have all group member addresses appear in the header for an outgoing message.

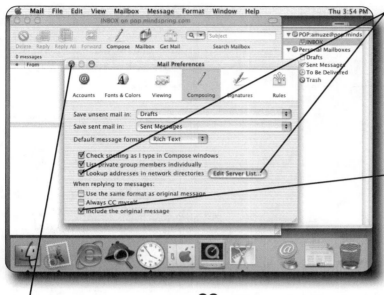

20. Leave the **Lookup addresses in network directories check box** checked if you're sending e-mail over a network, **and click** on **Edit Server List** to specify the server(s) hosting the network directory.

21. Leave the **Include the original message check box** checked if you want to include the text of the message to which you're responding in your reply.

22. **Click** on the **close button**. The Mail Preferences window will close and the settings you selected will take effect.

Sending Mail

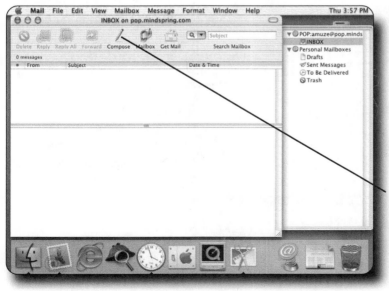

Sending an e-mail message requires two basic steps. You compose the message and then send your mail to the Internet. This section walks you through the ins and outs of each of these operations so that you'll be "e-mailing away" in no time!

1. **Click** on the **Compose button** on the toolbar of the main Mail window. The New Message window (also called the Compose window) will open.

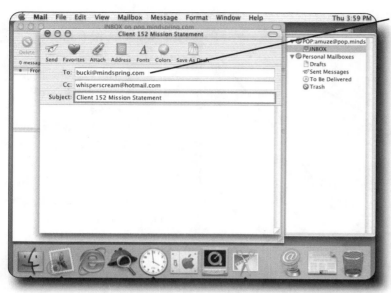

2. Type a **recipient's e-mail address** in the To text box, **and press Tab**. The insertion point will move to the Cc text box.

TIP

If you want to include more than one e-mail address in the To or Cc text boxes, type the first address followed by a comma and a space, and then type the next one.

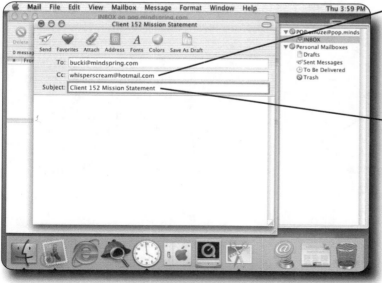

3. Type a **copy recipient's e-mail address** in the Cc text box, **and press Tab**. The insertion point will move to the Subject text box.

4. Type the **message subject** in the Subject text box, **and press Tab**. The insertion point will move to the message text area in the Compose window.

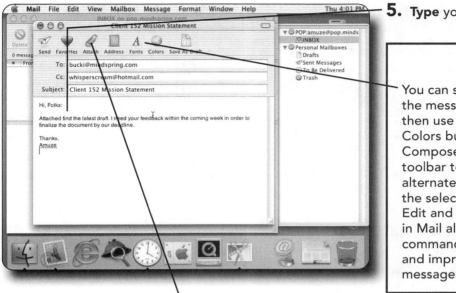

5. Type your **message text**.

TIP

You can select text in the message body and then use the Fonts and Colors buttons on the Compose window toolbar to apply alternate formatting to the selected text. The Edit and Format menus in Mail also offer commands for building and improving your message.

6. **Click** on the **Attach button** on the Compose window toolbar. A dialog will open so that you can select a file(s) to attach to the message.

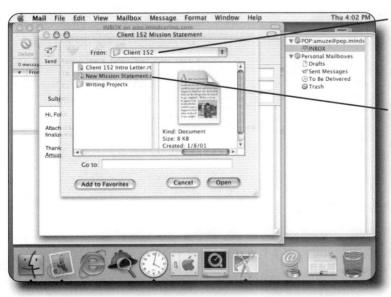

7. **Navigate to** the **folder** that holds the file(s) to attach. The folder's contents will be listed in the dialog.

8. **Click** on the **file** to attach. The file will be selected and a preview of the file will appear in the far-right column.

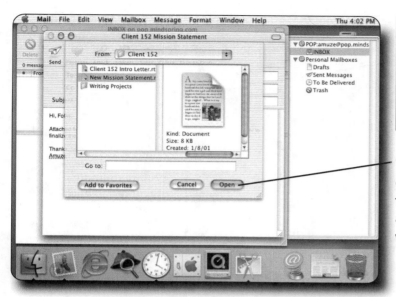

9. Click on **Open**. The dialog will close and an icon for the attached file will appear in the Compose window.

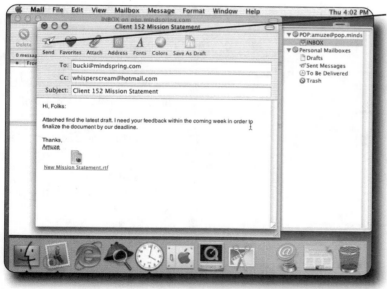

10. Click on the **Send button**. Mail will launch Internet Connect to connect to the Internet if needed and then send the message. A copy of the message will be placed in the Sent Messages folder (or the folder you specified in Mail Preferences).

CAUTION

If you attempt to send your e-mail without having first connected to the Internet or having configured Internet Connect to connect automatically as described in the chapter 11,"Setting up the Connection," you will see an Error message that Mail can't find the IP address of the Internet e-mail host, simply click on OK to close the message.

NOTE

If you want to reduce connect time, you can create messages, save them as drafts, and then open them later. To save a message as a draft, click on the Save As Draft button in the message window toolbar. To later send a draft, click on the Drafts folder (or the folder you specified to hold drafts in Mail Preferences). The Viewer window will list your message drafts. Double-click on a message in the list to open the message. Then click on the Send button on the Compose window toolbar.

Checking Mail

If you did not choose to set up Mail to check for incoming e-mail automatically, you can do so manually at any time. When you get your e-mail, Mail connects to the Internet if needed, checks for messages, and downloads messages into the

INBOX folder for your account, which appears in the Mailboxes window to the right of the main window.

1. **Click** on the **Get Mail button**. Mail will check for messages addressed to you. A copy of the message will be placed in the INBOX folder. If the INBOX folder is currently selected, the new message or messages will also be listed in the Viewer window.

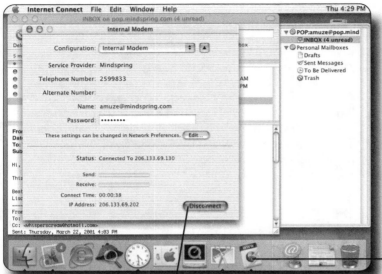

NOTE

If you have Mail set up to check multiple e-mail accounts, you can check a particular account by clicking on the Mailbox menu, moving the pointer to the Get New Mail in Account choice, then clicking on the account you want to check.

2. Click on the **Internet Connect icon** on the Dock. The Internet Connect window will become the active window.

3. Click on **Disconnect**. Internet Connect will hang up the Internet connection.

4. Click on **Internet Connect**. The Internet Connect menu will appear.

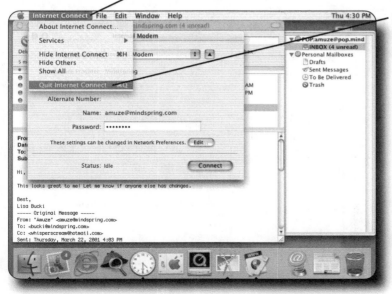

5. Click on **Quit Internet Connect**. Internet Connect will close.

NOTE

While you can read messages while your system is connected to the Internet, it's not necessary. I prefer to disconnect after getting e-mail, then reconnect to send any responses.

Reading and Responding to a Message

Any time you need to read your messages, you can display the list of messages in your INBOX in the main Viewer window in Mail. By default, that window will list the messages in chronological order, with the most recently composed message appearing at the bottom of the list. You can see who sent the message and its subject at a glance. After you read a message, you can decide how to respond to it, such as replying to the sender.

1. **Click** on the **INBOX** in the Mailboxes window. This will ensure that your received messages appear in the Viewer window. The bottom message in the list will be selected and its content will appear in the bottom pane of the Viewer window.

2. If needed, **click** on the **message** you want to read in the list. Its text will appear in the bottom pane.

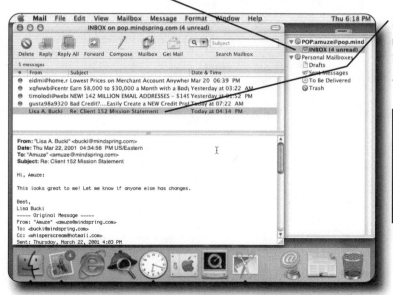

TIP

You also can double-click on a message in the list to open it in its own window.

If you want to respond to the message, there are three toolbar buttons from which you can choose:

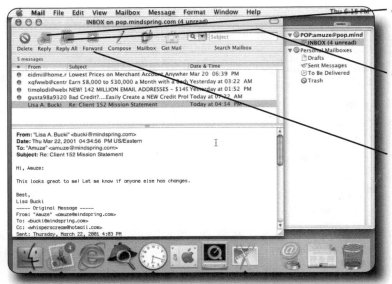

- **Reply**. Addresses the return message to the original sender only.

- **Reply All**. Addresses the return message to the original sender as well as all other recipients.

- **Forward**. Enables you to specify a recipient to whom you want to send a copy of the message and its attachments. Enter the recipient(s) in the To and Cc text boxes as needed.

After you click on of the toolbar buttons, a Compose window will open so you can type your response.

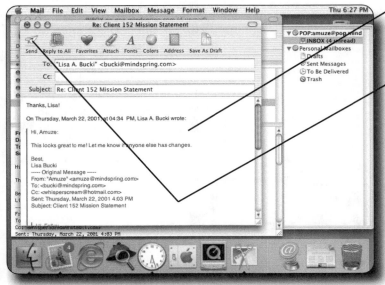

3. **Type** your **response and change** any other message **information** as needed.

4. **Click** on the **Send button**. Mail will use Internet Connect to connect to the Internet if needed, then send the message. A copy of the message will be placed in the Sent Messages folder (or the folder you specified in Mail Preferences).

Working with Address Book

The Address Book application in Mac OS X enables you to store contact information, especially e-mail addresses, to help you more easily address your Mail messages. Remember that Mail, to some degree, remembers e-mail addresses that you type into your outgoing messages. Address Book, however, enables you to capture much more information about a contact, such as a physical address and phone number, that you can use whenever needed. This section introduces you to Address Book so that you can begin to take advantage of its capabilities.

Starting and Quitting Address Book

You can start Address Book on its own or in conjunction with Mail. Mac OS X gives you three different ways to start Address Book, as follows:

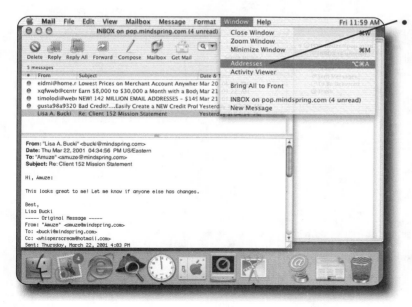

- In Mail, click on the Window menu, then click on Addresses.

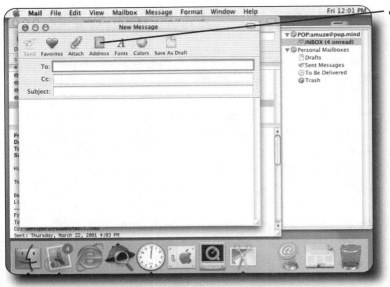

• In a Compose window, click on the Address button on the toolbar.

• Double-click on the Address Book icon in the Applications folder.

No matter which of the three methods you use, the Address Book window opens and its menu bar appears. When you want to close the Address Book, choose Quit Address Book from the Address Book menu.

Adding a Contact

When you add a contact, you store information about them in Address Book. The process works much like adding contact information into a paper address book.

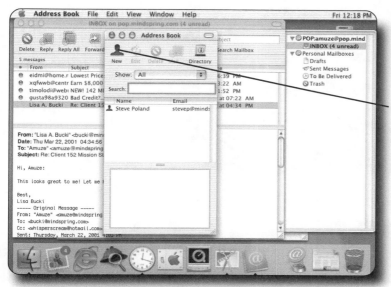

1. Double-click on the **Address Book icon** in the Applications folder. Address Book will open.

2. Click on the **New button** on the Address Book window toolbar. The untitled address card window will open.

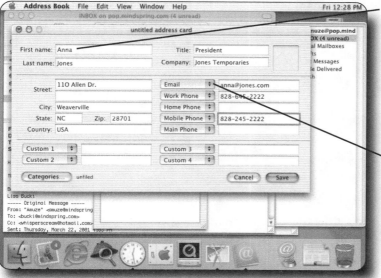

3. Type entries in the text boxes.

4. Press Tab. The cursor will move from field to field.

NOTE

When a field has a pop-up menu button beside it, you can use the pop-up menu to choose a different field name.

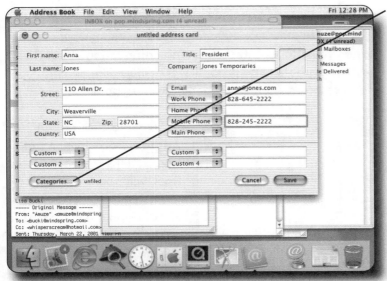

5. Click on **Categories**. The Choose Categories dialog will open.

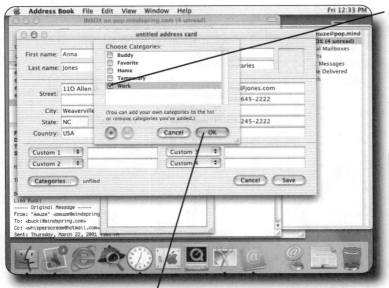

6. Click on the **check box** beside one or more categories. A check will appear in the boxes and the contact will be included in those categories for sorting purposes.

TIP

You can add or delete categories using the + and – buttons in the dialog.

7. Click on **OK**. The dialog will close and the category or categories will be assigned.

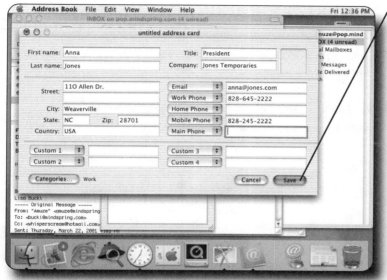

8. Click on **Save**. Address Book will save the new contact and close the untitled address card window. Your new contact will be listed in the Address Book window.

Once you've created a contact, you can click on the contact in the list in the Address Book window, then use the Edit and Delete buttons on the toolbar to change or remove it from the list. To view only contacts in a particular category, select that category from the Show list.

NOTE

You can organize two or more contacts into a group. Then, you can send an e-mail message to everyone in the group using the group listing in the Address Book. To create a group, use Shift+click to select contacts appearing contiguously on the list, or Command+click to select non-contiguous entries. Then, click on File and click on New Group. Enter applicable information to describe the group (such as a Group Name) in the window that appears, then click on Save. The group will be listed in the Address Book window.

Addressing a Message to a Contact

Sending a message to an Address Book process works quickly and easily.

1. Click on the **contact** (or group) to whom you want to send a message in the Address Book list. The contact will be selected.

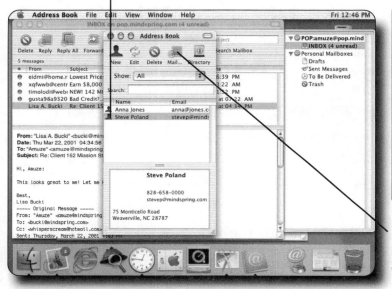

TIP

Use Shift+click to select contacts listed contiguously, or Command+click to select non-contiguous contact entries. The message will then be addressed to all of the selected contacts.

2. Click on the **Mail button**. A Compose window will appear, with the e-mail address for the selected contact appearing in the To text box.

13

Traveling the Web

Several years ago, my husband had a running joke with friends that the World Wide Web was "just a fad." Of course, his irony proved to be right on the mark and the World Wide Web evolved into a powerful and pervasive storehouse of information, products, and services. Twenty-four hours a day you can use the Internet to perform research, get news, play games, shop for products, browse auctions, and more. Mac OS X includes the Internet Explorer 5.1 Web browser program, which you can use to surf and search your way to the information you need. In this chapter, you'll learn how to:

- Start and exit Internet Explorer.
- Learn to navigate with links, URLs, and buttons.
- Visit and save favorite site locations.
- Search for more information about a particular topic.

Starting and Exiting Internet Explorer

Mac OS X offers easy access to Internet Explorer via the Dock.

NOTE

The first time you start Internet Explorer, you will see a dialog box asking if you want Internet Explorer to be your default Web browser. Click on the Yes button.

1. Click on the **Internet Explorer icon** on the Dock. Internet Explorer will open. Your home page will appear and you can begin browsing the Web.

NOTE

If your system connects to the Internet via a dial-up connection, and you have configured the system to connect automatically as explained in Chapter 11, "Setting up the Connection" your modem will dial your ISP when you start Internet Explorer.

2. **Click** on **Explorer**. The Explorer menu will appear.

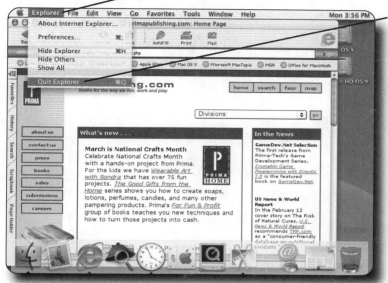

3. **Click** on **Quit Explorer**. Internet Explorer will close.

Now you will need to manually disconnect from the Internet.

4. **Click** on the **Applications button** on the Finder window toolbar. The contents of the folder will appear in the Finder window.

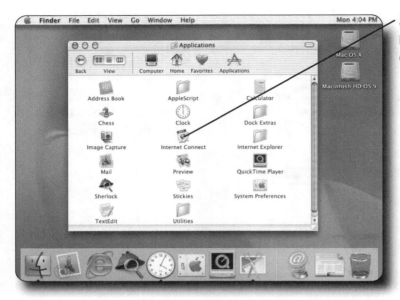

5. Double-click on **Internet Connect**. Internet Connect will open.

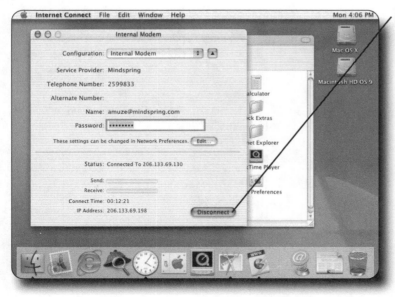

6. Click on **Disconnect**. Internet Connect will hang up the Internet connection.

7. Click on **Internet Connect**. The Internet Connect menu will appear.

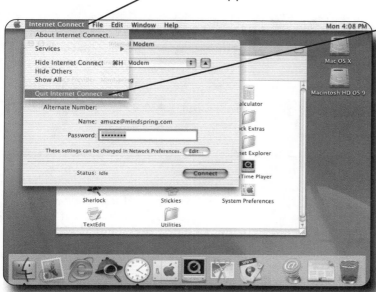

8. Click on **Quit Internet Connect**. Internet Connect will close.

Navigating Online

Graphical Web pages evolved to help users find and read information without having to remember esoteric commands and codes. Happily, Web page designs provide a lot of entertainment value and usually make pages more attractive and informative. They also provide you with a variety of ways to navigate between Web sites and pages. This section explains the various methods you can use to navigate online.

NOTE

A *Web site* includes a collection of individual Web pages that are published by a single source. For example, the Web address, http://www.prima-tech.com, leads to the main Web page for Prima Tech. The Prima Tech Web site includes many Web pages of information, such as http://www.prima-tech.com/books/featured/ (a page with featured books) or http://www.prima-tech.com/books/series/ (a page with descriptions of each book series published by Prima Tech).

Following a Link

Most Web pages feature distinctive text items that include special formatting such as underlining and special colors. This special formatting identifies the text as a *link* (or *hyperlink*) which leads to another Web page. Graphics, icons, or buttons on a Web page also often serve as links. Selecting a link is typically referred to as following a link or jumping to a link.

TIP

You can identify whether an item on the page is a link by moving the mouse pointer over the item. If the mouse pointer changes to a pointing hand, then the item under the pointer is a link.

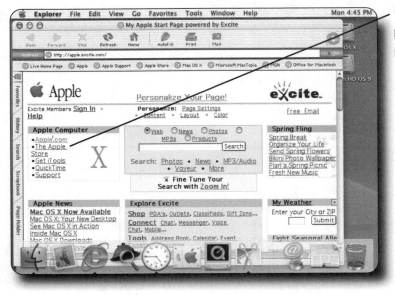

1. Click on a **text link**. The linked Web page will load in Internet Explorer.

2. **Click** on an **image link**. The linked Web page will load in Internet Explorer.

3. **Click** on a **button or graphical link**. The linked Web page will load in Internet Explorer.

TIP

If a message box appears after you follow a link, respond to the message so that the linked Web page can load.

Entering a URL

Each Web page has its own online address called its URL (*Uniform Resource Locator*). A full Web page address reads like this: http://www.prima-tech.com/index.html, where http:// identifies the content type, www.prima-tech.com identifies the domain or main page of the site, and anything following the final forward slash identifies a particular Web page. You can go to a particular Web page by entering its URL in Internet Explorer.

1. Click on the **current URL** in the Address text box. The entire contents of the text box will be selected.(If not, drag the mouse pointer over the existing address to select it.)

2. Type the **URL** to which you want to jump in the Address text box. A suggested completion for your entry and a drop-down list with suggested addresses will appear.

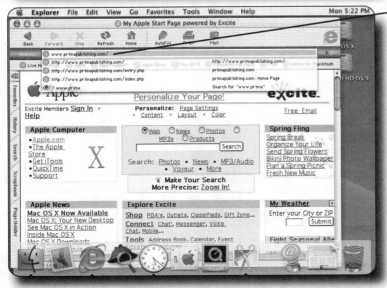

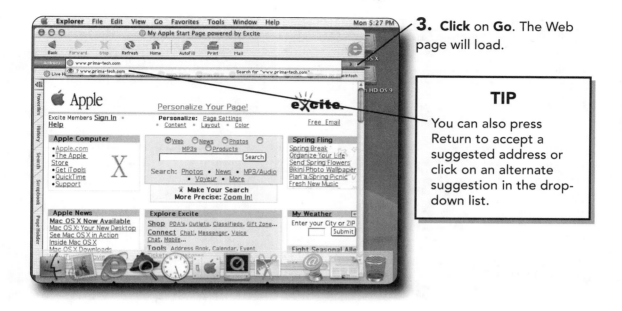

3. Click on **Go**. The Web page will load.

TIP

You can also press Return to accept a suggested address or click on an alternate suggestion in the drop-down list.

Backing up and Going Forward

At times, you may find that part of the information you want to view is on the current page, but other information you need is on a page you've viewed previously. The Internet Explorer toolbar offers buttons you can use to back up and move forward through pages you've already viewed.

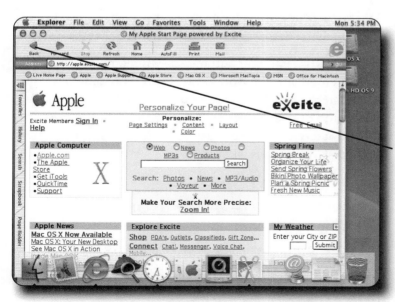

1. Click on the **Back button** on the toolbar. Internet Explorer will display the previous page you've viewed in the sequence of pages that you've browsed during this session. The Forward button will become enabled, as well.

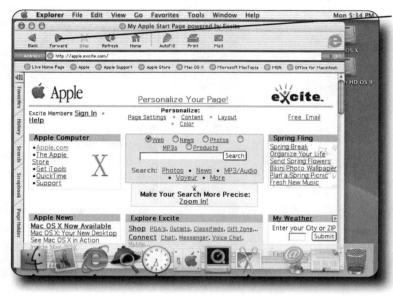

2. Click on the **Forward button** on the toolbar. Internet Explorer will redisplay the page from which you previously backed up.

TIP

Clicking on the Stop button on the toolbar stops a page from loading completely. You also can use it if there seems to be a problem with a page loading. Clicking on the Refresh button reloads the page contents from the Web server.

Working with Favorites

While Internet Explorer automatically remembers URLs that you've typed into the Address text box, you generally have to remember to retype at least part of the URL to take advantage of this feature. Internet Explorer offers an even easier feature that you can use to mark and return to particular Web pages—Favorites.

Marking a Page as a Favorite

When you mark a Web page as a Favorite, you add it to the list in the Favorites menu in Internet Explorer and the list in the Favorites pane, which is collapsed by default.

1. **Navigate to** the **Web page** that you want to mark as a Favorite. The page will appear in Internet Explorer.

2. **Click** on **Favorites**. The Favorites menu will open.

3. **Click** on **Add Page to Favorites**. The Web page will be added to the Favorites menu and list.

Organizing Your Favorites

Adding a Favorite places it at the end of the list on the Favorites menu or in the Favorites pane. If you mark many Web pages as Favorites, these lists will quickly grow so long that it'll actually be harder to find a Favorite that you want to visit. For this reason, Internet Explorer enables you to better organize your Favorites by grouping them into folders. You also can delete outdated Favorites that you no longer use to keep the list trim.

1. Click on to the **Favorites tab** at the left side of the window. The Favorites pane will open.

2. Click on **Organize**. The Organize menu will open.

3. Click on **New Folder**. A new folder will appear at the bottom of the list, ready for you to name it.

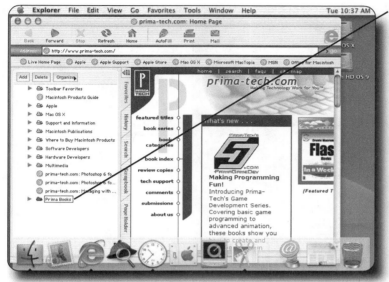

4. **Type a name** for the folder, **then press Return**.

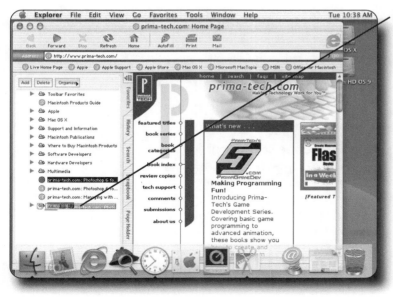

5. **Drag** a **Favorite** onto the folder. After you release the mouse button, the Favorite will move into the folder.

6. Drag a **Favorite or folder** to the Trash icon on the Dock. After you release the mouse button, the Favorite or folder (including its contents) will be deleted.

CAUTION

You cannot undelete a Favorite from the Trash.

7. **Click** on the **Favorites tab** that appears at the left side of the window. The Favorites pane will close.

TIP

You also can drag Favorites and folders to another position in the list.

Going to a Favorite Page

Now that you've set up your Favorites, you have two ways to access them: from the Favorites menu or the Favorites pane.

1. Click on **Favorites**. The Favorites menu will open.

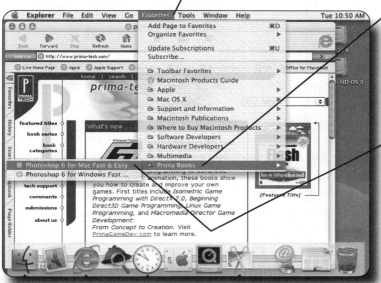

2. If needed, **drag** the **mouse pointer down** to the folder holding the desired Favorite. A submenu listing the Favorites in that folder will appear.

3. Click on the **desired Favorite**. Internet Explorer will display the specified Web page.

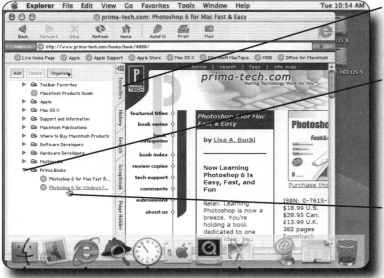

4. Click on the **Favorites tab**. The Favorites pane will open.

5. Click on the **arrow icon**, for the folder that holds the desired Favorite. The Favorites in that folder will appear below the folder in the pane.

6. Click on the **desired Favorite**. Internet Explorer will display the specified Web page.

Performing a Basic Web Search

As you might imagine, the early Web offered a lot of information but few easy roads for finding facts. You had to hear about the URL for a Web page of interest or browse and browse until you found the information you were after. Then, some smart groups of people simultaneously developed *search engines*. Basically, a search engine indexes information on Web pages, so that you can perform a search for topics of interest. The search engine typically returns a list of links to potentially-related Web pages, so you can review them and identify those that contain the information you need. Internet Explorer includes a Search pane that you can use to locate information on the Web.

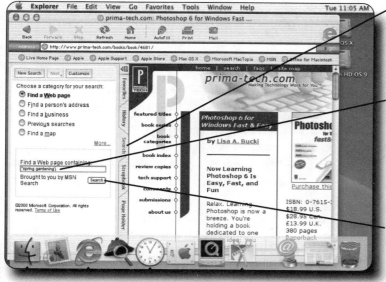

1. **Click** on the **Search tab** that appears at the left side of the window. The Search pane will open.

2. **Type** the **search term** into the Find a Web page containing text box. To search for an exact phrase, enclose the entire phrase in quotes.

3. **Click** on **Search**. The Search pane will list links to potentially matching Web pages.

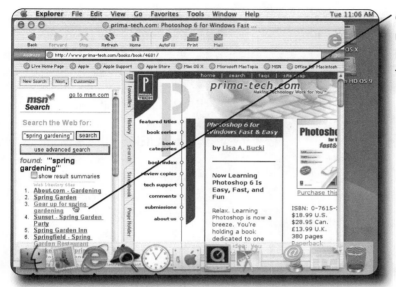

4. Click on a **link** in the results list in the Search pane. Internet Explorer will display the specified Web page.

Downloading Files

From time to time, you may encounter files that you want to download from the Internet, such as .PDF files or software updates from a support Web site or graphics files from another Web site. Internet Explorer includes the Download Manager to enable you to do so.

NOTE

To download a graphic file shown on any Web page, Control+click on the image and then click on Download Image to Disk.

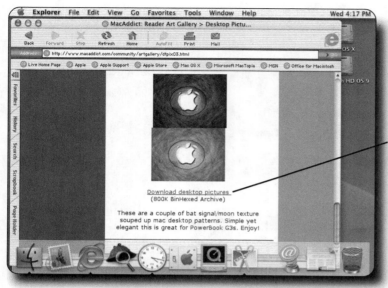

1. **Start Internet Explorer,** **connect** to the **Internet,** **and browse** to the **Web page** that holds the link for the file to download. The Web page will load.

2. **Click** on the **download link** on the Web page. The Web browser may display the *Download Manager* and start the download immediately, or you may have to proceed through several more Web pages to choose a download site and/ or provide payment information. If the latter is the case, simply follow the instructions.

NOTE

In some cases, there may not be a Download link. You may click on the file name link and see the Unhandled File Type dialog box to ask you how to handle the file. In most cases, you can click on the Save File As button, and then use the Save dialog box that appears to specify the folder where you'd like to save the file, if different from the Default Documents folder. After you do so, click on Save.

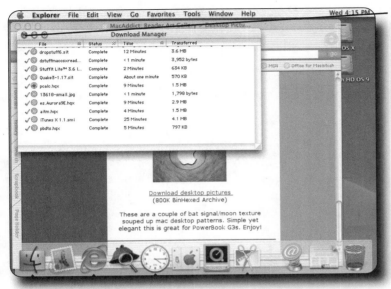

3. After the Download Manager in Internet Explorer finishes its downloading task, **click** on the **close button**. The Download Manager will close.

After the dowload is complete, another application may launch to decompress the downloaded file if it was an archive file. The file(s) will appear on the desktop. From there, you can copy the downloaded file into any folder within your Home folder. You can then continue browsing the Web or quit Internet Explorer and disconnect from the Internet.

14

Snooping for Content with Sherlock

Although Mac OS X provides a Home folder to help you organize your files, there may be times when you can't quite find a file that you need. It can be even more challenging to find information you need on the Web, even when using the Search Assistant in Internet Explorer. Mac OS X includes a more comprehensive search application called Sherlock. Sherlock can search for a particular file in your Home folder and any disks attached to your system. It also provides greater power for searching the Internet because it can use multiple search engines or Web sites in each search. In this chapter, you'll learn how to:

- Start and exit Sherlock.
- Find a file using its name, contents, or other attributes.
- Find Web information.
- Find a contact online.
- Search news resources.

Starting and Exiting Sherlock

You can start and leave the Sherlock application any time that you need to perform a find function.

1. Click on the **Sherlock icon** on the Dock. The Sherlock application window will open and its menus will appear on the menu bar.

2. Click on **Sherlock**. The Sherlock menu will appear.

3. Click on **Quit Sherlock**. The Sherlock application window will close.

Finding a File on Your System

Hard disks today store copious numbers of files. You might spend a lot of time looking for a particular file on your system's hard disk, on a partition of your hard disk, or on another disk attached to the system. The process will be even slower if you can't remember the exact file name. Sherlock will help you eliminate futility from the file search process. It can find a file based on the file name, file contents, or another attribute of the file such as its file type.

1. Click on the **Files icon** in the Sherlock window. The Files channel will appear in the Sherlock window.

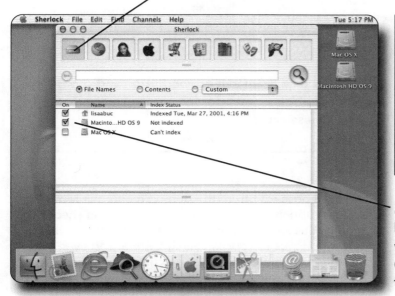

TIP

The icons at the top of the Sherlock window each represent a channel in Sherlock. You also can use the Channels menu to choose another channel.

2. Click on the **check boxes** as needed. Sherlock will search the checked disks (including partitions, Home folders and external drives) only. Clearing the check mark beside a disk that you don't need to search can make the search proceed faster.

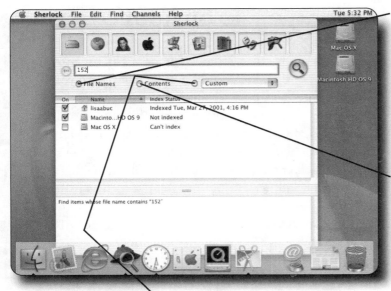

3a. **Click** on the **File Names option button** if you want to search for a file based on part of its file name. The option will be selected.

OR

3b. **Click** on the **Contents option button** if you want to search for a file based on information in the file, such as a key word or term. The option will be selected.

OR

3c. **Click** on the **Custom option button and choose** the **type of search** you want from the pop-up menu. The search type will be selected.

TIP

If you choose Edit from the pop-up menu, the More Search Options dialog box will open. You can check the various search types, then use the accompanying pop-up menus to specify search criteria, and even click on the Save As button to save a custom search that you create. It will then be added to the Custom pop-up menu. Click on OK to finish customizing the search and return to the Sherlock window.

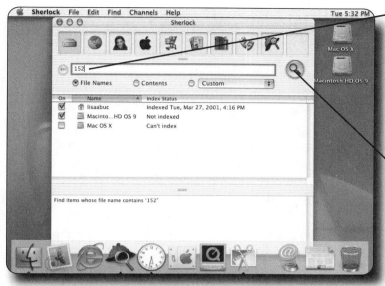

4. Enter the **search information** (the partial file name or search terms) in the text box. Sherlock will display a description of the search in the lower pane of the Sherlock window.

5. Click on the **Search button.** Sherlock will search the specified drives (or partitions) and display the search results in the Sherlock window.

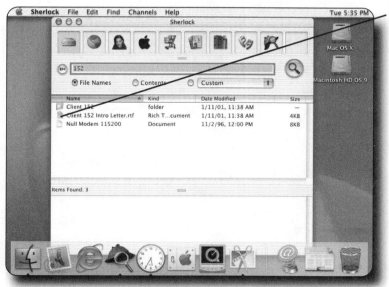

6. Double-click on the **file** you want to open. Mac OS X will open the file in the correct application.

You can now work with the file, close its application, and return to Sherlock as needed.

Finding Web Pages about a Topic

In the last chapter, you learned how to use the Search Assistant in Internet Explorer to find Web information pertaining to a particular topic. The Search Assistant defaults to using a single search engine for its search: MSN.com. Sherlock enables you to go further faster, searching multiple search engines and sites for the information you need.

1. **Click** on the **Internet icon** in the Sherlock window. The Internet channel will appear in the Sherlock window.

2. **Enter** the **word or phrase** (no need for quotes) for which you want to search in the text box.

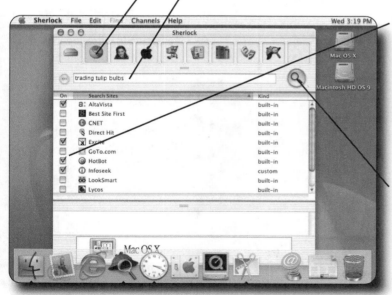

3. **Click** on the **check boxes** in the Search Sites list as needed. Sherlock will search checked sites only. Clearing the check mark beside a site that may not apply can make the search proceed faster.

4. **Click** on the **Search button**. If your system connects to the Internet via a dial-up connection, and you have configured the system to connect automatically as explained in Chapter 11, "Setting up the Connection," Internet Connect will launch and your modem will dial your ISP to connect to the Internet, then search for matching sites.

TIP

If a search is taking too long, you can click again on the Search button to stop the search.

NOTE

If Internet Connect stays open and in front of Sherlock at any time, just click on the Sherlock icon on the Dock to return Sherlock to the front.

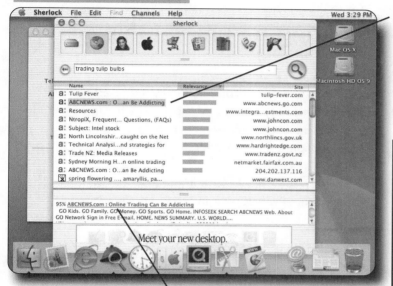

5. **Click** on a **Web page** of interest in the list. The bottom pane of the Sherlock window will display a more detailed description of the page, as well as its link.

TIP

If you drag an item from the search results and drop it onto the desktop, you can use the resulting icon to view the matching site at a later time.

6. **Click** on the **link** to go to the selected Web page. Mac OS X will launch Internet Explorer and display the Web site.

NOTE

You can download more search sites and resources (called plug-ins) for other channels from http://www.apple.com/sherlock/plugins.html. After you download a plug-in, use the Channels, Add Search Site command to add it into Sherlock.

Because Internet Connect does not disconnect automatically, you have to do so manually. Click on the Internet Connect icon on the Dock to bring Internet Connect forward, then click on the Disconnect button, open the Internet Connect menu, and choose Quit Internet Connect.

Locating a Person Online

Several online services now specialize in helping you find out information about friends, family members, and business colleagues. Some of these sites focus on helping you find e-mail addresses and others help you find additional contact information.

1. **Click** on the **People icon** in the Sherlock window. The People channel will appear in the Sherlock window.

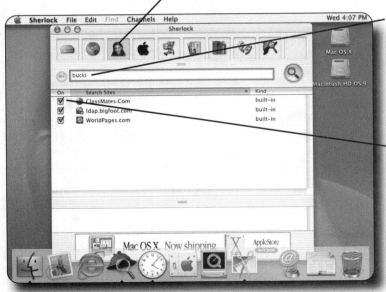

2. **Enter** the **name** for which you want to search in the text box. (Enter a last name only to increase the number of potential matches.)

3. **Click** on the **check boxes** in the Search Sites list as needed. Sherlock will search checked sites only. Clearing the check mark beside a site that may not apply can make the search proceed faster.

4. Click on the **Search button**. Sherlock will launch Internet Connect, if needed, to connect to the Internet, then search for matching persons. When the list of matches appears, you can use the appropriate e-mail address or phone number.

Searching for News

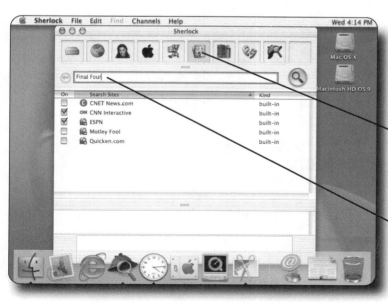

Searching for news works much like searching the Web in general. The News channel simply lists alternate search resources.

1. Click on the **News icon** in the Sherlock window. The News channel will appear in the Sherlock window.

2. Enter the **word or phrase** for which you want to search in the text box.

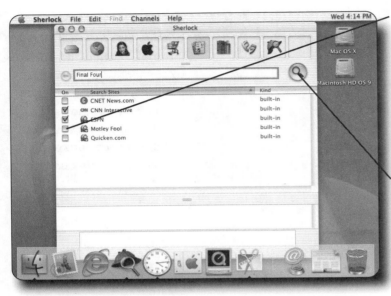

3. **Click** on the **check boxes** in the Search Sites list as needed. Sherlock will search checked sites only. Clearing the check mark beside a site that may not apply can make the search proceed faster.

4. **Click** on the **Search button**. Sherlock will launch Internet Connect to connect to the Internet, if needed, and search for matching sites.

5. **Click** on a **Web page** of interest in the list. The bottom pane of the Sherlock window will display a more detailed description of the page, as well as a link to the page.

6. **Click** on the **link** to go to the selected Web page. Mac OS X will launch Internet Explorer and display the page. You can switch between Internet Explorer and Sherlock to review additional matching pages.

15

Downloading and Installing Software

Every person has a distinct style for work and entertainment activities. For this reason, you can install new programs on your computer to get a job done more quickly, maintain the system, or just play around. (I won't tell!) Finding and installing a new program can be one of the most important skills for keeping your Mac useful. In this chapter, you'll learn how to:

- Find and download programs from online sources.
- Handle a program that's been compressed or "stuffed."
- Use a software installer.
- Run Software Update to keep Mac OS X up to date.

Downloading Applications

Today, computer users can purchase software applications from a variety of sources. You can visit your local computer, electronics, or office supply store and typically find a nice selection of boxed software. Even major discount stores carry some software these days. You also can order your software from a number of catalogs or direct from a software company. You may receive software along with a new piece of equipment like a scanner and will need to install that software in order for the new hardware to work. Or, if you've set up the Internet connection for your Mac, you can go online to find and download software. Following are just a few resources to check out:

- **http://www.apple.com/macosx/downloads**. The Mac OS X Web downloads page includes links to a number of downloadable new programs and demo software written expressly for Mac OS X.

- **http://www.macaddict.com**, **http://www. macdownload.com**, **http://www.tucows.com**. These sites also enable you to download shareware, freeware, and commercial software.

TIP

In Internet Explorer, click on the Favorites menu and look at the links in the Software Developers folder which is inside the Where to Buy Macintosh Products Folder. You can can jump directly to the Web sites for Macintosh product retailers and software developers.

---

1. **Start Internet Explorer, connect** to the **Internet, and browse** to the **Web page** that holds the link for the software to download. The Web page will load.

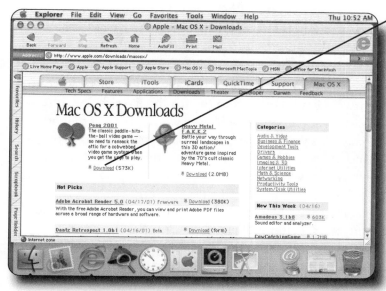

2. Click on the **download link** on the Web page. The Web browser may display the Download Manager window and start the download immediately, or you may have to proceed through several more Web pages to choose a download site and/or provide payment information. If the latter is the case, simply follow the instructions.

3. After the Download Manager in Internet Explorer finishes its downloading task, **click** on the **close button**. The Download Manager window will close.

You can then continue browsing the Web or quit Internet Explorer and disconnect from the Internet.

NOTE

By default, the Download Manager places downloaded files on the desktop. From there, you can move the downloaded file into any folder within your Home folder.

Unstuffing Files

NOTE

If the file has the .img or .smi file name extension, it's a disk image file. You don't have to unstuff such a file, but you do have to handle it a bit differently, as described in the later section "Running an Install Program."

To speed download time, many files that you download will be compressed or *stuffed*. Basically, this means that special software has been used to reduce the file size and in some cases compress multiple files into a single file, creating an *archive file* that transfers more quickly and is easier to handle. The most common stuffing format results in an archive file with the .sit, .hqx or .bin file name extensions.

In some cases, Mac OS X will unstuff the program or file immediately after download, placing the unstuffed (extracted) file or files on the desktop along with the downloaded archive. It uses the StuffIt Expander utility, which comes installed with Mac OS X. If the file doesn't unstuff automatically, you can do so manually.

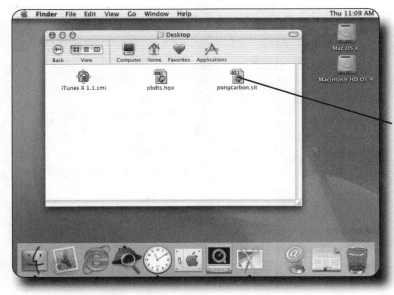

1. Minimize open Finder and file **windows** so you can see the full desktop. You will see the icon for the archive file on the desktop.

2. Open your **Desktop folder** in a Finder window **and Double-click** on the **downloaded file**. StuffIt Expander will open automatically, unstuff the archive, and place the extracted file(s) or folder on the desktop. StuffIt Expander will then close.

NOTE

Not all downloaded programs require installation. In some cases, you can simply go to the folder that holds the unstuffed files and double-click on the icon to start the program.

Running an Install Program

Once you've downloaded and unstuffed a software program or have pulled the CD-ROM out of its packaging, you can begin the install process immediately. A single file is used to start the installer program, which, in turn, guides you through all the installation steps. The install process varies a bit from program to program, and the process starts out a bit differently depending on whether you're installing from a CD-ROM or a downloaded file. What follows gives you an overview of the process so that you can get started no matter where the installer file is located.

1a. **Insert** the **CD-ROM** into your Mac's CD-ROM or DVD-ROM drive. An icon for the disc will appear on the desktop and a Finder window containing the installer program should appear automatically. If not, double-click on the disc icon on the desktop. The resulting Finder window should contain the installer file.

OR

1b. **Open** or **navigate** to the **folder** that holds the installer file you downloaded and unstuffed. The contents of the folder will appear in a Finder window.

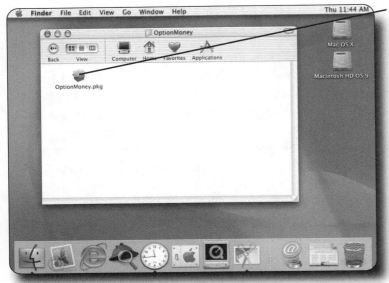

2. Double-click on the **installer file**. The install process will begin and the opening installer screen will appear.

In some cases, a downloaded program file may create a .img or .smi file when unstuffed. This type of file is a self-mounting disk image file. To use such a file, double-click on it. Mac OS X will use Disk Copy to *mount* the disk image. An icon for the mounted disk image will appear on the desktop. Double-click on the mounted disk image icon on the desktop and then double-click on the installer file in the resulting Finder window to start the install process.

NOTE

If the application is a Classic (Mac OS 9) application, the Classic environment will load so that the installation process can continue. This does not necessarily mean that the application itself will require the Classic environment; it may simply mean that the installer routine was written for the old environment.

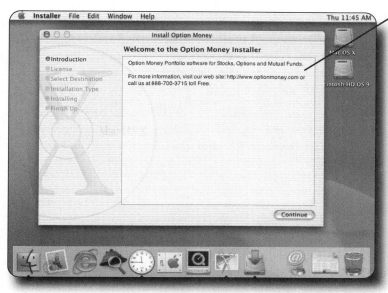

3. Follow the **instructions**, responding as required to each prompt.

Generally, the installer will ask you for a valid registration number and your user information for registration. It may also ask you to specify the folder in which you want to install the application. In addition, many applications will prompt you to agree to an End User License Agreement. Very simple programs may have no further installation steps.

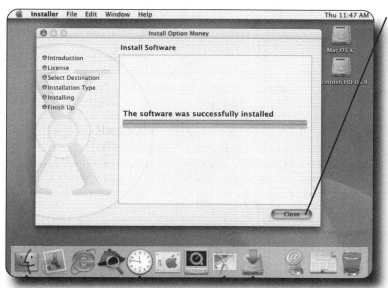

4. Click on **Close (or Quit)** when the installer informs you that it has completed the installation process. The installer will close.

Now you can navigate to the folder where you installed the program and double-click on it to begin using it.

TIP

The section called "Adding and Removing Dock Icons" in Chapter 8 "Setting up the Desktop" explains how you can add a program icon to the Dock for faster program access.

If the installer doesn't lead you through a registration process, you may be prompted to register the software the first time you start the application. Completing the registration helps the software developer keep you informed about product updates. For shareware, you should register the software and pay the shareware fee. Often, registering shareware and entering a registration number in the software enables features that are not available without registration.

Using Software Update

Mac OS X includes the Software Update pane, which enables your system to connect with Apple's Web site, determine whether your Mac OS X software requires any updates, and downloads and installs those updates automatically. In some cases, Software Update will start automatically when you start up your system. You also can start Software Update manually at any time.

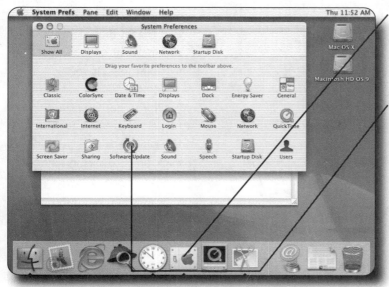

1. Click on the **System Preferences icon** on the Dock. System Preferences will open.

2. Click on the **Software Update icon**. The Software update pane will appear in the System Preferences window.

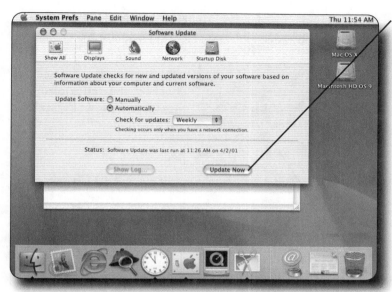

3. Click on **Update Now**. If your system connects to the Internet via a dial-up connection, and you have configured the system to connect automatically as explained in Chapter 11, "Setting up the Connection," Internet Connect will launch and your modem will dial your ISP and Software Update will check the Apple Web site for updates.

NOTE

You can click on the Software Update icon on the Dock if the Internet Connect application stays in front of Software Update.

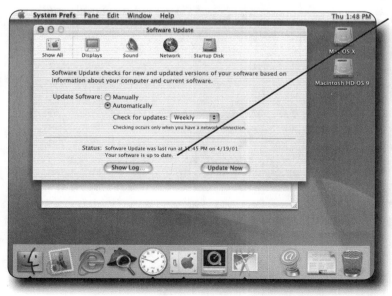

4a. If no updates are required, the Software Update pane will show that your software is up to date. You can **skip** to **Step 7**.

OR

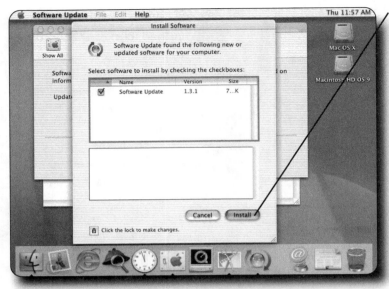

4b. If the Install Software dialog box appears to alert you of an update, make sure all the desired updates are checked, then **click** on **Install**. Software Update will continue.

NOTE

If a dialog box prompts you to enter an administrator password, type the password in the Password text box and then click on OK.

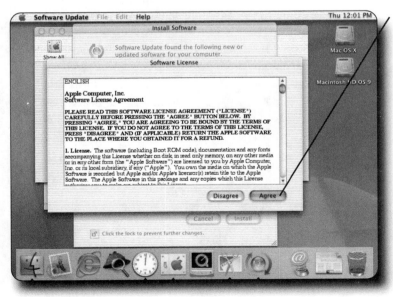

5. If the Software License dialog box appears, read its contents and then **click** on **Agree**. Software Update will continue.

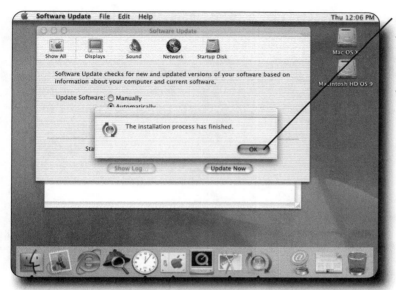

6. When all updates are finished, **click** on **OK** in the alert box. The alert box will close and Software Update will close automatically.

NOTE

In some cases, a message box may appear when a download starts reminding you that a particular update will require you to restart the system. Click on OK. Then, after the download completes and Software Update installs the downloaded software, another message box prompts you to restart the system. Click on Restart in the message box to do so.

7. Click on **System Prefs**. The System Prefs menu will appear.

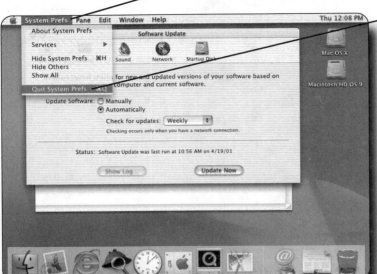

8. Click on **Quit System Prefs**. System Preferences will close. You should then use Internet Connect to disconnect from the Internet, as described in Chapter 11, "Setting up the Connection."

NOTE

In some cases, Software Update does not list all the available updates in the Install Software dialog box. Clicking on Update Now again before you close Software Update will alert you if there are additional updates to download.

Part IV Review Questions

1. How do I set up for the Internet? *See "Creating a Connection with Internet Connect" in Chapter 11.*

2. How do I hang up my Internet connection? *See "Connecting to and Disconnecting from the Internet" in Chapter 11.*

3. How do I create an send a Mail message? *See "Sending Mail" in Chapter 12.*

4. How do I get my e-mail? *See "Checking Mail" in Chapter 12.*

5. How do I deal with a message? *See "Reading and Responding to a Message" in Chapter 12.*

6. How do I go to a Web site? *See "Entering a URL" in Chapter 13.*

7. How do I mark a good Web page so that I can go back? *See "Marking a Page as a Favorite" in Chapter 13.*

8. How do I search the Web? *See "Performing a Basic Web Search" in Chapter 13.*

9. How do I find a file on my hard disk? *See "Finding a File on Your System" in Chapter 14.*

10. How do I find a friend online? *See "Locating a Person Online" in Chapter 14.*

PART V

Becoming a Multimedia Master

Chapter 16
Jamming with iTunes 251

Chapter 17
Using QuickTime Player 269

Chapter 18
Working with Other Features 287

16

Jamming with iTunes

Even the programmers for earlier computers looked for ways to have fun, developing computerized versions of chess and the arcade game, Pong. Computers have evolved to include many more personal entertainment capabilities. With the advent of ways to digitize music, your Mac can even work as your personal jukebox serving up your favorite tunes any time. To set up and use Mac OS X to play your audio CDs and other music files, you can download the free iTunes 1.1 software from Apple. In this chapter, you'll learn how to:

- Download iTunes.
- Start and exit iTunes.
- Play an audio CD.
- Create an MP3 file.
- Create and use a playlist.
- Control music playback.

Downloading and Installing iTunes

At the same time that it released Mac OS X, Apple released iTunes 1.1 for Mac OS X as a free download. You can download the software from Apple's site at any time. The download takes 20 to 30 minutes (depending on the speed of your Internet connection), so make sure to allow yourself enough time for the process.

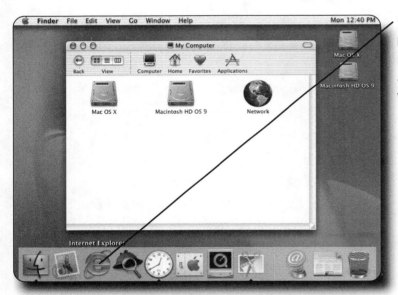

1. Click on the **Internet Explorer icon** on the Dock. Internet Explorer will open and your home page will load.

NOTE

If your system connects to the Internet via a dial-up connection, and you have configured the system to connect automatically as explained in Chapter 11, "Setting up the Connection" your modem will dial your ISP when you start Internet Explorer.

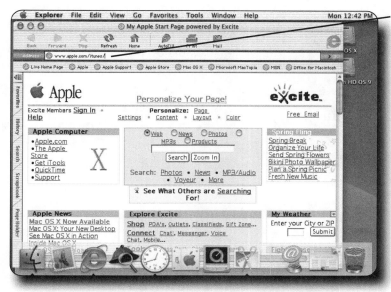

2. Type www.apple.com/ itunes into the Address text box **and press Return**. A page from Apple's Web site with information about iTunes will open.

NOTE

Because Web pages change over time, the download process may differ for you. Just be sure to download the correct version of iTunes—the one that's written for Mac OS X and is sometimes called iTunes X 1.1 (or a later version, if available).

3. Click on the **iTunes for Mac OS X link**. A Web page containing the download link will open.

4. Click on **Download**. (If you see a Security Notice dialog box, click on Send in the dialog box.) The Download Manager window will open to show you that it's downloading iTunes 1.1.

5. After the download finishes, **click** on the **close button**. The Download Manager window will close.

6. Click on **Explorer**. The Explorer menu will appear.

7. Click on **Quit Explorer**. Internet Explorer will close.

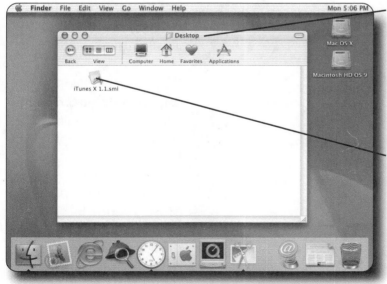

8. In a Finder window, **open** the **Desktop folder** within your Home folder. The Finder window will display the downloaded iTunes file, which is a disk image file.

9. Double-click on the **downloaded file**. Disk Copy will open the image file and the Software License Agreement window.

10. Read the **Software License Agreement** for iTunes, **and click** on **Agree** if you agree with its provisions. Mac OS X will mount the disk image. A disk icon will appear on the desktop and a Finder window for the iTunes disk will open.

11. Click on **File**. The File menu will appear.

12. Click on **New Finder Window**. A new Finder window will open.

13. Click on the **Applications button** on the Finder window toolbar. The contents of the Applications folder will appear.

14. Click on the **iTunes for Mac OS X title bar**. iTunes for Mac OS X will become the active window.

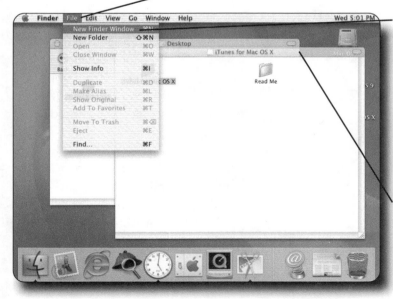

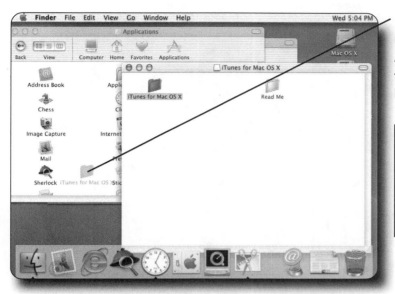

15. **Drag** the **iTunes for Mac OS X folder** into the Applications folder. The folder and its contents will be copied, installing iTunes.

TIP

You can drag the disk image icon to the trash to remove it from your desktop.

Starting and Exiting iTunes

After you copy the iTunes for Mac OS X folder into your Applications folder, you can go there to start iTunes.

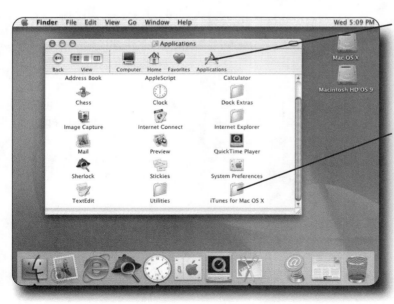

1. **Click** on the **Applications button** on the Finder window toolbar. The contents of the Applications folder will appear.

2. **Double-click** on the **iTunes for Mac OS X folder** in the Finder window. A Finder window containing iTunes will open.

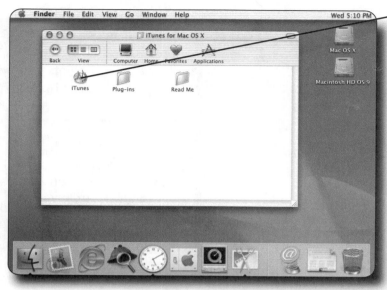

3. Double-click on **iTunes** in the Finder window. iTunes will open. The first time you start iTunes, the iTunes Setup Assistant window will open.

4. Click on **Next**. The iTunes Setup Assistant will ask you a few brief questions regarding your Internet connection and finding MP3 files on your system's hard disk.

5. Respond to the **questions** in the second window as needed, **then click** on **Next**. A final window of questions will appear.

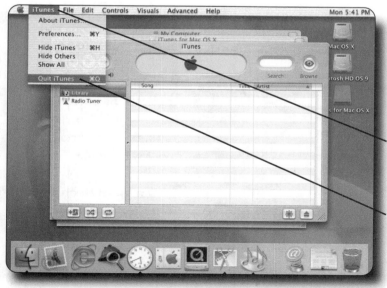

6. Respond to the **questions** on the third window as needed, **then click** on **Done**. The iTunes Setup Assistant will close and you can start using iTunes.

7. When you're ready to quit iTunes, **click** on **iTunes**. The iTunes menu will appear.

8. Click on **Quit iTunes**. iTunes will close.

NOTE

By default, iTunes connects to the Internet as needed (assuming you've set up your Internet connection to connect automatically as described in Chapter 11 "Setting up the Connection,") but it may fail to disconnect. In such a case, you will need to disconnect manually using Internet Connect.

Playing a CD

Many of us have made a substantial investment in an audio CD collection. iTunes doesn't make that collection obsolete. Instead, it gives you yet another way to listen to your music collection and even take advantage of extra playback features. It is simple to play an audio CD after you start iTunes.

1. Insert an **audio CD** into the CD-ROM or DVD-ROM drive. The iTunes window will list tracks by number in the playlist at the right.

You will see a message that iTunes is accessing the CDDB database (an online database that helps software like iTunes identify album titles, song titles, and artists). If your system connects to the Internet via a dial-up connection, and you have configured the system to connect automatically as explained in Chapter 11, "Setting up the Connection" your modem will dial your ISP. The specific album title, song titles and artist names will be listed.

TIP

If no information appears after iTunes has attempted to access the CDDB database, choose Get CD Track Names from the Advanced menu to try again. Sometimes you will need to select the correct album from the CD Lookup Results window, before the specific information is filled in.

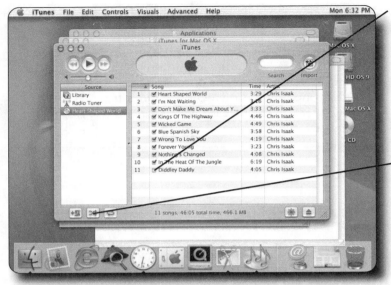

2. Click on the **check box** beside any song which you do not wish to listen to. The check will be removed and iTunes will skip the song.

TIP

Click on the shuffle button to turn shuffle mode on or off. iTunes will play through the selected songs in random order.

3. Click on the **Play button** to start playing the CD. Music playback will begin immediately.

4. Drag the **volume slider**. The volume will be adjusted.

As a song plays, you can see information about the song in the small pane that appears at the top center of the iTunes window. Drag the small diamond in the timeline bar to back up or fast forward within the song that's currently playing.

5. After playback finishes, **click** on the **Eject button**. iTunes will eject the audio CD.

Making MP3s and Adding Them to Your Library

If you want to build long playlists for your computer or play music on portable devices, then you may want to convert your CD audio tracks to the MP3 file format and save them in your iTunes Library. When you use software like iTunes to convert a CD track to an MP3 file, the software eliminates certain file information that humans can't hear. The resulting file is about 11 percent of the size of the original file (the MP3 file for a typical song is 3-4MB) and sounds great to most listeners using typical equipment.

1. Insert an **audio CD** into the CD-ROM or DVD-ROM drive for your system. The iTunes window will list the tracks by number in the playlist. You will see a message that iTunes is accessing the CDDB database, your modem will dial your ISP and the specific album title, song titles and artist name will be listed.

2. **Click** on the **check box** beside any song you do not wish to convert. iTunes will skip the import and MP3 conversion of any song you uncheck.

3. **Click** on the **Import button**. iTunes will start simultaneously playing and converting the tracks.

The process of converting the songs and importing them into your Library actually takes less time than the playback. A small green check mark appears beside each song in the playlist after iTunes has successfully converted and imported the file.

NOTE

iTunes stores the MP3 files in subfolders within the iTunes Music folder in your Documents folder, although the folders and files may not appear until you exit iTunes.

4. After the conversion and import operation is finished, **click** on the **Stop button**. iTunes will stop playing the CD.

5. **Click** on the **Eject button**. iTunes will eject the audio CD.

NOTE

To add other MP3 files to your Library, use the File, Add to Library command.

Building and Playing an MP3 Playlist

Most computers have a single CD-ROM or DVD-ROM drive, meaning you can play the contents of one audio CD at a time. When you've converted (or downloaded) and stored MP3 files on your Mac's hard disk, you can mix and match songs from different sources as needed to develop your own playlist file. This gives you control over not only which songs play, but also how many songs play so that you don't have to swap CDs every hour or so.

1. **Click** on the **New Playlist button**. A new playlist icon and file name will appear in the Source list at the left side of the iTunes window.

2. **Type** a **name** for the new playlist, then **press Return**. The new playlist name will appear in the Source list.

TIP

You also can open the File menu and then click on New Playlist to start a new playlist.

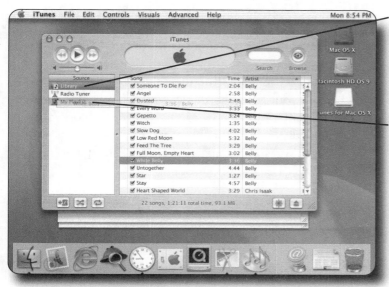

3. **Click** on **Library** in the Source list, if it isn't selected. The MP3s in your iTunes Library will appear in the playlist area at the right.

4. **Drag songs** from the existing playlist onto the new playlist named in the Source list. As you release the mouse button to drop each song onto the new playlist, iTunes will add the song to the new playlist. Repeat this step, as needed, to build the new playlist.

5. When you're ready to play a playlist, **click** on the **playlist name** in the Source list. The playlist will be selected.

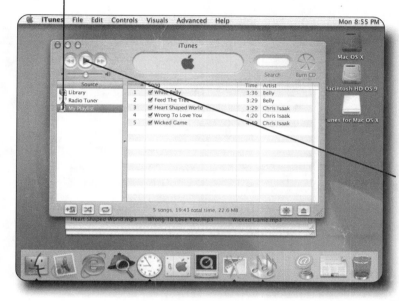

TIP

To delete a playlist, click on the playlist name in the Source list, then choose the Edit, Clear command.

6. Click on the **Play button**. iTunes will play the songs in the playlist.

TIP

Once you start playing your playlist, an animation file can also be played to accompany the music. To do so, choose Visuals, Turn Visual On.

Playing an Internet Radio Stream

iTunes doesn't limit you to music that's in your personal audio CD library. In addition to songs that you can purchase and download from online sources, you also can use iTunes to tune into streaming music broadcast by Internet radio stations and sources. iTunes works in conjunction with the Kerbango Tuning Service, which hosts a variety of Internet broadcasts featuring all types of content: music, sports, talk, news from a variety of locales, and more.

1. Click on **Radio Tuner** in the Source list. iTunes will connect to the Kerbango Tuning Service, if needed, and the list of stream categories will appear in the Stream list at the right side of the iTunes window.

2. Double-click on a **category** in the Stream list. The list of streams in the category that you selected will appear.

3. Click on the **desired stream**. The stream will be selected in the list.

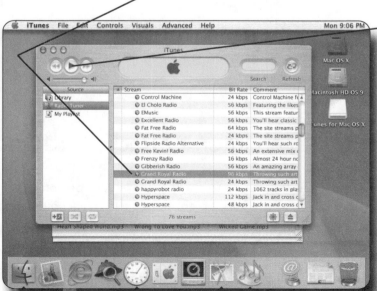

4. Click on the **Play button**. iTunes will *buffer* the stream (downloading part of the information to play in advance, so that playback can proceed smoothly), and then begin playing the stream.

Pausing and Muting Playback

When you're playing an audio CD, playlist, or stream in iTunes, you can control the playback as on a CD or tape deck. Use the following controls to manage playback of your CD or playlist:

- **Previous Song**. Backs up to the previous song in the CD, playlist, or pre-recorded stream.

- **Pause**. Stops the playback. (After you click on this button, it becomes the Play button, so that you can click on it again to resume play.)

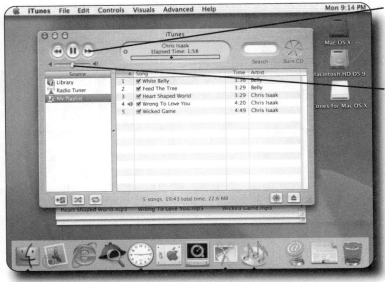

- **Next Song**. Moves forward to the next song in the CD, playlist, or pre-recorded stream.

- **Volume/Mute**. Drag the slider to adjust the volume, or click on one of the speaker icons at either end to mute (left) or maximize (right) the volume.

TIP

Pausing and moving between songs doesn't work for an Internet stream unless it was pre-recorded.

17

Using QuickTime Player

As computer processor speeds and video processor speeds increased, Macs emerged as one of the leading multimedia systems. Earlier Mac models were among the first to offer playback for video and other forms of media. While video playback initially was limited to small windows and jerky performance, today's Mac models offer smooth-as-silk playback for larger format video. Mac OS X includes QuickTime Player 5.0, which enables video playback from files stored on your system, video on CD-ROMs or DVD-ROMs, or even from Web sites. In this chapter, you'll learn how to:

- Start and exit QuickTime Player.
- Open a movie file.
- Control movie playback.
- View a Web movie.
- View and use QTV.
- Adjust QuickTime Preferences.

Starting and Exiting QuickTime

By default, the Mac OS X Dock offers an icon for starting QuickTime Player. You can start and quit the application any time that you need to use it.

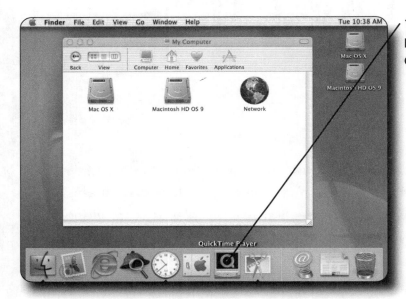

1. **Click** on the **QuickTime Player icon** on the Dock. QuickTime Player will open.

NOTE

The first time that you start QuickTime, a message box will ask you if you want to download and install QuickTime Pro. You can choose to install or skip the download. If you choose to download and purchase the full QuickTime Pro software (for $29.99 from http://www.apple.com/quicktime/download), you can edit and enhance your own movies rather than simply playing movies.

2. **Click** on **QuickTime Player**. The QuickTime Player menu will appear.

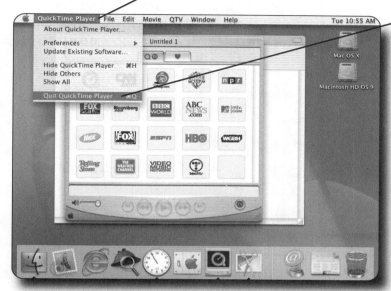

3. **Click** on **Quit QuickTime Player**. QuickTime Player will close.

Opening and Closing a Movie File

QuickTime Player can open and display or play hundreds of different file types, including graphics files, audio files, movie files, and even virtual reality files that simulate a 3D environment. Most often, you'll want to use QuickTime to view various types of movie files that combine audio and video.

The following table lists a few common movie file formats that you can play back in QuickTime:

Common Movie File Formats	
File Extensions	**Description**
.qt, .mov	QuickTime files
.mpg, .mpeg, .mp	Various MPEG (Motion Picture Experts Group) files
.avi, .wmv	Windows video files

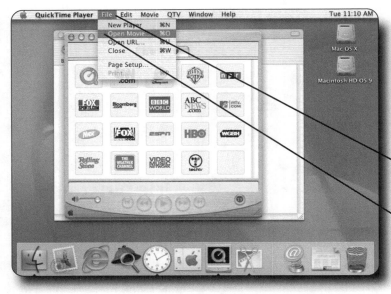

You may have copied a movie file from a CD-ROM or DVD-ROM and stored the file on your hard disk. In such a case, you can open and play the movie file with QuickTime Player.

1. Click on **File**. The File menu will appear.

2. Click on **Open Movie**. The Open dialog box will open.

TIP

If you have a sound file that won't play in iTunes, open and play it in QuickTime Player. Chances are that QuickTime Player can handle it.

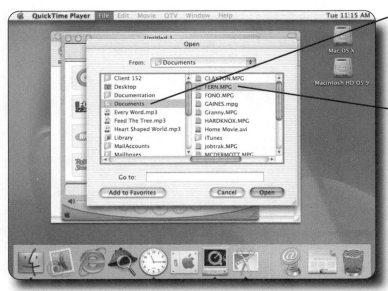

3. Navigate to the **folder** that holds the movie file. The Open dialog box will list movie files in that folder.

4. Click on a **movie file**. The file will be selected in the list.

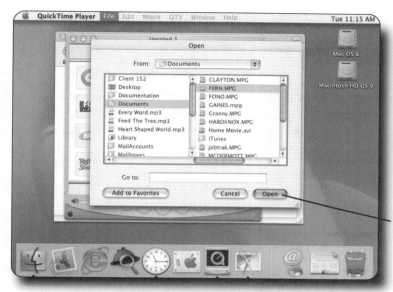

NOTE

When you click on a movie file in the list, the Open dialog box will display a preview frame if one is available. Often the preview feature won't work for older movie files.

5. Click on **Open**. The movie file will open in the QuickTime Player window and will start playing automatically. When you've finished watching the movie file, you can close it.

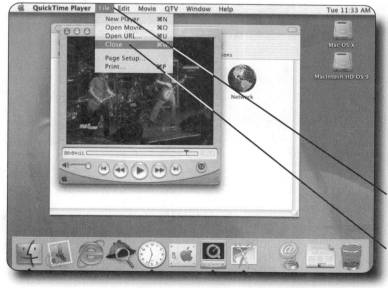

NOTE

Of course, if the movie file that you want to start is on an inserted CD-ROM, DVD-ROM, or removable disk, you can double click on the disk icon, navigate to the movie file you want to play and then double-click on the movie file to start playback.

6. Click on **File**. The File menu will appear.

7. Click on **Close**. The movie file will close.

Controlling Movie File Playback

If you've ever used a cassette tape deck or VCR, then the controls on the QuickTime Player window will look familiar to you. You can use these controls to start and stop movie playback, choose a playback location, and more.

- **Beginning**. Click on this button to move to the beginning of the movie file.

- **Rewind**. Click on this button to back up slightly. Click and hold the button to back up a greater distance in the movie.

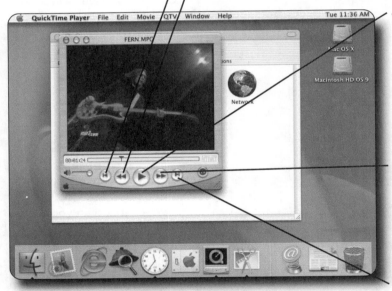

- **Pause/Play**. Click on this button to start movie play, at which time it changes to the Pause button (with a double bar). Click on the Pause button to temporarily stop movie playback.

- **Fast Forward**. Click on this button to move forward slightly. Click and hold on the button to move forward a greater distance in the movie.

- **End**. Click on this button to move to the end of the movie file.

TIP

Press the right arrow key to move forward by one frame. Press the left arrow key to move back by one frame.

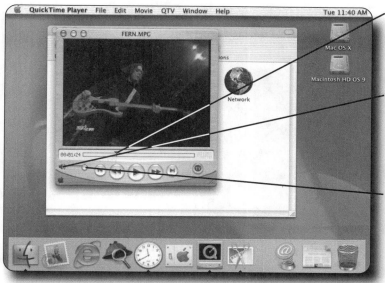

- **Timeline Bar**. Drag the small arrow above the bar to select a playback position in the movie.

- **Mute**. Click on the small speaker icon to mute the sound. Click on the icon again to turn the sound back on.

- **Volume**. Drag this slider to increase or decrease the sound playback volume.

NOTE

If you're playing a movie file that's embedded within another multimedia application, typically you'll click on a special icon to start the QuickTime Player and play the movie. In some cases, the controls for the movie may appear in a small bar across the bottom of the resulting movie pane.

Viewing a Movie from the Web

As more businesses and households enjoy high-speed Internet connections, more Web site developers are including movies along with other Web page content. For example, if you're on a site offering computer help, you may be able to play a demonstration video right from the Web site. QuickTime Player handles this for Internet Explorer via the QuickTime Player Plug-In. QuickTime Player need not be open.

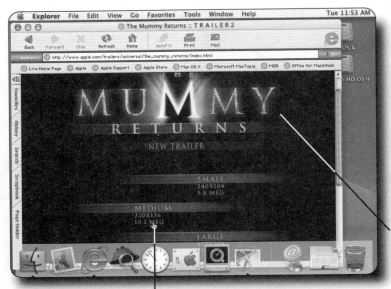

TIP

The QuickTime Web
site, http://
www.apple.com/
quicktime, offers links
to a variety of
QuickTime resources,
including sites with
QuickTime movies that
you can view.

1. Connect to the
Internet, **open Internet
Explorer** and **Navigate** to
the **Web page** that includes
choices to play the movie, which is typically a playback size.
(If you don't see any playback choices, skip ahead to Step
3.) The choices will appear in your Web browser.

2. Click on the desired **playback option**. The Web browser
will open a page with the appropriate playback box size.

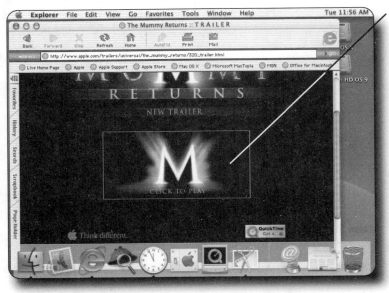

3. If prompted, **click** on the
box that will play back the
movie. The first frame of the
movie will appear in your
Web browser.

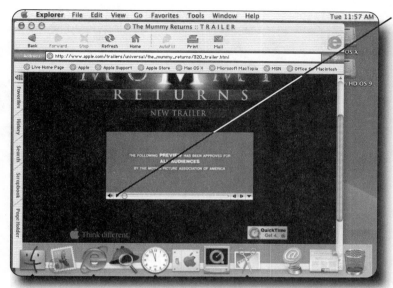

4. Click on the **Play button**. The movie file will start to play and the play control will change to the pause control so that you can play and stop the movie at will.

NOTE

If you don't have a high-speed connection, playback will be limited by your connection speed and you may have to click on the Play button numerous times to get through the whole video. In such a case, choose the smallest playback size. See the section titled "Setting QuickTime Preferences" to learn how to make sure that you've chosen the proper playback speed.

Viewing a QTV Channel

Many QTV (*QuickTime TV*) channels offer an interactive multimedia experience. When you use a QTV channel, you don't have to simply watch a movie from start to finish. You can choose from a variety of movies and view related content in your Web browser. Other QTV channels play a live audio stream or other broadcast content. QuickTime Player offers a number of predefined QTV channels, making it easy for you to get started with the variety of QTV resources.

1. Click on a **QTV channel** on the QTV tab in the QuickTime Player window. If your system connects to the Internet via a dial-up connection, and you have configured the system to connect automatically as explained in Chapter 11, "Setting up the Connection,"your modem will dial your ISP and QuickTime Player will display the main channel.

TIP

The first time you try to view a QTV channel, you may see a dialog box asking you to set your connection speed in the Quicktime pane of System Preferences. If you do, skip ahead to the section "Setting Quicktime Preferences" to find out how.

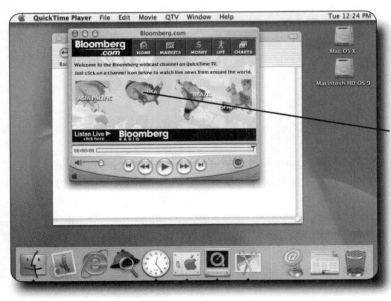

2. If you see a window with choices for various topics, **click** on a **topic button or link**. QuickTime Player will show the desired content.

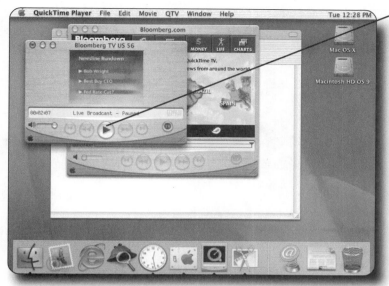

3. **Click** on the **controls** to play or pause QuickTime videos as needed. Sometimes the video opens in a separate QuickTime Player window (as shown here) and sometimes the video appears within the QuickTime Player window with separate controls below the movie box. The content will play or pause accordingly.

NOTE

Some links in a QTV channel will launch your Web browser and display related Web content. Other links will start playback of a live Internet radio broadcast.

Adding a Favorite QTV Channel

The main QuickTime Player window offers a second tab (with a heart on it) that's designated to hold additional QTV channels that you mark as Favorites. You can go to Apple's Web site to find additional QTV channels and mark them as Favorites.

1. Click on the **QuickTime Player icon** on the Dock. QuickTime Player will open.

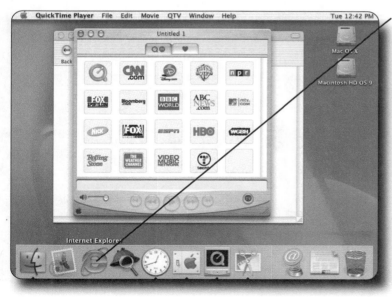

2. Connect to the **Internet**, **open Internet Explorer** and **Navigate** to **http://www.apple.com/quicktime/qtv**. A page from Apple's Web site with information about additional QTV channels will appear.

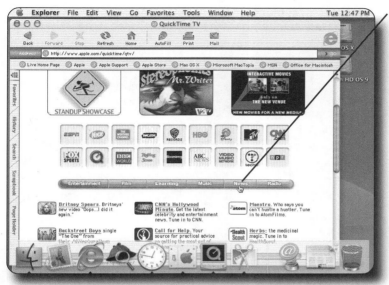

3. Scroll down the page **and click** on the **button** for a QTV category. A Web page listing channels in that category will appear.

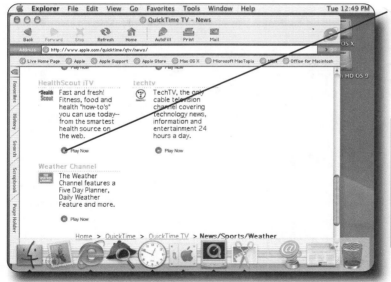

4. Scroll down the page, **and click** on the **Play Now button** for the QTV channel. The channel will open in QuickTime Player.

NOTE

If the QuickTime Player window and menu bar does not come forward, click on the QuickTime Player icon on the Dock.

5. **Click** on **QTV**. The QTV menu will appear.

6. **Move** the **mouse pointer down** to Favorites. The Favorites submenu will appear.

7. **Click** on **Add Movie As Favorite**. The QTV channel will be added to the Favorites tab and to the QTV, Favorites submenu.

NOTE

If an icon for the new Favorite doesn't appear on the Favorites tab, choose QTV, Favorites, Show Labels so that you can, at least, see its name.

To use a favorite QTV channel, display the Favorites tab and then click on the Favorite.

Setting QuickTime Preferences

QuickTime Player differs from other Mac OS X applications in that it includes two sets of preferences: one for the software itself and another for connection speed and other settings available in the Quicktime pane of System preferences.

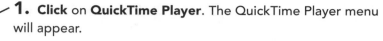

1. **Click** on **QuickTime Player**. The QuickTime Player menu will appear.

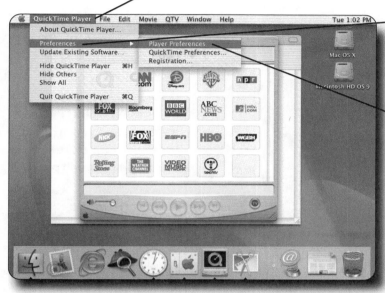

2. **Move** the **mouse pointer down** to Preferences. The Preferences submenu will appear.

3. **Click** on **Player Preferences**. The General Preferences dialog box will open.

The options in the General Preferences dialog control some of the basic settings controlling how Quicktime Player will handle multiple open movie windows.

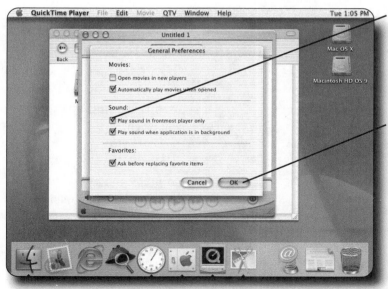

4. **Click** on the **check boxes**, as needed. Checks will appear or disappear in the boxes and the options will be enabled or disabled.

5. **Click** on **OK**. The General Preferences dialog box will close, applying your setting changes.

6. Click on **QuickTime Player**. The QuickTime Player menu will appear.

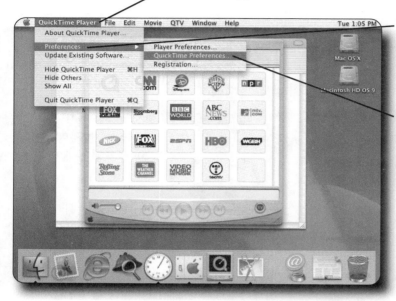

7. Move the **mouse pointer down** to Preferences. The Preferences submenu will appear.

8. Click on **QuickTime Preferences**. System Preferences will start and the QuickTime pane will open.

There are five tabs on the Quicktime pane allowing you to fully customize the way your Macintosh handles Quicktime media.

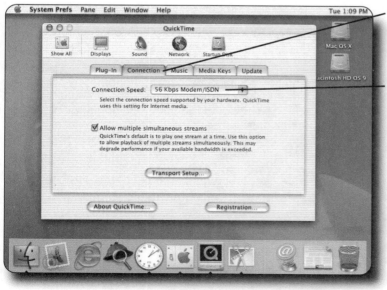

9. Click on the **Connection tab**. The Connection tab will come forward.

10. Click on the **Connection Speed pop-up menu**. The pop-up menu will open.

11. Click on your **connection speed**. Your connection when using Quicktime will be set for optimum playback.

12. **Click** on **System Prefs**. The System Prefs menu will appear.

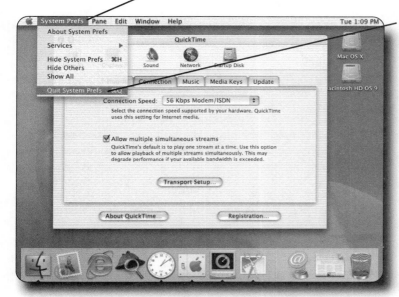

13. **Click** on **Quit System Prefs**. System Preferences will close, applying the new settings. You can then continue to work in QuickTime Player or quit the application if you are finished.

18

Working with Other Features

In addition to the applications that supply major areas of functionality within Mac OS X, a number of other applications supply other practical and fun functions. If you want to make a note to yourself, play chess, write a letter to a friend, and more, this is the chapter for you. In this chapter, you'll learn how to:

- Create Stickie reminders.
- Play chess against Mac OS X.
- Use the calculator.
- Create a text file.
- Take a picture of the screen.
- Use Preview to view graphics and PDF files.
- Add a graphic to a rich text file.
- Create your own PDF file.

Creating and Deleting a Stickie

If you need to make a temporary note to yourself and place it in a visible location, create a Stickie. As long as Stickies is open, your Stickies stay on the desktop—right where they can be seen until you discard them.

1. **Click** on the **Applications button** on a Finder window toolbar. The contents of the Applications folder will appear in the Finder window.

2. **Double-click** on **Stickies**. Stickies will start and a blank Stickie will open along with instructions on how to create a Stickie.

TIP

Once Stickies is open, choose File, New Note to add another new Stickie.

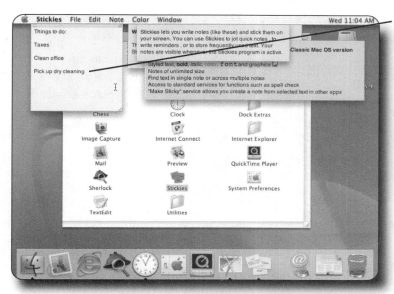

3. Type a **note**, pressing **Return** when needed.

TIP

You can use the Note menu to format any selected text in your Stickies.

4. Click on **Color**. The Color menu will appear. It features choices for changing the background color of the current Stickie.

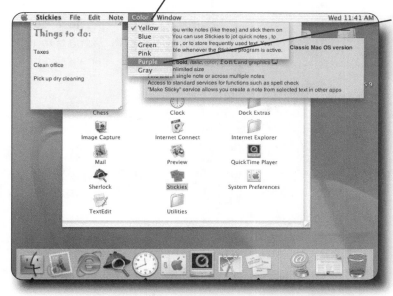

5. Click on a **color**. Stickies will apply the color to the current note.

6. Click on **File**. The File menu will appear.

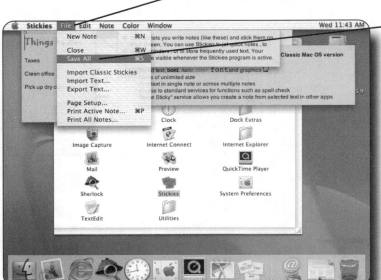

7. Click on **Save All**. Stickies will save all new notes that you've created.

TIP

If you want to close the tip windows that appear when Stickies is open, click on a tip window, then click on the small close box that appears in the upper-left corner of the window.

8. To discard a Stickie, **click** in the **Stickie**. The Stickie will become active.

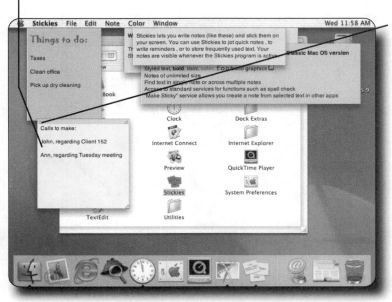

9. Click on the **close box**. If the Stickie has unsaved information, a message box will open.

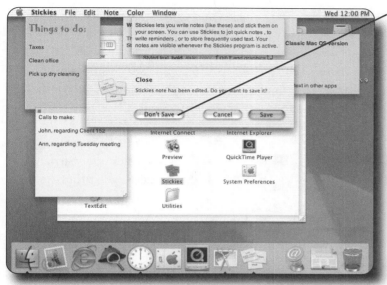

10. **Click** on **Don't Save**. The Stickie will be discarded.

Closing the Stickies application hides all of the Stickies without deleting them. Choose Stickies, Quit Stickies to close the Stickies application. To redisplay your Stickies, simply start Stickies again.

Starting and Quitting a Chess Game

If you want a bit of rest and relaxation (or an intellectual challenge), you can play chess against Mac OS X. While I can't teach you how to play chess, I can give you the basic steps for starting and ending a game.

1. **Click** on the **Applications button** on a Finder window toolbar. The contents of the Applications folder will appear in the Finder window.

2. **Double-click** on **Chess**. Chess will start and a new game will open.

You play the white pieces and Chess plays black. You move first.

3. Drag a **white chess piece** to the desired board position. The piece will move to that location, successfully eliminating another piece if you take it.

4. After Chess makes its move, **take** your **turn**. The game will progress in this fashion.

TIP

You may notice that a round window with a microphone icon appears when you start Chess. This window is for the speech (Speakable Items) feature, which enables you to give voice commands in certain applications. To turn on this feature, click on the down arrow that appears at the bottom of the round window, then click on Speech Preferences. See the section called "Working with Speakable Items" at the end of the chapter to learn more.

5. When you're ready to admit defeat, **click** on **Chess**. The Chess menu will appear.

6. Click on **Quit Chess**. Chess will close.

Performing a Calculation

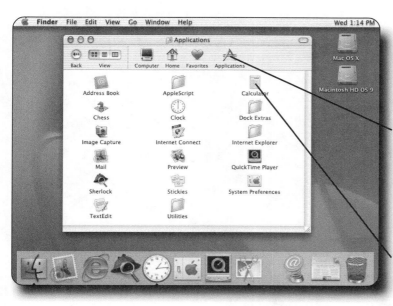

Mac OS X offers Calculator to help you out with math, which is particularly helpful in one of those moments when your mind just goes blank.

1. Click on the **Applications button** on a Finder window toolbar. The contents of the Applications folder will appear in the Finder window.

2. Double-click on **Calculator**. Calculator will start.

3. **Enter** your **Calculation**, either by clicking on the buttons in the Calculator window or by pressing keys on your keyboard's numeric keypad.

4. **Enter** an **= symbol** by clicking or typing. The Calculator will complete the calculation and display the result.

TIP

After you calculate the result, choose Edit, Copy to copy it to the clipboard. Then, you can switch to another application and choose Edit, Paste to paste that value into a document.

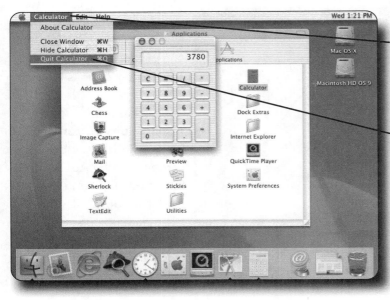

5. When you're finished calculating, **click** on **Calculator**. The Calculator menu will appear.

6. **Click** on **Quit Calculator**. Calculator will close.

Creating an RTF (Text) File

Mac OS X includes TextEdit for creating basic documents. Although you can use TextEdit to create plain text (TXT) documents, by default it creates RTF (*Rich Text Format*) documents. Rich text documents can include various text formats and graphics, capabilities that aren't available for plain text documents. As a bonus, most commercial word processors can open and read rich text format documents, so virtually any other user to whom you e-mail an RTF file will be able to open and use it.

1. Click on the **Applications button** on a Finder window toolbar. The contents of the Applications folder will appear in the Finder window.

2. Double-click on **TextEdit**. TextEdit will start and a blank document window will open.

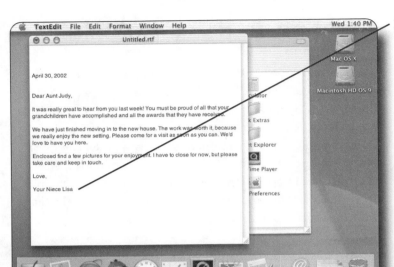

3. **Type** the **document text**.

4. **Drag** over **text** in the document. The text will be selected (highlighted).

5. **Click** on **Format**. The Format menu will appear.

6. **Move** the **mouse pointer down** to Font. The Font submenu will appear.

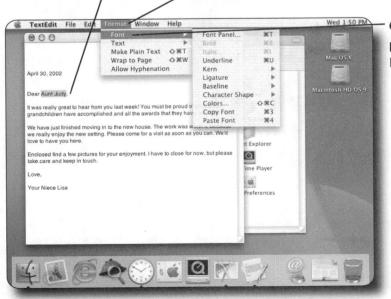

The following list identifies the most commonly used commands on the Font submenu:

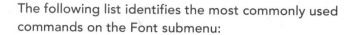

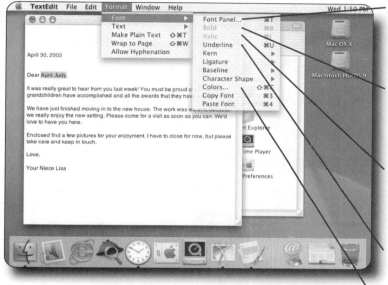

- **Font Panel**. This command opens the Font window and allows you to choose a font and size.

- **Bold**. This command makes the text bold, if that option is available for the current font.

- **Italic**. This command makes the text italic, if that option is available for the current font.

- **Underline**. This command adds underlining to the selected text.

- **Colors**. This command displays the Colors window and allows you to choose a text color.

TIP

If you make a mistake when creating a document, use the Edit, Undo command. (The command name changes to reflect the last action you performed in TextEdit.)

7. **Click** in a **paragraph** in the document (or drag over multiple paragraphs). The paragraph(s) will be selected.

8. **Click** on **Format**. The Format menu will appear.

9. **Move** the **mouse pointer down** to Text. The Text submenu will appear.

You can use the commands on the Text submenu to format the selected paragraph in the following ways:

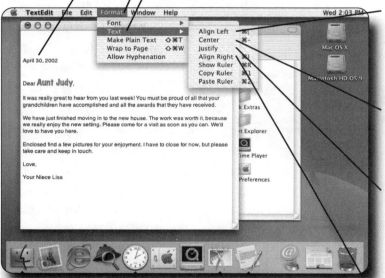

- **Align Left**. This command aligns the left side of each line to the left margin in the document, leaving a ragged right edge.

- **Center**. This command centers each line in the paragraph between the margins.

- **Justify**. This command aligns the left and right side of each line to its respective margin with space added between words within each line.

- **Align Right**. This command aligns the right side of each line to the right margin in the document, leaving a ragged left edge.

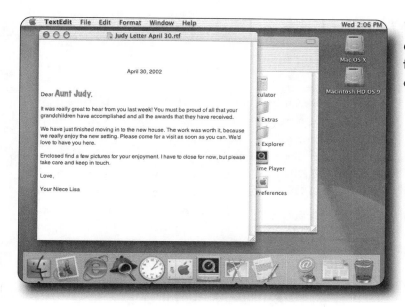

10. Save and print the **document** as needed. These functions will work just as in other applications.

11. When you're finished creating documents, **click** on **TextEdit**. The TextEdit menu will appear.

12. Click on **Quit TextEdit**. TextEdit will close.

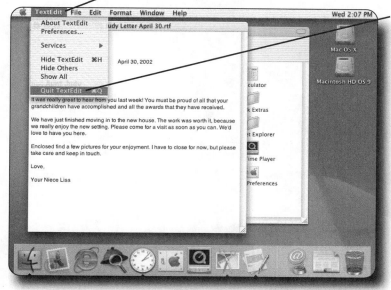

Shooting a Picture of Your Screen

There may be times when you want to take a picture of what's on the screen in Mac OS X. For example, you may be writing a "how to" procedure about a program to share with a friend; screen shots (pictures of the screen) can illustrate your steps. Or, you may be having a problem with an application. You can take a screen shot of the problem or error message, then e-mail the image or fax a printout to a tech support representative. No matter what your reason, you can use Grab to shoot the screen and save the shot as a TIFF graphic file.

1. **Click** on the **Applications button** on a Finder window toolbar. The contents of the Applications folder will appear in the Finder window.

2. **Double-click** on the **Utilities folder**. The contents of the Utilities folder will appear in the Finder window.

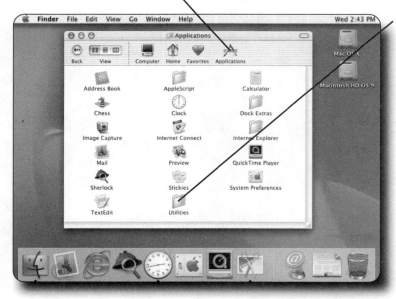

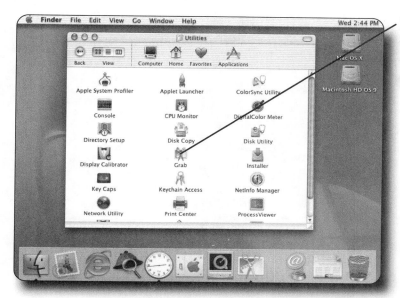

3. Double-click on **Grab**. Grab will start. It doesn't have an application window, but its menus will appear.

4. Click on **Capture**. The Capture menu will appear.

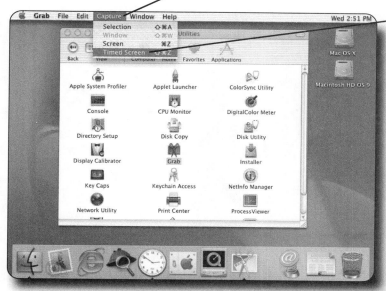

5. Click on **Timed Screen**. The Timed Screen Grab dialog box will open.

Choosing the Timed Screen option allows you 10 seconds to set up the screen for capture, helping you ensure that you get exactly the shot you want.

6. Click on **Start Timer**. The Grab timer will start counting down, so that you can navigate to the proper location for the shot. You will hear a camera sound and a window will open displaying the screen shot.

7. **Save and print** the **graphic file** as needed. These functions will work just as in other applications.

8. When you're finished creating screen shots, **click** on **Grab**. The Grab menu will appear.

9. **Click** on **Quit Grab**. Grab will close.

Viewing a Graphic or PDF File

So many graphics applications, so many file types. Preview helps you view graphics files in a variety of formats. In addition, Preview enables you to view Adobe PDF (*Portable Document Format*) documents. PDF has become a standard format for documents that include text and graphics. In fact, many downloadable electronic books (e-books) use the PDF format.

NOTE

In some cases, you can simply double-click on a graphic or PDF file in a Finder window to start Preview and open the file.

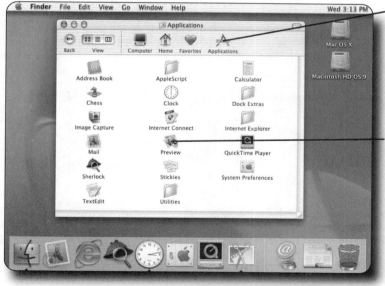

1. **Click** on the **Applications button** on a Finder window toolbar. The contents of the Applications folder will appear in the Finder window.

2. **Double-click** on **Preview**. Preview will start.

3. Click on **File**. The File menu will appear.

4. Click on **Open**. The Open dialog box will open.

5. Navigate to the **folder** that contains the graphic or PDF file. The Open dialog box will list the files in that folder.

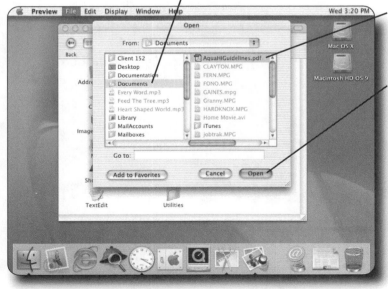

6. Click on a **graphic or PDF file**. The file will be selected in the list.

7. Click on **Open**. The graphic or PDF file will open in the Preview window.

Once a file is open in Preview, you can print it or save it under a new name. If the file is a graphic file, you can use the File, Export command to save it in another graphic format.

8. When you're finished working with graphics and PDF files, **click** on **Preview**. The Preview menu will appear.

9. **Click** on **Quit Preview**. Preview will close.

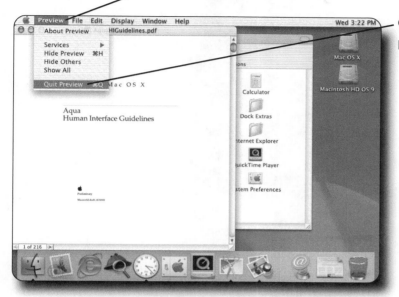

Adding a Picture to a Text File

You can use TextEdit and Preview together to jazz up an RTF document by adding graphics to it. You can get your graphics files from a variety of sources, such as a clip art collection or from an online resource. Be sure to respect copyright law whenever you use graphics from any source.

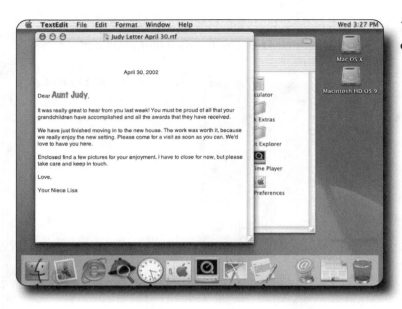

1. **Start TextEdit**, and **open or create** a **document**.

2. **Open or switch to Preview, and open** a **graphic file**. The graphic will appear in a window.

3. In Preview, **click** on **Edit**. The Edit menu will appear.

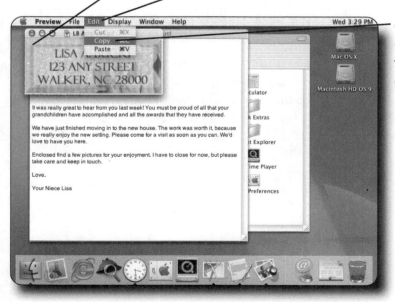

4. **Click** on **Copy**. The graphic will be copied into the system's memory, commonly called a *clipboard*.

5. Click on the **TextEdit icon** on the Dock. TextEdit and the open document window will come forward.

6. Click on the **location** where you'd like to insert the graphic. The *insertion point* (the blinking vertical line) will move to the location.

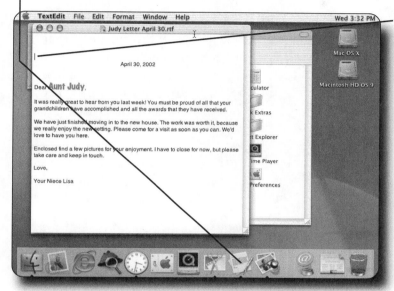

7. In TextEdit, **click** on **Edit**. The Edit menu will appear.

8. Click on **Paste**. The graphic will be pasted into the document at the insertion point location.

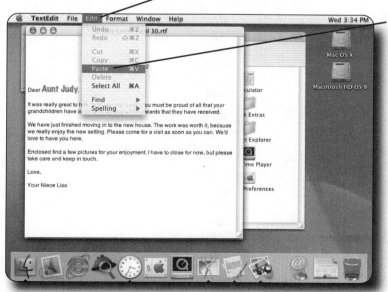

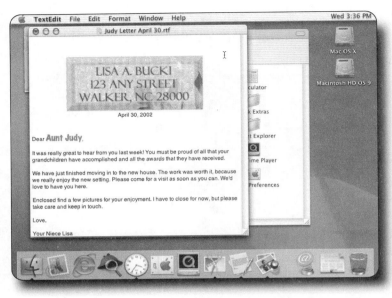

9. Save the **file**. The new file will be saved to the location you specify.

Now you can do further formatting to your document. For example, you can choose Format, Text, Center after inserting the graphic to center the graphic file in the document. You can also print the file or attach it to an e-mail.

Creating a Basic PDF File

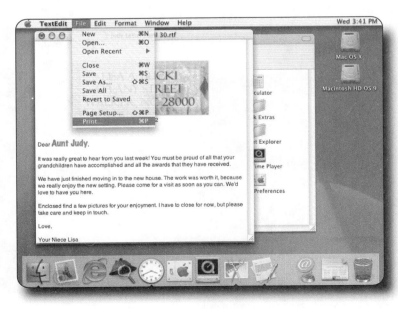

Because of the increasing popularity of the PDF format, Mac OS X enables you to save documents from many applications as PDF files.

1. Start the **application, and open or create** the **file** to convert to PDF. The application will launch and the file will appear in a window.

2. Click on **File**. The File menu will appear.

3. Click on **Print**. The Print dialog will open.

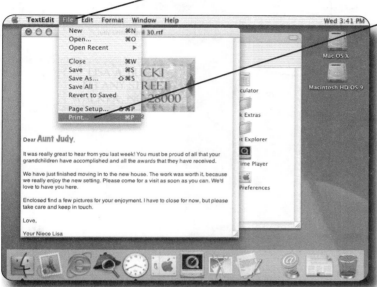

4. Click on the **Copies & Pages pop-up menu**. The pop-up menu will appear.

5. Click on **Output Options**. The Print dialog will change to display the output options.

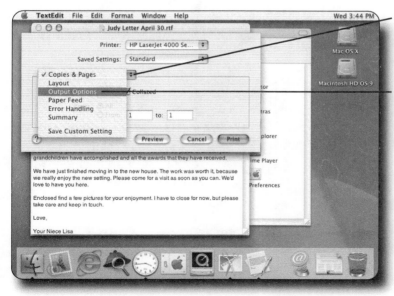

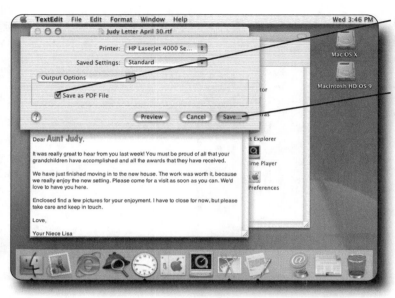

6. **Click** on the **Save as PDF File check box**. A check will appear in the box.

7. **Click** on **Save**. The Save dialog will open.

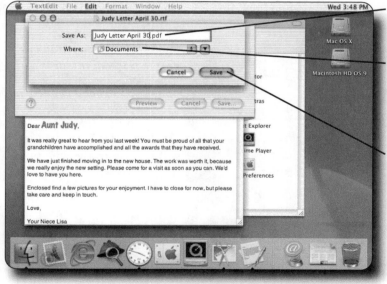

8. **Edit** the **file name** in the Save As text box as needed.

9. **Specify** the **folder** in which to save the file, if needed. The Where pop-up menu will display your choice.

10. **Click** on **Save**. Mac OS X will save the PDF file in the specified location. You can then use Preview to view the PDF file.

Working with Speakable Items

The Speakable Items feature in Mac OS X enables you to give voice commands in certain applications and to Mac OS X in general. Some applications may even be able to speak text back to you. This can be a great feature if you like to multi-task while you work or cut down on typing and mouse use due to some hand or wrist ailment.

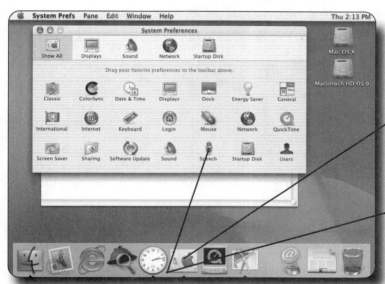

1. Click on the **System Preferences icon** on the Dock. System Preferences will open.

2. Click on the **Speech icon**. The Speech pane will appear in the System Preferences window.

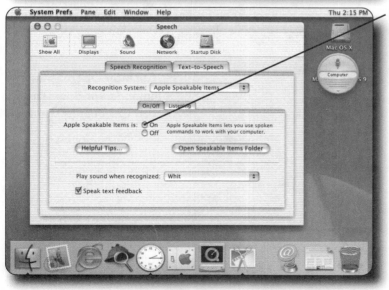

3. Click on the **On option button**. Speakable Items will start up, and a round feedback window will appear.

4. Click on **System Prefs**. The System Prefs menu will open.

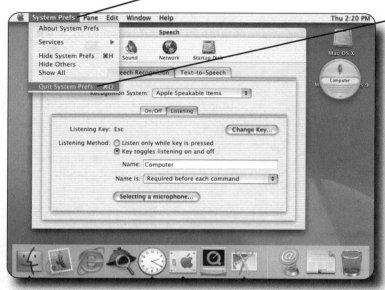

5. Click on **Quit System Prefs**. System Preferences will close, but Speakable Items will remain active.

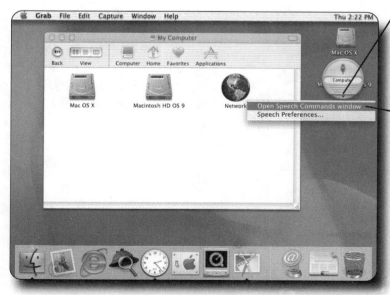

6. Click on the **down arrow** that appears at the bottom of the feedback window. A menu will appear.

7. Click on **Open Speech Commands window**. The Speech Commands window will appear.

You will see a list of the available speech commands and directions about how to proceed with Speakable Items.

8. Speak a **command**. Speakable Items will perform the desired action and the top pane of the Speech Commands window will display your command.

You could say, "Computer Switch to Clock," and Clock would become the active application. Sometimes the computer will also prompt you for additional input, if needed, such as if you asked Speakable Items to tell you a joke. To toggle listening on and off, press and hold the Esc key for about a second. Precede each voice command listed in the Speech Commands window with "Computer," as in "Computer, Tell Me a Joke."

9. When you've finished using Speakable Items, speak **"Computer Quit Speakable Items."** Speakable Items will stop and the feedback and Speech Commands windows will close.

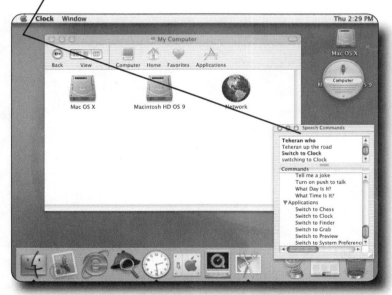

TIP

Don't pause between the lead-in name ("Computer") and the command itself. Otherwise, Speakable Items will not recognize your command.

Part V Review Questions

1. How do I get iTunes? *See "Downloading and Installing iTunes" in Chapter 16.*

2. How do I create my own MP3 files? *See "Making MP3s and Adding Them to Your Library" in Chapter 16.*

3. Can I tune in to Internet radio? *See "Playing an Internet Radio Stream" in Chapter 16.*

4. How do I play a movie file? *See "Opening and Closing a Movie File" in Chapter 17.*

5. How do I view QTV? *See "Viewing a QTV Channel" in Chapter 17.*

6. How do I play Chess? *See "Starting and Quitting a Chess Game" in Chapter 18.*

7. How do I create a letter? *See "Creating an RTF (Text) File" in Chapter 18.*

8. How do I open a graphic file? *See "Viewing a Graphic or PDF File" in Chapter 18.*

9. How do I save a PDF file? *See "Creating a Basic PDF File" in Chapter 18.*

PART VI

Basic Maintenance and Troubleshooting

Chapter 19
Emergency Startup Measures **317**

Chapter 20
Tackling Disk Issues **327**

Chapter 21
Managing Users **337**

19

Emergency Startup Measures

Macs enjoy an excellent reputation in terms of system reliability. They tend to be very stable with few instances where the system locks up or otherwise goes on the fritz. Despite such stability, you may encounter situations where Mac OS X locks up. If you have both Mac OS X and OS 9.1 (or 9.0x) installed on separate disks, you also may encounter situations where you need to boot from the disk with the older operating system, then return to the Mac OS X boot disk. In this chapter, you'll learn how to:

- Restart the system when it hangs.
- Start up the system from your Mac OS X CD-ROM.
- Boot the system from an OS 9.X disk (volume).
- Return to booting the system from the Mac OS X disk (volume).
- Rebuild the Classic Desktop if it hangs.

Restarting the System

In the process of writing this book, I spent many hours using the Public Beta version of Mac OS X. Even this test version worked reliably, with few, if any, instances where the system crashed. Nevertheless, all systems hang at some point or another. For example, you could install a piece of shareware that causes a problem or open a corrupt file that the system can't handle.

When the system freezes, you have a few ways to deal with the situation and restart the system:

- If something goes wrong but you still can use the mouse, click on the Apple menu, then click on Restart. The system should restart.

- If the mouse doesn't work, try the keyboard next. Press Command+ Control+the Power button. (For some systems, you may need to press Command+ Option+Shift+ the Power button.)

- If you have an iMac, you can press the Reset button. It's a small round button imprinted with a left arrow and is located along with the ports on the system—below the modem port.

- If none of the other methods work, press the Power button to turn the system off. Let it power all the way down until you can hear that the hard disk has stopped spinning. Then press the Power button again to restart the system.

Starting up from a CD-ROM

You may encounter situations so severe that Mac OS X won't boot at all from a hard disk. Or, you may have forgotten the password for the system. If you encounter such a problem, you may need to start up the system from the Mac OS X CD-ROM.

1. **Insert** the **Mac OS X CD-ROM** into the CD-ROM or DVD-ROM drive.

2. **Restart the system**, **pressing and holding** the **C key** as soon as you can.

3. Once you hear the CD-ROM spinning, **release** the **C key**. The system will continue restarting and the installer will appear.

Because most systems read data more slowly from a CD-ROM or DVD-ROM, restarting from the CD-ROM will take longer than starting normally.

4a. **Click** on the **Continue button and rerun** the **installer**. Mac OS X will be reinstalled, which should help any serious problems with the system. After the installer sequence finishes, the system will restart automatically.

OR

4b. **Click** on **Installer**. The Installer menu will appear.

4c. **Click** on **Reset Password or Disk Utility**. The utility you select will start.

Use Reset Password to create a new password, which is handy if you've forgotten the system password. Use the First Aid feature of Disk Utility to verify (check) or repair the selected hard disk. (Chapter 20, "Tackling Disk Issues," covers how

---

NOTE

Pressing C while restarting will also reboot to the CD-ROM if you've inserted an OS 9.x CD-ROM. However, in this instance the reboot process takes you to an OS 9.x Desktop.

Disk Utility works.) Be sure to quit each utility when you finish with it. Then choose Quit Installer from the Installer menu and click on Restart in the resulting dialog box.

Changing the Startup Disk

If you have Mac OS X and Mac OS 9 installed on separate disks or disk partitions, you can choose the disk or partition from which you want the computer to boot. Of course, booting from the Mac OS 9 disk starts up your Mac with the Mac OS 9 operating system and booting from the Mac OS X disk starts up your system with the Mac OS X operating system. This section covers how to reboot from disk to disk and system to system.

Changing to a Mac OS 9.1 Disk

You may want to boot to OS 9 (usually OS 9.1) if the Classic environment won't work correctly or if you want to work with an OS 9 application that won't work through the Classic environment for some reason. These steps assume that Mac OS 9.1 is installed on a separate disk volume.

1. **Click** on the **System Preferences icon** on the Dock. System Preferences will open.

2. Click on the **Startup Disk icon**. The Startup Disk pane will appear in the System Preferences window.

3. Click on the **System Folder** labeled Mac OS 9.1 in the Startup Disk pane. The icon will be selected.

4. Click on **System Prefs**. The System Prefs menu will appear.

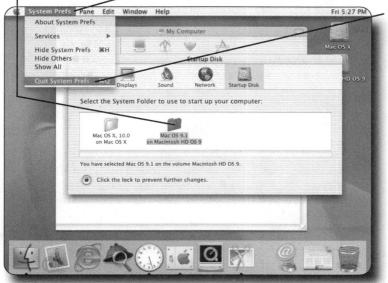

5. Click on **Quit System Prefs**. The System Preferences application will close.

6. Click on the **Apple menu**. The Apple menu will open.

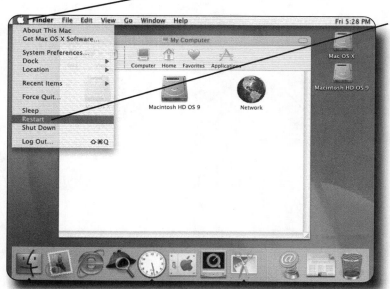

7. Click on **Restart**. The system will restart, rebooting into Mac OS 9.1.

Changing Back to a Mac OS X Disk

Rebooting into Mac OS X works a little differently from Mac OS 9.1, as you might expect due to the significant differences between the systems.

NOTE

To restart from a Mac OS 9 version that's older than 9.1, drag the Startup Disk Control Panel file from the Utilities folder on the Mac OS X CD-ROM into the Control Panels folder in the System Folder of the hard disk volume that holds Mac OS 9.x. Then you can use the Startup Disk control panel to switch back to Mac OS X.

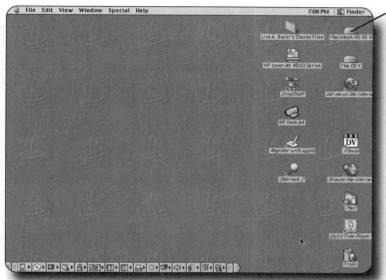

1. Double-click on the **Mac OS 9 hard disk icon** (your hard disk may have a different name) on the Desktop. A Finder window will open.

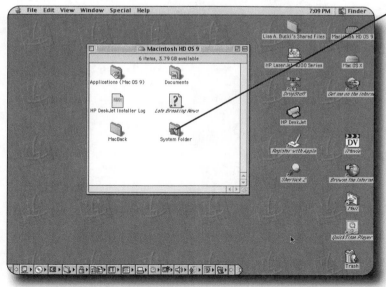

2. Double-click on the **System Folder**. A Finder window for the System Folder will open.

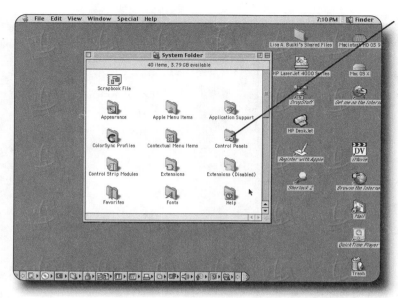

3. Double-click on the **Control Panels folder**. A Finder window for the Control Panels folder will open.

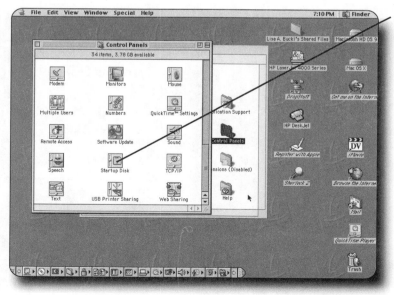

4. Double-click on **Startup Disk**. The Startup Disk window will open.

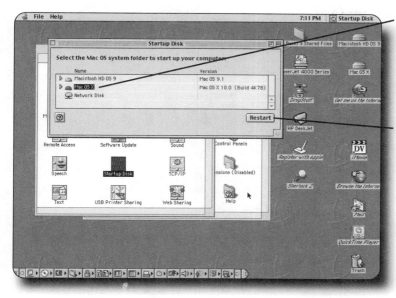

5. Click on the **hard disk** that holds the Mac OS X system in the list. The hard disk will be selected as the boot disk.

6. Click on the **Restart**. The system will restart, booting to Mac OS X.

Rebuilding the Classic Desktop

There may be times when you're working in the Classic environment and its programs start malfunctioning. In such a case, rebuilding the Classic Desktop within Mac OS X can cure some of the problems.

CAUTION

This process may change the application used by default to open certain types of files under Mac OS X.

1. Click on the **System Preferences icon** on the Dock. System Preferences will open.

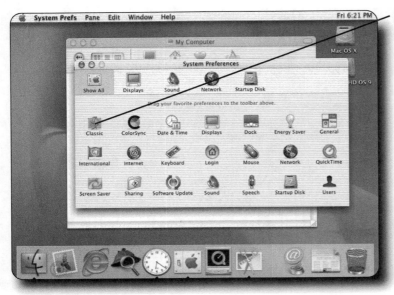

2. Click on the **Classic icon**. The Classic pane will appear in the System Preferences window.

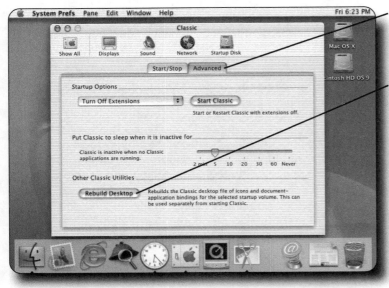

3. Click on the **Advanced tab**. The Advanced tab will come forward.

4. Click on **Rebuild Desktop**. The Desktop will be rebuilt, a process that takes a few minutes on most systems. You can then either close System Preferences or continue working.

20

Tackling Disk Issues

While Mac OS X offers a great deal of stability, sometimes you may not be as lucky with the disk media that you use. The surface of both hard disks and removable disks consists of magnetic material that can be damaged. If dust somehow gets in the disk case, it can cause damage. If the heads in a drive malfunction, it can cause damage. Other magnetic matter placed too close to the disk can also cause damage. In this chapter, you'll learn how to:

- Start and exit Disk Utility.
- Check a disk for errors.
- Repair a disk.
- Erase a disk.

Starting and Exiting Disk Utility

Earlier Mac operating systems also offered the Disk Utility application to enable users to eliminate disk problems. In Mac OS X, Disk Utility can verify and repair disks formatted as one of the following volume types:

- Mac OS Standard.

- Mac OS Extended.

- UFS.

Before you use Disk Utility, you should close all open applications. If you are not logged in as an administrator (using the original User Name you entered or another administrator User Name created as described in Chapter 21, "Managing Users,") you will need to unlock the Disk Utility settings. Alternatively, you will be prompted to log in as an administrator.

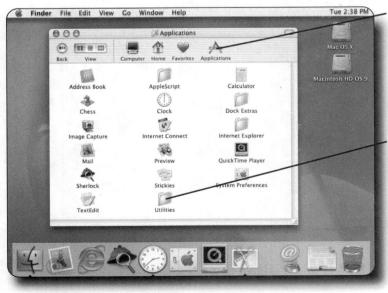

1. Click on the **Applications button** on a Finder window toolbar. The contents of the Applications folder will appear in the Finder window.

2. Double-click on the **Utilities folder**. The contents of the Utilities folder will appear in the Finder window.

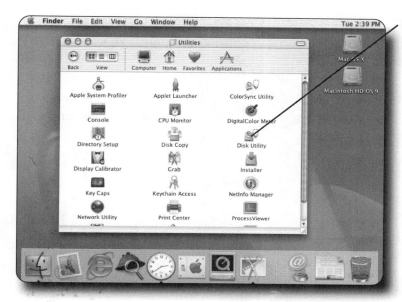

3. Double-click on **Disk Utility**. Disk Utility will start.

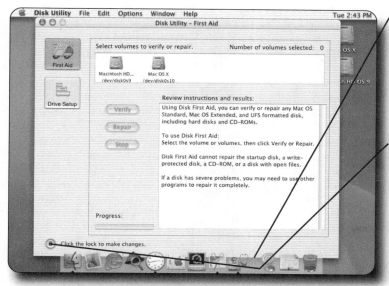

4. Drag the **vertical divider line** on the Dock down to make the Dock smaller. The Dock will shrink so that you can see the small lock icon.

5. Click on the **small lock icon**. A dialog box will appear to prompt you to enter the administrator password.

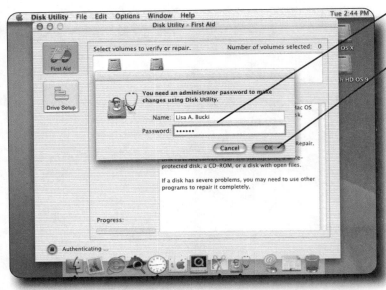

6. Type the **password** into the Password text box.

7. Click on **OK**. Mac OS X will verify that you have administrator privileges and unlock Disk Utility so that you can make changes.

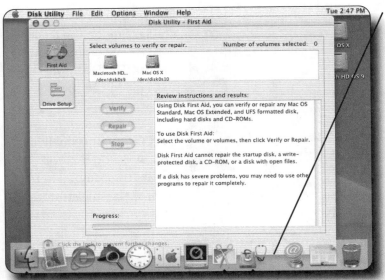

8. Drag the **vertical divider line** on the Dock up. The Dock will return to a larger size.

9. Once you've finished working in Disk Utility, **click** on **Disk Utility**. The Disk Utility menu will appear.

10. **Click** on **Quit Disk Utility**. Disk Utility will close.

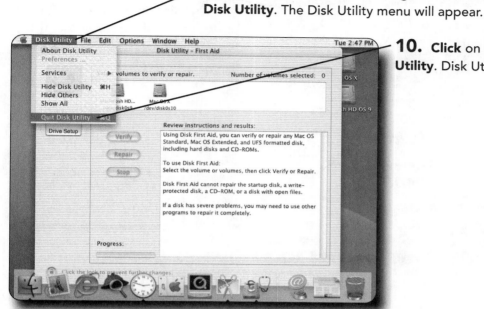

Verifying a Disk

Symptoms of a disk problem may vary. For example, using a particular document file or application may cause the system to hang or crash. Or, perhaps the system is experiencing slight problems when starting. If you ever suspect that you have a disk problem, use the Disk Utility application right away to check the disk.

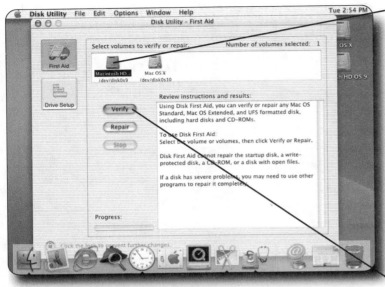

1. Click on the **volume (disk)** in the Select volumes to verify or repair list. The volume will be selected and the Verify and Repair buttons will become active.

TIP

Make sure that the First Aid button at the left side of the Disk Utility window is selected.

2. Click on **Verify**. Disk Utility will verify the disk and display a list of results.

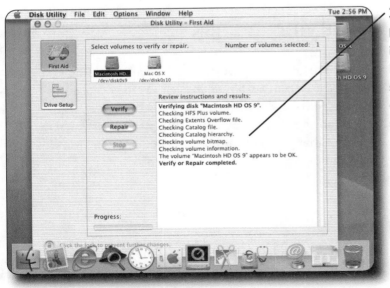

3. Review the **results**. If Disk Utility finds a disk error, it will be included on the list. If any errors are listed, you should repair the disk as described in the next section.

Repairing a Disk

If you verify a disk and find that it has problems or are advised by a technical support representative to repair a disk, then you can use Disk Utility to do so. However, Disk Utility does have a few limitations in this regard. It cannot:

- Repair a write-protected disk or CD-ROM.

- Repair a disk that has files open in other applications. (Close all open applications and files to eliminate this problem.)

- Repair the startup disk (boot disk or startup volume). To repair the startup disk, you can boot from the Mac OS X CD-ROM and then choose Disk Utility from the Installer menu.

If none of the above conditions exist, repairing a disk is simple.

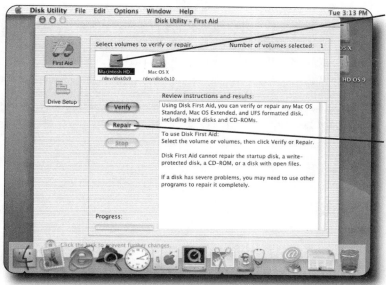

1. Click on the **volume (disk)** in the Select volumes to verify or repair list. The volume will be highlighted and the Verify and Repair buttons will become active.

2. Click on **Repair**. Disk Utility will repair the disk and display a list of results.

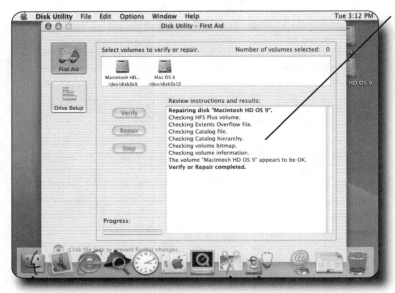

3. Review the **results**. If Disk Utility finds a disk error, it will be listed along with the corrective action that was taken.

TIP

If you click on the Drive Setup button at the left side of the Disk Utility window, Disk Utility displays options for repartitioning the system hard disk—that is, dividing the physical disk into multiple logical or functional disks. Avoid using this capability unless you have expert help or are confident that you have a recent backup of your system.

Erasing a Disk

You can erase a disk if you no longer need its contents and want to reformat it. Typically, you'll only want to erase some type of external disk: a floppy or Zip disk or an external hard disk, for example. You cannot erase the current startup disk (volume).

1. Insert the **disk** into the drive, if needed.

2. Click on the **volume (disk)** in the Select volumes to verify or repair list. The volume will be highlighted.

3. Click on **Options**. The Options menu will appear.

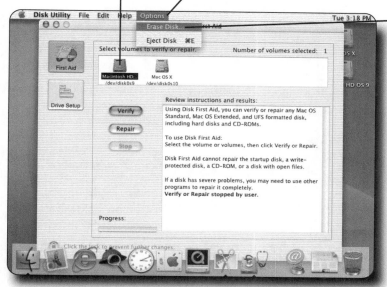

4. Click on **Erase Disk**. The Erase Disk dialog will open.

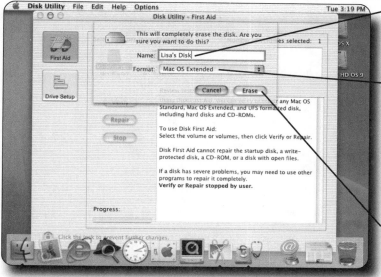

5. Type a **new name** for the disk, if required, in the Name text box.

6. Click on the **Format pop-up menu**. The pop-up menu will open.

7. Click on a **disk format**. The new format choice will appear.

8. Click on **Erase**. Disk Utility will erase and reformat the disk.

CAUTION

You can't undo a disk format operation, so be sure that you've selected or inserted the proper disk before you proceed.

21

Managing Users

Mac OS X was designed to accommodate multiple users. Mac OS X creates separate Home folders for each user and, restricts that user's hard disk access to his or her own Home folder and its subfolders. By employing this and other special features in Mac OS X, not only do you protect each user's files but you also streamline each user's ability to operate his or her system. In this chapter, you'll learn how to:

- Add or delete a user.
- Change a user's password.
- Change a user's administration privileges.
- Use Keychain Access.
- Turn automatic login on or off.

Setting up Multiple Users

To add and work with the multiple user features in Mac OS X, you will use the Users pane in System Preferences. To work with user information, you must be logged in as an administrator or you must unlock the Users pane by providing an administrator's user name and password.

1. Click on the **System Preferences icon** on the Dock. System Preferences will start.

2. Click on the **Users icon**. The Users pane will appear in the System Preferences window.

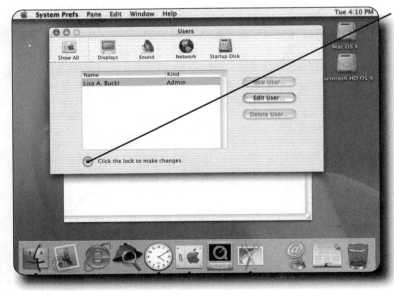

3. Click on the **small lock icon**. A dialog box will open prompting you to enter the administrator password.

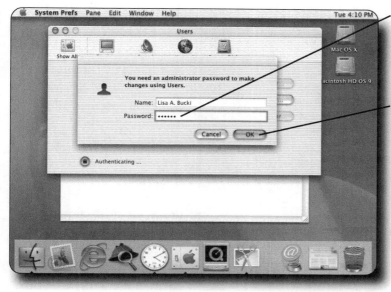

4. Type the **password** into the Password text box. A dot will appear in the text box for each letter you type.

5. Click on **OK**. Mac OS X will verify that you have administrator privileges and will then unlock the user's preferences.

Adding a User

Once you've opened the Users pane in System Preferences and have unlocked its settings, you can set up additional users. For each user, you'll specify a separate user name and password, as well as additional, optional information. The user can then use the assigned user name and password to log in to the system and access his or her new Home folder.

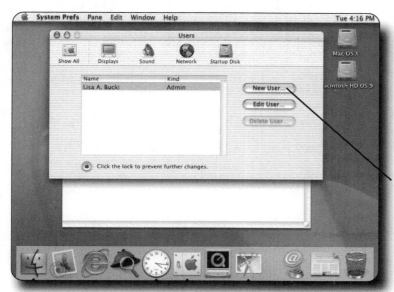

1. Click on **New User**. The New User dialog box will open.

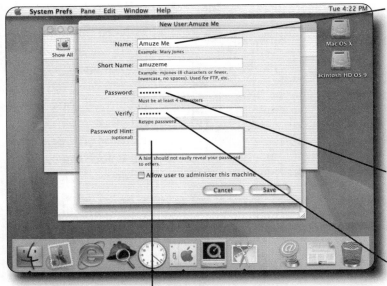

2. Type a **new user name** in the Name text box, **and press Tab twice**. The new user name will appear in the Name text box and Mac OS X will automatically make an entry in the Short Name text box.

3. Type a **new password** in the Password text box, **and press Tab**. The cursor will move to the Verify text box.

4. Type the **password** again in the Verify text box, **and press Tab**. The cursor will move to the Password Hint text box.

NOTE

Remember that user names and passwords are case- and punctuation-sensitive, so the user must enter the name and password exactly as you did.

5. Type a **hint** in the Password Hint text box.

If the user tries to log in to Mac OS X and fails three times, Mac OS X automatically displays the password hint to help the user.

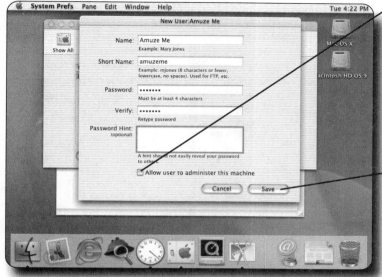

6. **Click** on the **Allow user to administer this machine check box** to select it, if needed. The user will have administrator privileges and will be able to change key system settings when logged in.

7. **Click** on **Save**. Mac OS X will create the new user, close the New User dialog box, and return to the Users pane in System Preferences where the new user will be listed. The process may take a few minutes as Mac OS X creates the folders for the user.

NOTE

If you enter a password hint and that feature is not currently available, a message box will ask whether you want to turn on password hints. Click on Yes to do so. After this, you may again need to click on Save in the New User dialog box.

Deleting a User

If a user no longer needs to work on the system, you can delete that user's login information. (The only user that you cannot delete is the first user created under Mac OS X.) The user's files will not be deleted. Instead, you can grant access to the files to one of the administrators, with the thought that that person can then cull through the files and keep or discard files as needed.

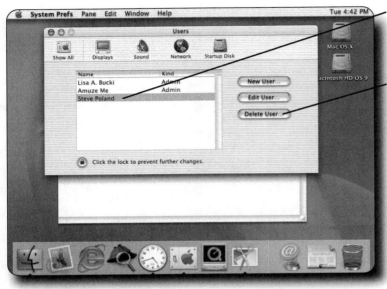

1. Click on a **user name** in the list. The user will be selected.

2. Click on **Delete User**. A dialog with options for reassigning the user's folders will open.

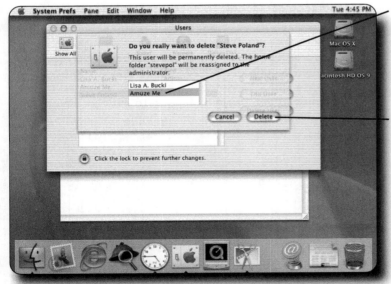

3. Click on the **administrator's name** in the list to whom you want to assign the user's folders. The administrator will be selected.

4. Click on **Delete**. Mac OS X will delete the user.

CAUTION

Mac OS X gives no further warning about deleting the user, so be careful when deleting users.

Updating a Password or Administration Privileges

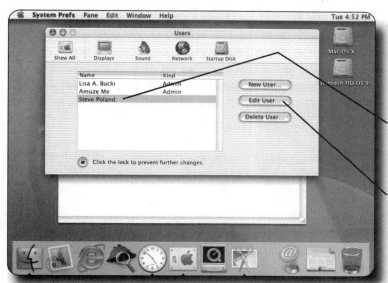

User information isn't set in stone. You can update a user name, password, and administration privileges at any time.

1. Click on a **user name** in the list. The user will be selected.

2. Click on **Edit User**. A dialog box with the user information will open.

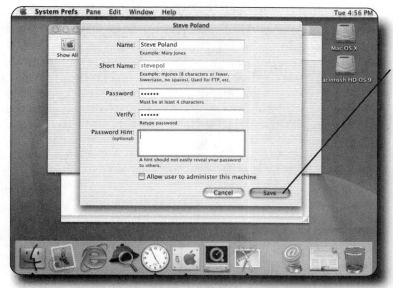

3. Make any **changes** to the users' login or privileges.

4. Click on **Save**. Mac OS X will save your changes.

NOTE

Any user that does not have administration privileges is considered part of the "staff" group under Mac OS X. Users with administration privileges are part of the "administrator" group.

Working with Keychain Access

Keychain Access existed in previous Mac operating systems, so you may already be familiar with it. Basically, you can use the keychain file to track passwords such as a password for a particular Web site, application, or network server. When you go back to the location that requires the password, Keychain Access enters the password for you automatically, assuming that the software in use (such as your Web browser) is keychain-enabled.

Mac OS X automatically creates a basic keychain file for each user you add. You can then use Keychain Access to add additional keychains as needed.

1. **Click** on the **Applications button** on a Finder window toolbar. The contents of the Applications folder will appear in the Finder window.

2. **Double-click** on the **Utilities folder**. The contents of the Utilities folder will appear in the Finder window.

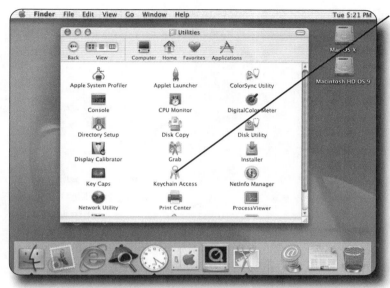

3. Double-click on **Keychain Access**. Keychain Access will start.

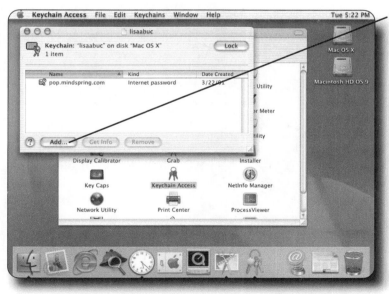

4. Click on **Add**. The New Password Item dialog box for creating a new keychain will open.

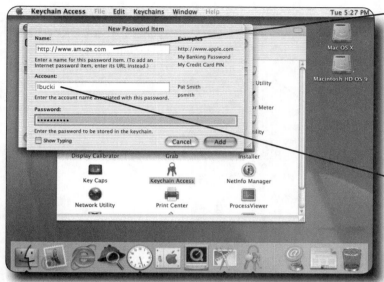

5. **Type** a **name** for the new keychain item (the name of the Web page or location that uses the keychain) in the Name text box, **and press Tab**. The cursor will move to the Account text box.

6. **Type** the **account name** you use for the location or site in the Account text box, **and press Tab**. The cursor will move to the Password text box.

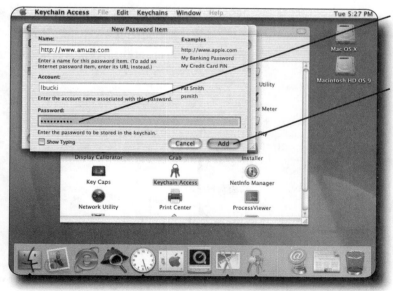

7. **Type** the **password** you use for the location or site in the Password text box.

8. **Click** on **Add**. The New Password Item dialog box will close and Keychain Access will add the new item to its keychain list.

9. Click on **Keychain Access**. The Keychain Access menu will appear.

10. Click on **Quit Keychain Access**. Keychain Access will close.

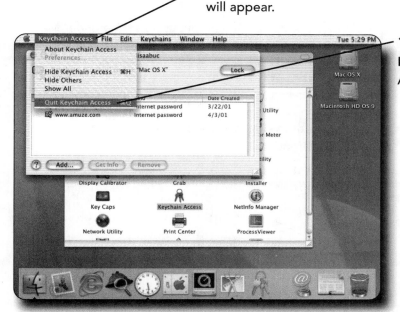

NOTE

Keychain Access creates a file to hold your keychain items. The file uses your eight-character user name (such as lisaabuc, short for Lisa A. Bucki) as the file name. You can typically find this file in the Library, Keychains subfolder of your Home folder. If you copy this file to the same folder on another Mac that also uses Mac OS X, that Mac can also use the keychains you've set up.

Setting up Automatic Login

If you're the only user on your system, you can enable automatic login (this feature is enabled by default), so that you no longer need to type your user name and password each time you start the system.

NOTE

Obviously, if you have multiple users set up under Mac OS X, you should take the opposite approach and leave the automatic login feature turned off so that all users can log in separately.

1. **Click** on the **System Preferences icon** on the Dock. System Preferences will start.

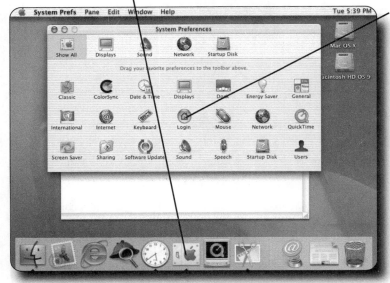

2. **Click** on the **Login icon**. The Login pane will appear in the System Preferences window.

NOTE

If the small icon in the lower-left corner is locked, click on the icon, enter an administrator user name and password, then click on OK to continue.

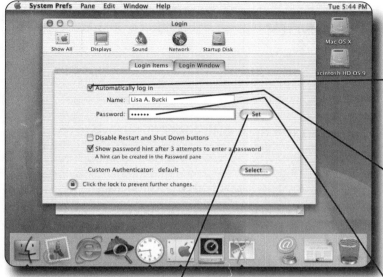

3. Click on the **Login Window tab**. The tab will come forward.

4. Click on the **Automatically log in check box**. Automatic login will be selected.

5. Type a **user name** into the Name text box, **and press Tab**. The cursor will move to the Password text box.

6. Type the **user's password** into the Password text box. A dot will appear for each character in the password.

7. Click on **Set**. The user name and password will be applied, and Mac OS X will automatically log in that user when it starts up.

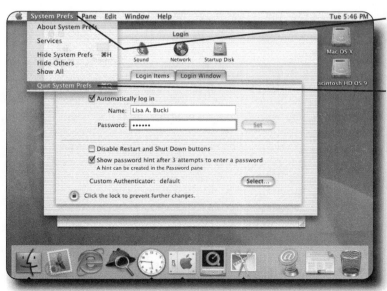

8. Click on **System Prefs**. The System Prefs menu will appear.

9. Click on **Quit System Prefs**. System Preferences will close.

Part VI Review Questions

1. How do I restart my Mac? *See "Restarting the System" in Chapter 19.*

2. What if I can't start up from the hard disk? *See "Starting up from a CD-ROM" in Chapter 19.*

3. I have Mac OS 9 and OS X on separate partitions. How do I boot from one or the other? *See "Changing the Startup Disk" in Chapter 19.*

4. How do I repair a disk? *See "Repairing a Disk" in Chapter 20.*

5. How do I authorize more Mac OS X system users? *See "Adding a User," in Chapter 21.*

6. How do I change a password? *See "Updating a Password or Administration Privileges" in Chapter 21.*

7. Can I log in automatically? *See "Setting Up Automatic Login" in Chapter 21.*

Appendix
Installation Notes

The Mac OS X CD-ROM includes both the Mac OS X program files and an installer program that walks you through the installation process. To complete the installation process, you boot using the installation CD-ROM (see the section "Starting up from a CD-ROM" in Chapter 19 "Emergency Startup Measures,") and then follow the instructions. While *that* part of the process is simple, there are some issues to consider before and after you install Mac OS X.

Considering Installation Options

If you're installing Mac OS X on a system that already uses an older Mac operating system, you have a few decisions to make before you begin the installation process. You need to pause and consider your options before diving into the install process. Here are the key points you should consider:

- Before you do anything, open and read the READ BEFORE YOU INSTALL.PDF file on the Mac OS X CD-ROM. (If needed to read the document, install Adobe Acrobat Reader from the CD-ROM.) This document covers important considerations such as the system requirements for Mac OS X, where to check to see if you need to upgrade your firmware before installing Mac OS X, and more. This document also reviews how to start the Mac OS X installer.

- Before you can install Mac OS X, you need to upgrade any Mac OS 9.x version to 9.1. That's because Mac OS X requires Mac OS 9.1 to run any non-OS X (now called Classic) applications. A Mac OS 9.1 CD-ROM is included with Mac OS X.

- You need to decide whether to install Mac OS X over your current Mac OS 9.1 installation, or whether to partition the disk and install Mac OS X in a separate partition. You may want to take the latter approach, for example, if you have some mission-critical Classic applications and want to guarantee that you'll still be able to run them.

- If you do want to partition the hard disk, be aware that the partitioning process erases everything currently on the disk. Therefore, you'll need a good backup of your files.

You should also record any important information (such as TCP/IP settings, Internet connection and e-mail account settings, and dial-up connection settings) before beginning the partitioning process. If you use a good backup program, you should be able to restore all information to the Mac OS 9.1 partition after you partition the disk.

- If you're not sure how to partition your hard disk, you can get help from http://www.apple.com. On the Web site, click first on the Support tab and then the Tech Info Library link. Now search for Article ID (article number) 19286 so that you can read instructions for partitioning the disk in prior Mac OS versions.

- Once you start the installer, it will prompt you to select the partition on which you want to install Mac OS X. Be sure to select the proper partition.

- Consult Chapter 19 "Emergency Startup Measures" to learn how to boot between the two partitions (and operating systems).

Completing the Mac OS Setup Assistant

After the installer program finishes copying files, it launches the Setup Assistant. The Setup Assistant gathers additional information from you to help configure Mac OS X. All you need to do is respond to each of the Setup Assistant screens.

The Create Your Account Screen is perhaps the most important. There, you enter the user name that you want to use in the Name text box. In addition, you're asked to enter the password that you want to use in the Password and Verify text boxes, along with any Password Hint. Then click on Continue to proceed with the Setup.

NOTE

The first eight characters (the Short Name) of the user name that you set up in this way designate the first administrator for the system. When you need to work with administrator settings, enter this user name and password.

Once you establish the initial user name and password information, the Setup Assistant will prompt you to establish other key settings such as setting up your Internet account. Respond to each screen, as required, to complete the Setup Assistant.

Glossary

A

Active Window. The window in which the insertion point appears. Click on a window to make it active.

Alias. A shortcut that helps you jump to a file or folder stored in another location. For example, an alias might be on the desktop, while the file or folder to which it refers is in the Documents subfolder of your Home folder.

Alt Key. (see Option key).

Application (Program). A software program that adds specific functionality to your computer, such as a particular game or word processing program.

Aqua. The name for the new user interface featured in Mac OS X.

Archive File. A file that holds a number of files, which may be compressed. Generally, you create an archive file with special compression software such as DropStuff from Aladdin Systems. Archive files often enable you to more quickly e-mail or download a number of files, because you can "group" all of those files within a single archive file.

Auto Hide. A feature that, when enabled, hides the Dock until you move your mouse pointer over it.

B

Browser. (see Web browser).

C

Channel. In QuickTime Player, a channel delivers interactive QuickTime TV content, which can include streaming video, streaming audio, and links to related information on the Web.

Check Box. In a window or dialog box, a check box element allows a user to enable or disable an option. To use a check box, click in the box to place a check mark in it, which enables or selects that setting. Click on a check box again to remove the check mark, which disables, unchecks, or clears the setting.

Classic Application. An application written for Mac OS 9.1 or earlier. The Classic environment must load in Mac OS X so that you can use a Classic application.

Classic Environment. The Mac OS 9.1-based environment that runs applications written for earlier Mac OS versions.

Click. To press and release the mouse button.

Column View. A Finder window view that displays information in multiple columns. Generally, the leftmost column indicates upper-level locations (disks) and the rightmost column identifies a single file. The columns in between identify the folders and subfolders leading to the file.

Command Button. In a window or dialog box, you click on a command button to perform a command. In some instances, a subsequent dialog box is displayed.

Command Key Combination. (see shortcut key combination).

Contextual Menu. In Mac OS X, a menu that appears when you Control+click on an item.

Crash. (see hang).

Current Window. (see active window).

D

Delete. (see also Trash). To remove an item from a folder or disk and place it in the Trash, from which you can permanently delete or retrieve the item.

Desktop. The working screen area of Mac OS X, from which you launch applications and use the Finder to manage files.

Disabled. An item that's dimmed on-screen indicating that it's not available for selection or use.

Disk Image. A special type of file that represents a disk volume. The Disk Copy utility typically mounts any disk image file after you double-click on the file. A removable disk icon for the disk image appears on the desktop. You can use the Finder to navigate to folders on the disk image just as you would navigate to a folder on a physical hard disk.

Disk Utility. An application that enables you to check and repair disks.

Dock. The bar that appears at the bottom of the Mac OS X desktop. The Dock contains icons for launching applications. You also can minimize an open file and window to an icon on the Dock, then click the icon on the Dock to reopen the window.

Document. (see file).

Double-click. To press and release the mouse button twice in quick succession.

Download Manager. This utility works in conjunction with Internet Explorer to display the progress of a file being downloaded from the Web.

Drag. To drag, move the mouse pointer over an item, and then press and hold the mouse button as you move the mouse on your desk. When the mouse pointer (or the item you're dragging) reaches the desired location, release the mouse button.

Driver. A file that provides extra functionality to your system such as a file needed to enable Mac OS X to use a particular printer.

E

E-mail. A means of sending messages, sometimes including attached files, electronically, commonly over the Internet.

E-mail Rule. A means of specifying how Mail should handle messages from a particular source, such as instantly deleting a message from a source that sends junk mail.

F

Favorite. In the Finder or Internet Explorer, a folder or page that you use frequently and therefore mark for easy access.

File. The named set of information that you create in an application. For example, you use the TextEdit application to create RTF files such as letters and memos.

File Name Extension. A period plus an identifying suffix that appears at the end of a file name. The extension typically identifies the file type. While extensions weren't necessary in older Mac operating systems, they are used in Mac OS X because it's based on new UNIX source code.

Finder. The application that helps you manage system disks, folders, and files.

Finder Menu. In the Classic Environment and older Mac operating systems, this menu appears at the far-right of the Desktop menu bar and allows you to switch between applications.

Folder. Similar to a physical file folder, a folder is a named location on a disk in which you typically store files that are related in some way.

Freeware. Software written by a programmer for free distribution. You typically download freeware from the Web or receive it on a demo disk.

Freeze. (see hang).

G

Graphical User Interface (GUI). A computer operating system user interface that is graphics-based, including elements such as pull-down menus and icons that enable you to interact using a mouse. Because a GUI enables you to give commands by working with items that you can see on-screen (rather than having to remember obscure commands), GUIs are considered to be more user-friendly than command-line interfaces.

H

Hang. To have an application or the operating system stop responding to input for some reason.

Hard Disk. A computer component that consists of a sealed metal box housing spinning disks coated with magnetic material for data storage.

Help Button. A button labeled with a question mark found on some Help screens. Clicking a Help button displays the Help Viewer.

Help Viewer. The application that enables you to browse for Help in Mac OS X.

Highlight. (see select)

Home Folder. The folder set up to store the files for your user name. The Home folder contains a number of subfolders. Each user has access only to his or her Home folder contents as well as one Shared folder that all users can access.

Home Page. The page that, by default, loads first when you start Internet Explorer.

I

Icon View. A Finder window view that represents each file and folder as an icon.

Internet Service Provider. A company that sells Internet time via a dial-up (phone line), DSL, or other broadband connection.

iTunes. An audio application that enables Mac users to play audio CDs, create MP3 files, and build playlists.

ISP. (see Internet Service Provider).

K

Keyboard Repeat Rate. When you hold down a key, this rate controls how quickly the system duplicates the character.

L

Link (Hyperlink). A connection to another location (typically a Web page) on which you can click to jump to the destination page or location. On Web pages, a link can appear as specially formatted text, a graphic, or a button.

List View. A Finder window view that lists each file and folder along with basic information about the file or folder, such as the date it was last modified.

Log In. To enter your user name and password to gain access to Mac OS X after you start up your system.

M

Magnification. A Dock feature that causes an icon to increase in size when you move the mouse pointer over the icon.

Menu. (see pull-down menu)

Menu Bar. The list of menus that appears at the top of the screen when you start a particular application.

Minimize. To reduce an open window to an icon on the Dock.

Mount. When Disk Copy opens a disk image file and creates an icon for it on the desktop.

Mouse. An input device for your system, which is designed to work with the graphical user interface. You move the mouse on your desk to move the mouse pointer in the corresponding direction and distance on-screen. Then, use the mouse button to click, double-click, and drag.

MP3. (MPeg Audio Layer 3). A technology resulting in a special music file with a compact file format yielded by discarding frequencies and tones not perceptible to the human ear.

O

Operating System. The software that enables computer system components to communicate and accomplish tasks, as well as enabling the user to give input to the computer.

Option Button (Radio Button). In a window or dialog box, a round button on which you can click to select an option. Typically, option buttons appear in groups and are mutually exclusive, meaning that only one option in the group can be selected at any time.

Option key. A modifier key on Mac keyboards that's typically used in shortcut key combinations.

P

Password. A secret word or group of characters that you enter to log in to Mac OS X, certain Web sites, and other locations. Passwords limit access to authorized users (those with the password).

Path. The full list of folders and subfolders that identify a file's location.

Playlist. In iTunes, a custom list of songs that you create to control playback order.

Program. (see application).

Pop-up Menu. A menu that opens after you click on a double-arrow button in a window or dialog box.

Print Center. The Mac OS X application that enables you to install and remove printers and control printing.

Print Queue. The list of documents being sent to the printer by Print Center.

Pull-down Menu. A menu that appears when you click on a menu name on the menu bar.

Q

QuickTime TV (QTV). Special QuickTime-based Web sites that provide both streaming QuickTime content and Web-based information.

R

Repair Disk. To use Disk Utility to find and fix problems on a disk.

Rich Text Format (RTF). The default type of document created in TextEdit. RTF documents can include text formatting and some graphics, unlike plain text (TXT) files.

Root. The base location on a disk outside of any folders contained on the disk.

Rule. (see e-mail rule).

S

Scroll Bar. A bar at the right side or bottom of a window or list that enables you to view other sections of the window or list contents. For example, click on the up arrow on a vertical scroll bar to scroll up in a document or list.

Search Engine. An application that searches for information (data) based on criteria generally supplied by the user. Typically, search engines are Web-based services that catalog Web pages, so that you can search the pages by topic. After you run the search, the search engine presents a list of links to potentially matching pages.

Select. To choose an icon by clicking on it or to choose text by dragging over it.

Shareware. Software distributed on the honor system. You typically download shareware from the Web or receive it on a demo disk, and are expected to send a modest fee to the developer if you plan to continue to use the software.

Shortcut Key Combination. Multiple keys pressed simultaneously to execute a command or action. Typically, these combinations include the use of the Control, Shift, Option, and/or Command (Apple) keys. In some cases, one of these keys is pressed while clicking with the mouse to execute the shortcut. The right side of most menus lists the shortcut key combination associated with a particular command.

Shut Down. To open the Apple menu and choose the Shut Down command to close Mac OS X and power down your Macintosh.

Signature. Closing information that Mail can automatically append to each of your outgoing e-mail messages.

Sleep (Sleep Mode). A power-conserving mode that can activate for your system's screen, hard disk, or both after a period of inactivity (when you haven't used the system at all).

Slider. In a window or dialog box, a knob or *thumb* that you drag to the left or right to increase or decrease a setting.

Stickies. Desktop notes that you can create and view using Stickies.

Stuffed. Another term for a compressed archive file.

T

Tab. In a window or dialog box, a graphical element representing another page (collection) of settings. Click on a tab to display its settings.

Text Box. In a window or dialog box, a rectangular area in which you type an entry.

Toolbar. A group of icons typically found at the top of a Finder window in Mac OS X. You can click on an icon to perform a command or go to a particular folder.

Tracking Speed. When you move the mouse on your desk, correspondingly the tracking speed refers to how far and fast the mouse pointer moves on-screen.

Trash. The Mac OS X feature that enables you to temporarily or permanently delete files from disks. You move a file to the Trash to delete the file temporarily. Empty the trash to permanently delete its files.

U

URL (Uniform Resource Locator). The Internet address for a Web page, usually in the format http://www.domainname.ext/foldername/filename.html.

USB (Universal Serial Bus). A type of port that enables you to connect and set up attached devices (like a printer) quickly and easily.

User Interface. The means of communicating with the operating system and your computer.

User Name. The name that you use to log in to Mac OS X and that is used to identify your Home folder.

Utility. A program or feature that typically performs some kind of system maintenance or repair feature.

V

Verify Disk. An activity performed by Disk Utility to check for problems on a disk

W

Web Browser. An application that enables you to view pages on the World Wide Web.

Web Page. A document on the World Wide Web coded in HTML (*HyperText Markup Language*). Web pages are viewed using a Web browser.

Web Site. A collection of related Web pages published by a single source on the World Wide Web.

Window. A frame that holds a document or collection of options on-screen.

Word Processor. A program that creates text-based documents such as letters, memos, and reports. TextEdit is a basic word processor.

World Wide Web. A collection of servers on the Internet that store and distribute interactive, graphical content in the HTML format.

Index

... (ellipsis) in menu commands, 18

A

Accounts pane, Mail, 187–189
active window, 355
  selecting, 29–30
Address Book, Mail, 7
  contacts, 201–203
    addressing messages to, 203–204
    groups, 203
  starting/quitting, 199–200
Advanced settings (Classic environment), 104–107
aliases, 68–71, 355
alignment, TextEdit, 298
Alt key, 355
analog clock, setting, 126
animation, Dock icons, 119
Apple key, 318
Apple menu, 12
  Dock commands on, 119
  System Preferences, displaying, 128
Apple Tech Info library, 230
AppleTalk, printing and, 156
applications, 355
  Classic, 240
    opening and closing, 102–104
  closing, 55, 95–96

  cycling through with keyboard, 88
  deleting accidently, recovering, 59
  displaying, 48
  downloading, 236–237
    install programs, 239–242
  files
    creating, 88
    saving from, 88–90
  Help Viewer, 75
  hiding, 92–93
  locked, forcing to quit, 96–97
  preferences, setting, 91–92
  starting from Dock, 86
  switching among, 87–88
Applications (Mac OS 9) folder, 102
Applications button (Finder toolbar), 32
Aqua, 355
  desktop, 3
archive files, 355
arrows in menu commands, 18
attachments to Mail messages, 193–194
audio
  CDs
    muting playback, 267–268
    pausing playback, 267–268
    playing, 259–261

    streaming, 265–267
auto hide, 355
automatic login, users, 347–349

B

back button, 27
Back button, Internet Explorer, 213–214
Battery Monitor (Dock Extras), 123
bold text, TextEdit, 297
Bring All To Front command, 38
browsers, 355, 360
  URLs, entering, 212–213
browsing Help Viewer, 76–78
buffering stream, radio, 266

C

Calculator, 7, 293–294
CD-ROM drive, starting from, 319–320
CD-ROMs, ejecting, 58–59
CDDB database, 259–261
CDs, audio, 259–261
channels, 355
check boxes, 355
  dialog boxes, 22
check mark, menu commands and, 18
checking for Mail messages, 195–196

Chess, 7, 291–293
Choose Categories dialog box, 202
Classic applications, 240, 355
Classic environment, 355
closing, 107–108
preferences, adjusting, 104–107
starting, 100–101
clicking (mouse), 8, 356
Clipboard
Calculator and, 294
graphics and, 306
clock, appearance, 125–126
close button, 26
closing
applications, 95–96
Classic applications, 104
Classic environment, 107–108
files, 55
QuickTime, 271–273
Help Viewer, 80–81
locked applications, 96=97
windows, 41–42
color
number of, setting for display, 136
Stickies, 289
TextEdit, 297
Column view, 356
Column view button (Finder toolbar), 34
Command button
command buttons, 23
Command key, 318
commands
arrow in, 18
changing with Option key, 17
check marks and, 18
closing menus without selecting, 19
ellipsis in, 18
keyboard shortcuts for, 19–20
selecting, 16–17
special, 18

compatibility, Classic environment, 99–108
Compose window, Mail, 192–194
composing Mail messages, 189
compressed files, unstuffing, 238
Computer button (Finder toolbar), 31
connections, Internet, 179–181
Internet Connect, 175–178
preferences, 172–175
QuickTime movies and, 283–284
conserving power, 8–9
contacts, Address Book (Mail), 201–203
addressing messages, 203–204
groups, 203
contextual menus, 20–21, 356
copying
files, 55–58
folders, 54
crashing, 318, 356
current window, 356

D
date and time preferences, 133–135
deleting, 356. *See also* Trash
Mail messages, 189
users, 341–342
desktop, 4, 356
aliases, adding, 68
Classic, rebuilding, 325–326
displaying, 98
Dock, 6
Finder window, 5
folders, displaying, 116
Help Viewer, 74
icons, adjusting size, 116
icons, arranging, 116
menu bar, 5
original picture, restoring, 115
picture, choosing new, 115

dialog boxes
options, responding to, 22
question marks and, 23
resizing, 23
tabs, 360
digital clock, 126
disabled items, 356
disconnecting from Internet, 179–181
Disk Utility, 7, 356
starting/exiting, 328–331
disks
displaying on desktop, 116
erasing, 334–336
images, 356
repairing, 333–334
verifying, 331–332
displays preferences (monitor settings), 135–137
Displays (Dock Extras), 123
Dock, 6, 356
animating icons, 119
Apple menu commands, 119
application names, displaying, 93
applications
starting, 86
switching among, 87–88
Classic environment, starting, 100
clock, appearance, 125–126
Dock Extras, adding, 123–124
folder contents, viewing, 122–123
Help Viewer, 80–81
hiding, 119
icons, adding and removing, 120–121
magnification, 118
preferences, setting, 117–120
Trash, 58—63
windows
expanding, 40
minimizing to, 94–95

documents
closing, 42
saving during shutdown, 10
storing, 44
Documents folder, 44
Download Manager, 222, 356
applications, 237
downloading, 221–223
applications, 236–237
install programs, 239–242
graphics files, 114
help, 77
iTunes, 252–257
unstuffing, 238
dragging mouse, 17, 356
drivers, 356
duplicating. *See* copying

E

Edit menu, 14
ejecting floppy disks and CD-ROMs, 58
ellipsis in menu commands, 18
e-mail, 356. *See also* Mail
Energy Saver preferences, setting, 137–138
erasing disks, 334–336
error messages when saving files, 45

F

Favorites button (Finder toolbar), 32
Favorites, Internet Explorer, 214–215, 356
aliases, adding, 70–71
organizing, 215–218
selecting, 218–219
features overview, 6–7
File menu, 13
creating files from applications, 88
New Finder Window command, 28
file name extensions, 68, 357

file sharing, 45
privileges, checking, 64
files, 43, 357
aliases, 68–71
archive files, 355
closing, 55
creating with applications, 88
downloading, 221–223
applications, 236–237
unstuffing, 238
graphics, 303–305
downloading, 114
information about, displaying, 62–66
movie files, 271
moving, 55
multiple, selecting, 56
opening, 54–55
PDF, 303–305
creating, 308–310
previewing, 66
QuickTime, 271–273
recovering from Trash, 59–60
removing (Trash), 58–59
renaming, 66–67
RTF (text), 295–299
saving
during shutdown, 10
from applications, 88–90
new name, 89
Finder, 7, 13, 357
Bring All To Front command, 38
preferences, changing, 47
pull-down menus, 12–16
toolbar buttons, 26
Finder window, 5, 26–27, 357
folder contents, 179
folder icons, adding to toolbar, 33
opening additional, 27–28
toolbar, 30–33
view, changing, 33–35
Finder window toolbar, 5

floppy disks
displaying on desktop, 116
ejecting, 58
folders, 43, 46, 357
aliases, 68–71
Applications (Mac OS 9), 102
copying, 64
creating, 50–51
creating when saving files, 90
displaying on desktop, 116
Documents, 44
Favorites, adding aliases to, 70–71
Finder window, 179
finding, 46–50
Home, 44–46, 357
name for, 32
information about, displaying, 62–66
Library, 44
Movies, 45
moving, 51–53
Music, 45
naming conventions, 51
Pictures, 45
Public, 45
recovering from Trash, 59–60
removing (Trash), 58–59
renaming, 66–67
Sites, 45
Users, 46
viewing contents from Dock, 122–123
fonts, TextEdit, 297
Force Quit command, 97
Forward button
Internet Explorer, 213–214
Mail, 198
freeware, 357
freezing, 318, 357

G

general preferences, 138–139
Go menu, 15
Grab, 7, 301–302

graphics files, 303–305
  downloading, 114
    from Web page, 221
  new desktop picture,
    choosing, 115
**GUI (Graphical User
  Interface),** 357

H

hanging, 318, 357
hard disk, 357
  name, default, 6
  name, default in UFS
    format, 47
help. *See also* Help Viewer
  dialog boxes and, 23
  downloading, 77
  printing, 78
Help button, 357
Help menu, 16
Help Viewer, 357. *See also* help
  applications, 75
  browsing, 76–78
  closing, 80–81
  desktop, 74
  dialog boxes, 75–76
  searching, 78–80
hiding
  applications, 92–93
  Dock, 119
highlighting. *See* selecting
**Home button (Finder
  toolbar),** 31
Home folder, 44–46, 357
  name for, 32
home pages (Web), 357
hyperlinks. *See* links

I

Icon view, 357
Image Capture, 7
image links, 211
images. *See* graphics files
INBOX folder, Mail, 195
Info dialog box, 63

inkjet printers, 152
install programs, running,
  239–242
installation
  iTunes, 252–257
  options, 352–353
  partitioning hard drive and,
    352–353
  upgrades and, 352
interface. *See* desktop
international preferences,
  140–141
Internet
  connection preferences,
    172–175
  disconnecting from, 179–181
  downloading files, 221–223
  radio stream, 265–267
  searches, Sherlock, 230–232
Internet Connect, 7, 175–178
  Sherlock and, 231
Internet Explorer, 7
  Back button, 213–214
  Favorites, 214–215
    organizing, 215–218
  Forward button, 213–214
  starting/exiting, 206–209
**ISP (Internet Service
  Provider),** 172, 357. *See
  also* connections; Internet
italic text, TextEdit, 297
iTunes, 357
  downloading, 252–257
  installation, 252–257
  Library, MP3s, 261–263
  radio stream and, 265–267
  starting/exiting, 257–259

J–K

Kerbango Tuning Service, 265
keyboard
  aliases, creating, 69
  applications, cycling through, 88
  files
    closing, 55

  copying, 58
  deleting, 59
  selecting multiple, 56
  folders
    copying, 54
    deleting, 59
  locked applications, closing, 97
  menu commands, changing, 17
  menus, navigating among, 17
  Option key, 358
  preferences, 142–143
  repeat rate, 358
  shortcuts, menu commands,
    19–20
  startup process, 4
  undoing deletions, 59
Keychain Access, 7, 344–347

L

launching. *See* opening
Library folder, 44
**license agreements, iTunes
  downloads,** 256
links, Web pages, 358
  following, 210–211
  image links, 211
  searches and, 220
List view, 358
**list view button (Finder
  toolbar),** 34
locked applications, closing,
  96–97
log in, 358

M

**Mac OS 9.1 System folder,
  updating,** 101
magnification, 358
Mail, 7
  accounts, 187–189
  Address Book
    addressing messages,
      203–204
    contacts, 201–203
    starting/quitting, 199–200

attachments to messages, 193–194

checking for messages, 195–196

Compose window, 192–194

composing messages, 189

deleting messages, 189

Forward button, 198

INBOX folder, 195

Internet Connect and, 184

preferences, 187–191

reading messages, 197–198

Reply button, 198

replying to messages, 197–198

saving messages, 190
  as drafts, 195

sending messages, 191–195

settings, 186–191

sound, 188

spelling check, 190

starting/exiting, 184–186

maximize button, 38

menu bar, 358
  desktop, 5

menus, 358. *See also* toolbars
  active window, selecting, 30
  Apple, 12
  closing without selecting
    commands, 19
  commands
    changing, 17
    keyboard shortcuts for, 19–20
  contextual, 20–21, 356
  Edit, 14
  File, 12
  Finder, 13
  Go, 15
  Help, 16
  navigating among, 17
  pop-up, 22
  special commands, 18
  View, 14
  Window, 15

minimize button, 26, 39–40

minimizing windows, 358

mounting, Disk Copy and, 358

mouse, 11, 358
  clicking, 8
  Dock, resizing, 120
  dragging, 17
  files
    copying, 58
    selecting multiple, 56
  folders, moving, 52
  icons, adding to Dock, 121
  menu commands, selecting, 16–17
  new windows, opening, 28
  preferences, 143–145

movie files (QuickTime)
  formats, 271
  opening/closing, 271–273
  playback, 274–275
  QTV channels, 277–279
    favorites, 279–282
  Web, watching on, 275–277

Movies folder, 45

moving
  files, 55
  folders, 51–53
  windows, 36–37

MP3s, 358
  playlist, 263–265
  recording, 261–263

Multiple Users, 7

Music folder, 45

muting playback, audio CDs, 267–268

N

naming
  files, when saving, 89
  folders, rules for, 51
  hard disk, default name, 6
  renaming files and folders, 66–67

navigating Web pages, 209–214

navigation
  folders, finding, 46–50
  menus, 17

networks
  date and time preferences, setting, 134
  file sharing privileges, checking, 64
  Public folders, 45

New Finder window command, 28

news, searches (Sherlock), 233–234

O

opening
  applications from Dock, 86
  Classic applications, 102–103
  files, 54–55
    QuickTime, 271–273

operating system defined, 358

Option button, 358

option buttons, 23

Option key, 358

Output Options, PDF files, 309

P

Page Setup dialog, 158–161

partitioning hard drive, installation and, 352–353

passwords, 358
  Keychain Access, 344–347
  updating, administrator and, 343

path, 358

pausing playback of audio CDs, 267–268

PDF (Portable Document Format) files, 303–305
  creating, 308–310

people searches, 232–233

phone number, Internet Connect, 175

Pictures folder, 45

pictures in text files, 305–308

pictures of screen. *See* screen shots

playlist, MP3s, 263–265, 358

pop-up menus, 359
 dialog boxes and, 22
power
 conserving, 8–9
 shutting down, 9–10
 starting up, 4
Power button
 shutting down, 10
 starting up, 4
preferences
 Classic environment,
  adjusting, 104–107
 Date and Time, 133–135
 Displays settings, 135–137
 Dock settings, 117–120
 Energy Saver, 137–138
 Finder, changing, 47
 General, 138–139
 International, 140–141
 Internet connections,
  172–175
 Keyboard, 142–143
 Mail, 187–191
 Mouse, 143–145
 panes
  displaying, 128–130
  locking and unlocking,
   130–132
  redisplaying preference
   icons, 132
 QuickTime, 282–285
 screen saver, 145–147
 setting for applications, 91–92
 software update, 147–148
 sound, 148–149
 speech, 149–150
Preview, 7
previewing files, 66
Print Center, 7, 153–157, 359
print queue, 164, 359
printers
 AppleTalk and, 156
 default, 162–166
 inkjet, 152

removing from queue, 164–166
 selecting, 156, 157–161
 setup, 153–157
printing
 help, 78
 page setup, 158–161
 paper size, 158
Public folder, 45
pull-down menus, 359.
 See menus

Q
QTV (QuickTime TV), 359
 channels, 355
  favorites, 279–282
  viewing, 277–279
**question marks (?), dialog
 boxes and,** 23
QuickTime
 files, 271–273
 movie playback, 274–275
 preferences, 282–285
 starting/exiting, 270–271
QuickTime Player, 7

R
radio stream, Internet music,
 265–267
reading Mail messages,
 197–198
**Rebuild Desktop (Classic
 environment),** 106
rebuilding Desktop, 325–326
renaming files and folders,
 66–67
Repair Disk, 359
repairing disks, 333–334
Reply button, Mail, 198
replying to Mail messages,
 197–198
resizing
 desktop icons, 116
 Dock, 118
 windows, 37–38

**resolution (monitor settings),
 preferences,** 136
restarting system, 318
 Mac OS 9.1 disk volume, 320–
  322
 Mac OS X disk from OS 9.1
  volume, 322–325
root, 359
 contents, displaying, 47
RTF (text) files, 295–299, 359
rules (Mail), 356

S
saving
 documents when closing
  windows, 42
 error messages, 45
 files
  during shutdown, 10
  from applications, 88–90
  with new name, 89
 Mail messages, 190
  as drafts, 195
screen saver preferences,
 145–147
screen shots, 300–302
scroll bar, 359
scrolling windows, 38–39
Search Assistant
 Web searches, 220
search engines, 220, 359
searches. *See also* Sherlock
 Apple Tech Info library, 230
 files, 227–229
 Help Viewer, 78–80
 Internet, Sherlock, 230–232
 people searches, 232–233
 Sherlock, 233–234
 Web-based, 220–221
selecting, 359
sending Mail messages,
 191–195
Session Options dialog box,
 177–178

Setup Assistant, 353–354
shareware, 359
Sherlock, 7
  file searches, 227–229
  Internet Connect and, 231
  Internet searches, 230–232
  news searches, 233–234
  people searches, 232–233
  starting/exiting, 226
shortcut keys, 19–20, 359
shortcuts. See also aliases
Show Info command, 62
shutdown, 9–10
shutting down, 359
Signal Strength (Dock
    Extras), 123
signatures, 359
Sites folder, 45
size box, 27, 37
sleep feature, 8–9
  setting preferences, 138
Sleep Mode, 359
  Classic environment, 106
slider controls, 23
sliders, 359
Software Update, 242–246
  preferences, 147–148
sound
  Mail, 188
  preferences, 148–149
Speakable Items, 311–313
speech recognition, 311–313
  preferences, 149–150
spelling in Mail messages, 190
starting Mail, Address Book,
    199–200
startup
  CD-ROM startup,
    319–320
  disk, changing, 320
  Mac OS 9.1 disk volume,
    320–322
startup process, 4
Stickies, 7, 288–291, 359

stuffed files, 360
  unstuffed, 238
Stuffit Expander, 7
symbols, keyboard keys, 20
System Folder, 101
system freezes, 318
System Preferences, 7
  displaying preference panes,
    128–130
  icons, redisplaying, 132
  panes, locking and unlocking,
    130–132
  Software Update and, 242–246

T
tabs, dialog boxes, 360
text boxes, 360
  entering information in, 22
text files
  pictures, adding, 305–308
  RTF files, 295–299
TextEdit, 7, 295–299
timed screens, Grab, 301
title bars, 26
  minimizing windows, 40
  windows, moving, 37
toolbars, 360. See also menus
  Finder window, 5, 30–33
  Finder, buttons on, 26
  folder icons, adding, 33
tracking speed, 360
Trash, 360
  emptying, 61
  files and folders
    recovering, 59–60
    removing, 58–59

U
UFS format (hard drive), 47
underlined text, TextEdit, 297
Unhandled File Type dialog
    box, downloading files
    and, 222
unstuffing files, 238

updating software, 242–246
URLs (Uniform Resource
    Locators), 360
  entering in browser, 212–213
USB (Universal Serial Bus), 360
user interface, 360. See desktop
user management
  adding users, 338–339
  automatic login, 347–349
  deleting users, 341–342
  Keychain Access, 344–347
  multiple users, 338–339
  password updates, 343
  privileges, 343
user name, 360
Users folder, 46
utilities, 360
  displaying, 47

V
Verify Disk, 360
verifying disks, 331–332
view buttons, 27
View menu, 14
  Finder toolbar, displaying, 31
  window views, changing, 35
views
  Column view, 356
  Icon, 357
  List, 358
volumes, verifying, 331–332

W
Web pages, 209, 360
  favorites, 214–215
  graphics, downloading, 221
  links, following, 210–211
  navigating, 209–214
  QuickTime movies, 275–277
  searches, 220–221
Web sites, 209, 360
Window menu, 15
  Bring All To Front
    command, 38

windows, 25, 360
  active, 355
    selecting, 29–30
  back button, 26
  close button, 26
  closing, 41–42
  current, 356
  Finder, 5
    changing view, 33–35
  Finder toolbar, 30–33

  maximize button, 38
  minimize button, 26
  minimizing, 39–40
    to Dock, 94–95
  moving, 36–37
  resizing, 37–38
  scrolling, 38–39
  size box, 37
  System Preferences,
    172–175

  System Preferences panes,
    displaying, 128–129
  title bar, 26
  zoom button, 26
word processor, 360
WWW (World Wide Web),
    360. *See also* Web

X–Y–Z
zoom button, 26